STEAM CUISINE

Before her marriage Tessa Hayward worked in publishing and when her children went to school she returned to work to edit and produce the Magimix cookery books which combined her publishing experience with her enthusiasm and love of cooking. While she was with Magimix she wrote the instruction books for their various products as well as *The Magimix Cake Book* and, having edited the original *Magimix Cookery* by Marika Hanbury Tenison, she revised and updated it for a new edition. Tessa Hayward is also secretary of the André Simon Memorial Fund and organises their annual awards to the authors of books on food and drink.

STEAM CUISINE

TESSA HAYWARD

DK

Dorling Kindersley London

A Jill Norman Book

First published in Great Britain in 1988
by Dorling Kindersley Limited,
9 Henrietta Street, London WC2E 8PS

British Library Cataloguing in Publication Data
Hayward, Tessa
Steam cuisine.
1. food : Dishes for steaming – Recipes
I. Title
641.5'87

ISBN 0-86318-282-8
ISBN 0-86318-332-8
Typeset by Goodfellow and Egan, Cambridge
Printed in Great Britain by
The Bath Press, Avon

ACKNOWLEDGEMENTS

In writing this book I have had encouragement
from many people but there are some whom I
would especially like to thank: my family, Derek,
Leo and Natasha for the continual interest they
have shown; Julian Cotterell who started me off by
letting me experiment with electric steamers when
he first imported them; Michael Schneideman and
Divertimenti from where I obtained much informa-
tion about equipment. I have also drawn on the
experience of Patricia Lousada, Claudia Roden
and Grania and Alan Munro, whose help on the
couscous section I am most grateful for. My
particular thanks to Jill Norman whose wise comments on the manuscript I have found very illumi-
nating. Finally, I would like to dedicate the book to
my father and to the memory of my mother;
between them they taught me to enjoy and
appreciate good food.

CONTENTS

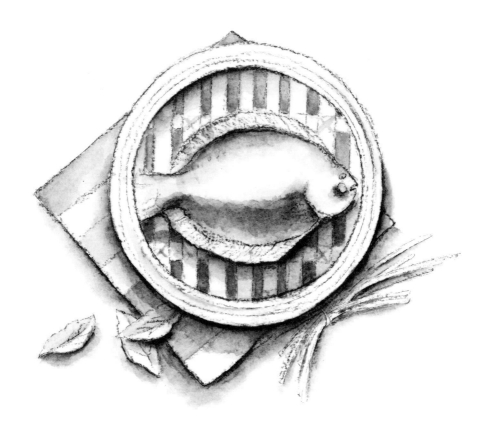

INTRODUCTION

Cooking food with steam is a simple way of cooking, which seems to me to be totally relaxed and natural. Food that is steamed cooks by itself in its own juices, thereby retaining its own individual personality and flavour along with many of the vitamins and minerals that are so frequently lost when using some other method.

For many years steaming has been thought of in the context of either fattening and stodgy puddings or of a little bit of easily digestible, and often overcooked and tasteless, cod served up to recuperating patients in hospital. The advent of nouvelle cuisine and cuisine naturelle has done much for steaming, for they both attach great importance to the natural taste of food and the limited use of fat. This quest for low fat, lighter, healthier food has now spread from its beginnings in France, through the London restaurants, to the British domestic kitchen. Steaming is an easy way of cooking; all you need is some boiling water and a basket to hold the food. Vegetables, fish and meat can be steamed and eaten just as they are (perfect for those on a low fat diet), but you can, of course, add a sauce or other flavourings to them and I have tried, in this book, to cover both the simple, the ethnic and the more elaborate 'entertaining' food.

This is not a health food book; I am not a fanatic about eating or rejecting any particular food. I believe that a mixed balanced diet is probably as healthy as anything, but, in common with most people, my own cooking includes far less fat, cream and butter than it did a few years ago. However I don't altogether ban anything, and think that a steamed pudding eaten, perhaps not too often, after a low stodge first course and in reasonable quantities, should not do any healthy individual any harm. Many of the recipes I give have stuffings or sauces, but as these are best served in small quantities, and as no additional fat is used in the basic cooking, this does not detract from the modern ethos of being careful with egg and fat consumption – all things in moderation.

Steaming, as a method of cooking, can trace its origins far into antiquity. It is thought to have first been used by the Chinese as long ago as 5000 BC and the British Museum has, in its collection of bronzes, a well developed and sophisticated *hsein*, or two part steamer, from the Shang dynasty (12th – 11th century BC). Chinese bronzes are very beautiful objects, with marvellous workmanship, and one feels that the food that was steamed in them must also have had a remarkable degree of sophistication. Unfortunately no records seem to exist of what was cooked in these *hsein*, but the holes are quite large which leads one to think that perhaps they were used for vegetables or fish rather than for grains or rice.

Civilization at this period covered the northern part of China and did not stretch down to the south or Pearl River delta, which, being hot and damp, is now the main rice growing area. It is known, however, that the climate has undergone a change and that between 3000 and 1400 BC the average annual temperature on the north China plain was 3 – 4°C hotter than it is now and that rice as well as millet, sorghum and winter wheat were grown there. The rice was presumably cooked in some way (steamed?) and used as a staple food alongside the other grain products.

Steaming spread from its origins in the north China plain to South East Asia and then on to Japan and India; each country adding its own individuality in the shape of spices, sauces, stuffings or a change in the timing or way of steaming. The cuisines of all South East Asian countries include a variation of the Chinese clear steamed fish. The fish is placed in a shallow dish which is, in turn, placed on a trivet in a wok which contains boiling water. The whole is then covered with the lid of the wok and left simmering until the fish is cooked. The fish thus retains round it the juices that flow out of it while cooking and which can themselves mix with any sauce or flavouring that has been sprinkled over the fish. The use of a dish also means that the heated oil, which is frequently poured over at the last minute to give extra taste and lustre to the fish, does not drain away.

The European approach is quite different. The fish is placed directly in the steaming basket and then served simply or perhaps with a sauce made from the reduced steam water which will contain the juices that flowed from it during cooking.

As far as steaming is concerned, the other important facet of Chinese cuisine is the dimsum or snack. These, a variety of which are often eaten for lunch or individually between meals, consist of savoury or sweet stuffed buns, wuntun, dumplings and stuffed omelettes or eggskins. They are traditionally cooked in a bamboo steamer and, as many people know from eating in Chinese restaurants, are brought to the table still steaming in the basket.

Steaming, historically, was also used in Britain, and wrapping puddings in floured cloths and steaming them, very often suspended on a string over the stew, was an indigenous development which followed naturally from wrapping food in the gut of the animal, as is still done today with a traditional haggis.

The French, always great cooks and gourmets, were by the 18th century using heavy copper fish kettles or poissionières. At the height of the revolution the famous gourmet Grimod de La Reynière's complaint was that there was not a single turbot to be had in the Paris market; if there had been, no doubt he would have steamed or lightly poached it in a turbotière. However, the rise of the new bourgeoisie seemed to lead to a flowering in French cuisine and the publication in the early 19th century of many books on food and cookery, La Reynière, who was also a well known wit, saying in one that 'a well-made sauce will make even an elephant or a grandfather palatable'.

Fish kettles became the established utensil for cooking fish and the Victorian English also continued to steam traditional suet and sponge puddings. There were few changes until after the First World War, when many good cookery books were published. All of them seem to give recipes for steamed puddings and custards and the more sophisticated ones included steamed soufflés, which, looking at the liberal use of shellfish and sole, was probably an idea that came from France.

Since the last war, we have seen many fads and fashions in food and we are now returning to the very sensible thought that nothing should be overdone and that the flavour of the food itself should be allowed to dominate. Steaming suits this idea perfectly; the food retains its taste and its shape and can be steamed to serve on its own with a little butter and some lemon juice, or with a light sauce that blends with and enhances the original base. You can also add herbs, spices or other flavourings to the food; their taste and aroma will be steamed into it.

I have tried, in this book, to show how very versatile a steamer is and to demonstrate how it can be used in many different ways. I have given timings and instructions for cooking foods on their own, and, especially with fish and poultry, I have based many of the recipes on nouvelle cuisine. However, I have also included traditional dishes such as steamed puddings, and ones that cook especially well in a steamer, such as custards.

Like all cookery books, this one is meant to be read and used, but it is also meant to be experimented with; there is no reason why you should not swop the sauces, flavourings or spices around. Once you are familiar with steaming food, your imagination will, I hope, be sparked, and you will find yourself adapting some of your old, tried and trusted recipes to your new found friend, the steamer.

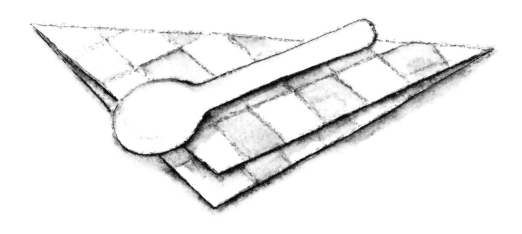

GENERAL RULES

The steaming water

In recipes for steamed food it is often suggested that the steaming water is made up of a stock or that it is flavoured with herbs. I have found that, except for the use of a strong herb infusion which I discuss below, additions to the water can make a marvellous smell in the kitchen but that the steam carries little of the flavour with it. Therefore, I normally use plain water in the base of my steamer. However, when I want to use the steaming liquid to make a sauce for the food, I will add the fish or chicken bones and an onion or a bunch of herbs to the water and, after the food has cooked, strain the liquid into a small saucepan and bubble it down to reduce it well before proceeding with the sauce.

Some of the more powerful herbs can be used to make an infusion which is then used for steaming and will give a delicate flavour to fish or meat. For some reason rabbit seems to take up the flavour of an infusion particularly well: Frances Bissell steams it over lavender and Michel Guérard over hyssop. Other herbs that can be used in this way are rosemary, sage or very aromatic thyme. With all of them you need to use a good sized bunch of the fresh and preferably flowering herb. The herb is dropped into rapidly boiling water, which is then removed from the heat and left to infuse for 20 minutes before being reheated and used as the steaming liquid. The infusion after use will be very strong, probably very bitter and of no use for sauce making; just throw it away.

Salt is definitely not carried by steam. There is no point at all in salting the water: the steam disperses, leaving the salt in the base; the liquid, which will naturally have reduced, will then be too salty to use for a sauce or stock.

Seasoning the food

As you read through the recipes you will notice that quite often, especially with vegetables, I have suggested that salt should be added half way through the cooking. This is because it is best to season wet food; salt sprinkled onto dry florets of cauliflower will just tumble off into the steaming water, but salt sprinkled onto wet, partially cooked florets will stick to them, melt and then season them.

Cooking times

I have given cooking times in all the recipes and have based them on using an electric steamer set on its lower setting which keeps the water at a constant simmer. Steam is always at the same heat, but a full pan of fast boiling water produces a lot more of it than a pan of simmering water that is only a quarter full, therefore the fast boiling pan will cook the food considerably faster, a fact worth remembering when you are calculating your timings.

A full steaming basket will also take longer to cook than a comparatively empty one. My timings have been based on cooking for four and using a large basket; if you fill your basket up with, for instance, new potatoes, you will have to increase the steaming times.

If you have a double steamer you will find that anything cooked in the top basket will take considerably longer, probably about twice as long; if the top basket is over a full bottom basket, which lets little steam through, it may take three times as long. Most double steamers have interchangeable baskets which means that you can swop them round to slow down the cooking of one and speed up the other.

Steaming cloths

I have often recommended wrapping food in a cloth before steaming it; this serves to keep an item such as a whole cabbage in shape or to prevent a whole fish from breaking up. It also keeps the item moist and makes it easier to lift out of the steamer. I suggest using 'J' cloths, as most kitchens have a supply of these, while butter muslin or old string bags are more difficult to come by. However, don't use pink ones as they are apt to give off their colour; blue or yellow both seem to be fast dyed.

Cooking en papilotte

One often sees recipes for wrapping food in a foil parcel and then steaming it or cooking it in a bain marie. I haven't included any papilotte recipes for, good as they are, I don't think of them as steaming. Food en papilotte can be cooked just as well in an oven as in a steamer, and the way everything is enclosed in an impermeable wrapper has much more in common with cooking en croûte or in a salt crust than cooking above boiling water.

Measurements

I give all measurements, using a standard conversion table, in both imperial and metric. Use whichever set you prefer but don't mix them up.

TYPES OF STEAMERS

These notes and comments cover the main types and makes of steamer that are reasonably easy to find in cook shops or ethnic shops. Many manufacturers frequently seem to be adding steaming baskets and sets to their ranges and I am sure that there are many excellent ones that I have not touched upon.

The main choice is what type to buy. This will be influenced by your budget, kitchen cupboard space, how many people you cook for, the type of food you like cooking and how often you think you will use it. I have tried to point out the disadvantages as well as the advantages of each type of steamer and can only add that, like everything else, the better the quality the more use you will get from it.

Petal steaming baskets and basket inserts

The petal steaming baskets which fold out to fit inside a saucepan are very cheap and take up little storage space, but they have a limited life. They come in different sizes and it is best to choose one with regard to the diameter of the saucepan you intend to use it in. The biggest one is not always the best choice as you want to let it fold out to make the bottom as flat as possible. Most petal steamers have a central spindle which acts as a handle to lift the basket and its contents from the saucepan; the spindle also unscrews to give extra space in the basket and to enable the lid to be put onto the saucepan. The cheapest are in aluminium but the stainless steel ones are still inexpensive and worth the extra.

The petal steamer works well for vegetables and can be used for pieces of fish or joints of chicken, and if you are cooking for several people it does not matter if the food overlaps a little, just remember to increase the steaming time. There is not too much room for water underneath these steamers and this makes them impractical for cooking joints or large steamed puddings as the water would have to be constantly replenished.

I feel that these are really the bedsitter steamer and are only practical if you want to steam infrequently and not for too many people. One of them would also perhaps make a good starter for somebody who has never steamed food before and wants to experiment before investing in something larger and longer term.

You can also find collapsible wire baskets on feet to put inside a saucepan; these are really an extension of the blanching baskets we all used to use at the height of the freezing fashion. Yet again they are cheap and easy to store but would be best for occasional rather than daily use.

Baskets for the top of saucepans

Separate steaming baskets and lids come in either aluminium or stainless steel; the metal being reflected in the price. It is best to use them in a saucepan of the same metal. I find that an aluminium one used in a stainless steel saucepan expands when in use and is then very difficult to remove from the pan. These baskets are usually at least as deep as a saucepan and therefore have plenty of room for vegetables; several different ones could be cooked together. Place those that take longest to cook, such as potatoes, at the bottom, then carefully layer the others in order. The top ones, being protected from the steam, will cook slowly so, with luck, all of them will be ready at the same time.

Metal steaming baskets usually come with ridged bottoms so that they will fit, with no air holes or wobbling, two, three or four different sizes of saucepan. The ridging does, however, mean that the diameter of the bottom of the basket is considerably smaller than the diameter across the top; this makes it difficullt to cook fish or chicken joints as they not only have to be overlapped or placed on top of each other but the decreasing diameter and the depth of the steamer makes it difficult to remove them after cooking. I would not recommend using them for a whole fish.

You would not be able to cook a soufflé in one because in order to leave enough steam holes free and uncovered, the diameter of the soufflé dish would have to be considerably less than that of the bottom of the basket. However, a pudding basin, with its small bottom diameter, would happily fit into one.

These baskets can also be used for pulses and placed over a good sized saucepan would make an excellent couscousière.

A ridged bottom steaming basket is considerably cheaper than a complete stacking set, and, if you are into vegetables more than other forms of steamed food, one of these would be practical, long-lasting and good value. You could otherwise, of course, buy a flat bottomed steaming top from one of the ranges I discuss in the section on stacking steamers and use it in a saucepan.

Stacking steamers

Innumerable ranges of saucepans now include a steaming basket, sometimes just one, sometimes two, sometimes with a ridged bottom or with a metal ring to fit it into different sizes of pan. These saucepans and steamers are sometimes sold as sets, and sometimes separately to enable you to make up the combination you require. They come in a variety of materials, stainless steel, aluminium or enamel being the most usual.

I can't describe in great detail all that are available, but I give comments on some, which may or may not be relevant to any particular make that you might find.

The cheapest I found was an Eastern European enamel saucepan with one basket and a lid. The diameter was small, just over 6in/15cm, but it came in various colours and seemed to be robust and exceedingly good value. It would not be practical for family cooking, but it would be adequate for vegetables or chicken breasts or salmon steaks for two.

The kitchen department of one chain store sells a very large diameter aluminium steamer, made in China and of the type frequently used nowadays in China rather than the much prettier bamboo baskets. It has a base and two baskets, and a diameter of 11in/28cm. This would work well for family cooking or larger amounts and one could easily curl a 3 or even 4 lb (up to 2 kg) fish into one of the baskets. It is not at all expensive but I slightly wonder how long it would last. It is made of comparatively light gauge aluminium and the bottom might quite quickly loose its flatness and start to wobble around on the stove.

Stacked stainless steel steamers are hard wearing and multi-purpose, the bottom part is most frequently sold as a saucepan with a choice of steaming baskets sold separately. They are sometimes packaged together as a steaming set and although this is cheaper than buying the items separately you will only be supplied with one lid to fit the top basket; if you then buy the extra two lids separately you will find that it will be more expensive. The quality of the stainless steel is yet again reflected in the price: the cheapest come with a saucepan with a plain aluminium base; the middle range with a sandwich base of aluminium and stainless steel (the more you pay the heavier the base will be); and the top range with a copper core or, most expensive of all, copper sandwiched between silver alloy which is in turn sandwiched between stainless steel.

None of the non-stick ranges of pans have steamer inserts and it is quite difficult to find steamer sets or inserts in the cheaper stainless steel ranges. I did in the kitchen department of a high street chain store find some German pans; the range was not large, but they were very good value and a separate steamer insert was available. There is also a widely distributed Norwegian make that has a steamer set; they do not sell inserts on their own.

A good quality heavy gauge stainless steel French make is widely available, but they are pricey. They have simple clean lines and clever handles that always remain cool. There are flat bottomed steamer inserts, often with a choice of one or two handles, in five different sizes. They also make a well thought out steaming set which consists of a fairly deep, two handled casserole with two steamer inserts to go over it. The inserts neatly balance into the pan below and then widen out to a larger diameter. The inserts are not so deep that you have to peer into them but hold quite enough for most purposes, although they would be a little shallow for a soufflé dish or a whole fish. The lid that is included in the set only fits the largest top basket but it seems to balance on either the casserole or the bottom basket, and even without a snug fit enables you to use the casserole as a saucepan or just to steam in the smaller bottom basket. There is an Italian range which is similar in price and design, but the range is not so large and the steaming inserts all have ridged bottoms.

I also found an expensive but impressive Swiss range in which the sandwich core, which one normally only finds on the base, is carried throughout the saucepan. This means that the heat conductivity is excellent and much akin to that obtained with a copper pan. The design of the saucepans and inserts is simple and sensible.

The Rolls Royce of pans is a very heavy professional gauge range from Italy with the sandwiched copper, silver alloy, stainless steel base. They also come at Rolls Royce prices and are a lifetime investment rather than something to buy, try out and then shove to the back of the cupboard. Yet again there is a choice of sizes and there is also available a separate ring to enable a steamer insert to fit a pan with a large diameter. These pans are functional looking and beautifully finished in a non shiny stainless steel. They also make an oval casserole or small fish kettle which I discuss in great detail in the section on fish kettles.

The stainless steel pans I have discussed are all high quality and should give long and good service. However, a look round any kitchen shop may reveal other makes, but check carefully before you buy; ask if the base is sandwiched and, if so, which metals are in it, pick the saucepan up to feel the weight and make sure that the lid fits properly. You may come across a large stainless steel casserole that has a perforated liner for steaming. This liner sits right on the bottom of the pan, and although it would be useful for lifting fish or vegetables out, it could not really be used as a steamer as there is no space underneath it for water.

In one specialist shop I found an imported American range of hard anodised aluminium, which is pure aluminium that has had its molecular structure changed by placing it in an electro-chemical solution and subjecting it to a current. The resulting metal is of a non-stick-looking grey colour, is very hard, much harder than most base metals and, like ordinary aluminium, has marvellous heat conductivity. The range is large and included four practical looking steaming inserts. Needless to say, it is expensive.

Saucepan ranges are becoming wider and much more versatile, giving many choices in many different sizes. It could be worth looking at several different makes, then choosing a range that you like, and adding to it bit by bit, as your cooking demands it or your bank balance allows it.

Fish kettles

Fish kettles come in aluminium, stainless steel or enamel and in various sizes. The biggest is about 40 in/100 cm long and is made of aluminium – it would be unbelievably expensive to have something of this size in stainless steel. Before the advent of foil a fish kettle was almost a necessity, but a large fish can so easily be wrapped up and cooked in a slow oven that fish kettles are now really only for the very enthusiastic and for those with storage space.

All fish kettles have a perforated steaming platform with handles at the side to make for easy removal of the fish. Traditionally a fish cooked in a fish kettle is poached; the fish is placed in the fish kettle with a court bouillon and is then simmered very gently until cooked. A well poached salmon is delicious, but if you do not have the time and inclination to make a proper court bouillon you can steam the fish. The trouble is that most platforms rest on the bottom of the fish kettle, meaning that you will either have to replenish the water frequently (do this with boiling water) or arrange some forks or spoons in the fish kettle to hold the platform off the bottom. If you do find an easy way of keeping the platform off the bottom you can then use your kettle for other forms of steaming and it would be marvellous for cooking for a party.

The Italian range I mention in the paragraphs on stacking steamers includes a lovely oval casserole or small fish kettle. It is 8 × 15 in/20 × 37 cm and has a basket with handles and a separate stand for the basket which holds it off the bottom of the pan. It also has a deep lid to give it extra height. It is the perfect shape and size for cooking a medium sized fish or a couple of trout and can be used as a multi-purpose steamer for vegetables, meat, fish, soufflés or puddings or as a casserole, saucepan or covered roaster. Its only drawback is its price.

Steam ovens

Steam ovens have been used commercially for some years, mainly for baking the long lasting, plastic wrapped loaf. One or two small, plug-in and portable domestic models are now available and I was quite impressed by one that I used, finding that the very wet heat that they cook with was excellent for fish, stuffed vegetables and soufflés. Provided the timings and oven settings were worked out, I see no reason why many of the recipes in this book should not be cooked in a steam oven.

Asparagus steamers

Around May every year there is a flurry of advertisements and editorial write-ups for asparagus steamers. Marvellous if you have a large and productive asparagus bed, but for lesser mortals who buy asparagus as a treat three or four times a year, perhaps rather an extravagant space-wasting pot to own.

These steamers do cook asparagus perfectly, can very easily be used for other vegetables, and, as the assistant in one shop pointed out to me, their shape means that they are perfect for use as a stock pot. If you are going to buy one I would recommend looking for one with a basket that has a small mesh and a reasonable clearance underneath it, making it easier to convert to a steamer. They come in different metals and in various sizes and depths. Those with a fine mesh basket are sometimes sold as asparagus/pasta steamers.

Pasta steamers

Pasta steamers can usually be doubled up and used as asparagus steamers. They are tall with a small diameter and excellent for cooking pasta. The height makes it easy to add spaghetti and the basket makes for very easy removal and solves the problem I usually seem to have of strands of tagliatelle or delicious little tortellini sliding irretrievably out of the colander and down the sink. Choose one that has a basket with a fine enough mesh to stop spaghetti escaping through it and to make it suitable for other foods.

Colanders or home-made steamers

There is no need to rush out and spend a lot of money on a steamer or steaming basket; you can always use a metal colander set into a saucepan, though if you do start to steam regularly you will probably then buy a steamer of some sort. You will need a saucepan of fairly large diameter and, needless to say, the better the colander fits the more effective a utensil you will have, but if there are gaps round the edge just stuff them with a 'J' cloth or damp tea towel. If possible, your colander should go well down into the saucepan, making it easy to fit the lid over the top.

Some of the colanders or strainers stocked by kitchen shops fit very snugly into a saucepan, but you might find that you already have absolutely the right combination in your kitchen cupboards.

Electric steamers

Perhaps the most convenient and easiest of the steamers available. An electric steamer is quite an expensive piece of equipment, but if you compare it with a good quality stainless steel tiered steamer its price is put into perspective. However, a stainless steel steamer can be used for other things – the bottom part is an extra saucepan – while the electric steamer is just a steamer.

The electric steamer undoubtedly has many advantages. It is large, and if you buy one with a domed rather than flat lid it has lots of clearance. The oval shape means that it can easily accommodate a 4 lb (2 kg) fish, a good sized chicken or a leg of lamb and its second tray (they are of the same size and interchangeable) is big enough to hold both potatoes and a green vegetable. Steam the potatoes for 10 minutes or so, then pile them up at one end, put the vegetable in the other end and continue the steaming.

The electric steamer has a thermostat, which keeps the water at a constant temperature and releases the cook from the endless task of checking and then turning the heat up or down. A problem I found with one electric steamer that I tried, was that the thermostat kept the water at a fast boil and there was no way of turning it down. This meant that everything cooked very quickly (more quickly than the timings I give throughout the book) and that there was really too much steam for the more delicate foods. This can be overcome by steaming foods such as fish, chicken or custards in the top basket; you can then steam the vegetables or potatoes in the bottom, or just leave it empty, as the space disperses the steam and reduces its strength.

One electric steamer that I tried had an alarm which went off if the water should boil dry; very useful, especially if you are steaming a pudding or something that takes a long time.

The one disadvantage I have found with an electric steamer is a slight difficulty when washing up the base. The trays are just like any saucepan and, if you are willing to give them the room, can be put in the dishwasher. The base, having the element inside it, cannot be immersed in water and the inside has to be washed with detergent and water while care is taken to stop it slopping down the sides or round the bottom. However, this is a minor inconvenience and one that is applicable to all electric kitchen equipment.

An electric steamer with its good sized oval baskets is suitable for family cooking or larger quantities of food. It takes up quite a lot of space if kept on the work top, and would be better in a larger kitchen. It would, conversely, be a very good piece of bedsitter equipment as complete meals can be cooked in one and it can be plugged in anywhere.

Chinese baskets

Bamboo Chinese baskets, from the small 3–4 in/7-10 cm to the most usual 7–8 in/18–20 cm, through to the large 11–12 in/28–30 cm diameter are, I think, very attractive and a real bonus among the clinical and sensible metals of other cooking utensils. They need to be set in water in a steady wok, and the water, when boiling, will bubble up in the centre under the basket. The woven lid of the basket is of an almost perfect design; the excess steam escapes through the weave giving no problems with dripping or condensation, but the escape is slow and does not seem to lower the temperature in the basket or increase the cooking time when compared with other steamers.

If you are into Chinese food one of these baskets is a must, for it gives the right feel and look to the food, but it is perfectly good for other forms of steaming and can be used for vegetables, fish or meat dishes or custards. They do not have much depth so you would not be able to cook a whole chicken, a soufflé or a steamed pudding in one.

The baskets are pretty if brought to the table, but make sure to stand them on a plate in case they drip through the bottom. They can be bought from a Chinese shop, but they are often stocked by kitchen shops. They need careful looking after and washing and slow drying after use (don't put one in a dishwasher), but their life is limited and they are perhaps more for occasional fun rather than everyday cooking.

Couscousière

The capacity of a couscousière is large and, when made in aluminium, often increased by having a bulbous shape. The large bottom part is used as a casserole to cook the vegetable, fish or meat stew and the top basket is placed over the simmering stew to steam the couscous itself. Couscousières are available in both aluminium and stainless steel, with stainless steel (especially if you buy one with an aluminium sandwiched base) being the more expensive but the most long lasting.

There is nothing to stop you using a couscousière as an ordinary steamer, but the bottom 'saucepan' part is large and it means boiling up a lot of water. This is wasteful for a single vegetable and probably only worthwhile if you are going to steam a pudding or something like a chicken, perhaps surrounded by vegetables. The bottom part of a couscousière can also be used for any stew or casserole and the meal can be completed by steaming vegetables, rice or perhaps a covered pudding in the top basket. If you do buy a couscousière it is quite a good idea to augment it with a petal steamer which could be used for small amounts of vegetables or put into the base to transform it into a double basket steamer.

All recipes serve 4 unless otherwise stated.

SOUPS

It is usual for the first chapter in a cookery book to be about soups. You may think that, in a book on steaming, the chapter is included entirely for the sake of convention. However, that is not so, for there are many soups that are as good, if not better, when made with steamed, rather than fried then simmered, vegetables.

Cold summer soups, especially, benefit from the use of young steamed vegetables, for the delicate tastes are retained and not masked by the flavour of butter or oil. Butter gives a richness to a thick winter vegetable soup but its flavour is inclined to jar, and sometimes coagulate, if used in a cold soup.

It also goes without saying that steaming is the ideal way of making soups for those on a low fat diet, and the only stage that needs omitting from most recipes is the initial frying of the vegetables: just steam them over stock, put them through a blender or food processor and season, or flavour as you wish.

I like soups that start with a recipe or a thought, are cooked to a plan and end with a definite flavour. I am frequently caught out, and I suspect a lot of other people are, by turning out all my leftovers, whizzing them up and landing up with a muddled tasteless mess. The recipes in this chapter all have a definite idea and flavour, and I hope that in their variety they will show how steaming and steamed vegetables can be put to effective and imaginative use in soup making.

Avgolemono – Greek Egg and Lemon Soup

This soup is a perfect candidate for the steamer; the rice is cooked in stock, the egg and lemon are added and the whole is steamed gently to thicken the soup with very little risk of it separating. If your steamer will hold a dish big enough to contain all the soup so much the better, but you can always heat up any remaining stock separately and stir the two together just before serving.

2 oz/50 g long grain rice
1½ pt/900 ml chicken stock
zest and juice of 1 large lemon
2 eggs
salt and pepper

Wash the rice, place it in a deep bowl with ¼ pt/150 ml of the stock and the zest of the lemon and steam it for 12–15 minutes or until it is just al dente and most of the stock has been soaked up by the rice.

Beat the eggs and lemon juice together and add them to the rice with as much of the remaining stock as the steaming bowl will hold. Steam until the soup is hot; if the added stock was warm this will take 5–8 minutes and if cold, rather longer—up to 15 minutes. Stir and check the seasoning before ladling it into hot bowls.

Cold New Potato Soup
with Raw Tomato and Basil

I like the mixture of cooked and raw, and it goes without saying that the soup improves with the use of really sweet and fresh tomatoes. If you want a smoother, richer soup you can replace a proportion of the stock with single cream; if you do that you may find that this recipe is enough for 6 people.

12 oz/375 g new potatoes
3 shallots, peeled
1 pt/600 ml chicken stock
salt and pepper
8 oz/250 g tomatoes, peeled and deseeded
4 tablespoons double cream
a few fresh basil leaves, shredded

Wash the potatoes and put them on to steam. After 15 minutes lift the lid, salt the potatoes and add the shallots. Continue steaming for another 15–20 minutes or until they are both cooked. Leave the vegetables to cool a little, then using a sharp knife scrape the peel off the potatoes. Either put the potatoes and shallots through a mouli or process them with a little of the stock in a food processor or blender. You should finish up with a very smooth purée. Stir the purée into the remaining stock, season to taste, and put the bowl, covered, in the coldest part of the refrigerator.

Cut the tomatoes into cubes and stir them, reserving a few cubes for decoration, into the soup. Serve the soup in individual dishes decorated with a swirl of cream, the reserved tomato cubes and the shredded basil leaves.

Variation

The basic potato and shallot soup is also good served hot with a large bunch of finely chopped parsley stirred or, even better, processed into it.

Cucumber Soup with Dill

A thin soup that is at its best eaten ice cold on a hot summer's evening; preferably sitting outside, surrounded by the sight and smell of roses, sweet geraniums and herbs. However, in cold, wet and windy circumstances you can serve it hot but, if you do so, it improves if it is thickened as described below with a little beurre manié.

1 large or 2 small cucumbers
6 small or 3 large spring onions
1½ pt/900 ml light chicken stock
salt and pepper
3 fl oz/75 ml thick Greek style yoghurt
bunch of fresh dill, or 1 teaspoon dried dill weed

Peel the cucumber and cut it into chunks, and trim the outside leaves from the spring onions. Use the stock as your steaming liquid and steam the cucumber and onions for 18–20 minutes by which time the onions should be soft. Purée the vegetables in a food processor or blender, then stir them into the stock and season to taste. If the stock has reduced a lot and the flavours have concentrated you may need to dilute it with a little water. Refrigerate until very cold. Serve in bowls with a swirl of yoghurt, sprinkled with dill, in the centre of each one.

To serve hot: make a beurre manié by working ½ oz/15 g plain flour into 1 oz/25 g butter. Heat the soup to a simmer and drop the paste into it in pieces the size of a hazelnut. Whisk constantly to allow it to melt and thicken the soup. Stop when you feel the soup is thick enough and serve it piping hot with the yoghurt and dill.

Chilled Beetroot and Cucumber Soup

A lovely cold soup with, like all beetroot dishes, a ravishing colour. The stock or base should taste fairly strongly of beetroot and its slight sweetness is set off well by using raspberry or other fruit vinegar.

1 lb/500 g raw beetroot
4 oz/125 g onion
2 pt/1.2 litres light beef or chicken stock
½ cucumber
3 tablespoons fruit or wine vinegar
salt and pepper
3 tablespoons sour cream or yoghurt
1 tablespoon horseradish

Garnish
snipped chives (optional)

Peel 12 oz/375 g of the raw beetroot and the onion and either grate them or chop them finely and add them to the stock in the base of your steamer. Wash the remaining beetroot and steam them above the stock for up to an hour or until cooked.

Strain the stock, pressing as much water out of the vegetables as you can; discard the vegetables. You should have just over 1 pt/600 ml stock and if there is less you can make it up with more plain stock or water. Run the steamed beetroot under cold water and peel it. Cut 4 slices from the cucumber and keep them in cling film to use as a garnish. Peel the rest of the cucumber, deseed it and grate both it and the beetroot. Add the vinegar to the cooled stock, season it, stir in the beetroot and cucumber and refrigerate until needed.

Mix the sour cream or yoghurt with the horseradish and season with salt and pepper. Serve the soup in bowls with a tablespoon of the sour cream mixture in the centre, topped with a slice of cucumber and, if you have them, a few snipped chives.

Asparagus Soup

For soup, you can buy the cheaper, loose ungraded asparagus: ½ lb/250 g makes a good soup for four people, 1 lb/500 g makes a memorable one. If you are making the Asparagus and Crème Fraîche Tartlets (p. 126), which use only the top 2–3 in/5–7 cm of the spears, use the ends with a few whole spears and the steaming water to make this soup.

½–1 lb/250–500 g asparagus
2 shallots or spring onions, chopped
1½ oz/40 g butter
1 oz/25 g flour
salt and pepper

Cut any woody stems from the asparagus, wipe it clean and steam it (see p. 125) until tender. Carefully strain the water, measure it and, if necessary, make it up to 1¼ pt/750 ml by the addition of some light chicken stock or water. Cut the tips from the asparagus and put on one side.

Sauté the shallots or spring onions in the butter. When the onions are transparent stir in the flour, then gradually incorporate the steaming liquid and season with salt and pepper. Stirring continuously, bring it to the boil and simmer for 5 minutes. Add the asparagus stalks, simmer for a further 5 minutes and leave to cool slightly. Strain off most of the liquid and reserve, then purée the remainder in a food processor or blender. Strain the purée through a fine sieve, rubbing hard with a wooden spoon so that everything other than the stringy bits goes through, stir in the reserved liquid and keep until needed.

Just before eating slowly reheat the soup, checking the seasoning and adding the reserved asparagus tips no more than 5 minutes before serving.

Summer Vegetable Soup

The chopped mixed vegetables in this soup could be cooked in water with the tomato purée just being stirred in at the last minute, but I like to cook them in the steamer, for it gives one more control and makes it easier to finish with each vegetable just cooked but slightly crisp.

The pesto does give the soup a nice lift. When fresh basil is unobtainable an acceptable substitute is to use a little jar of ready made pesto.

2 small carrots
2 small courgettes
3 spring onions
4 oz/125 g french beans
5 tomatoes
1 tablespoon tomato purée
salt and pepper
pesto
12 large basil leaves
1 oz/25 g pine nuts or walnuts
1 clove garlic
2 tablespoons olive oil
½ oz/15 g butter
1 oz/25 g Parmesan cheese, grated

Peel the carrots and chop them and the courgettes quite finely, you can do this in a food processor, but keep the vegetables separate. Chop the spring onions and top and tail the beans, de-string them and cut them into ¼–½ in/5 mm–1 cm lengths.

Set the steamer to boil and start by steaming the tomatoes for a minute or so, peeling them, then deseeding and roughly chopping them. Steam the vegetables individually, until they are just cooked. The carrots and green beans will take about 5 minutes, the onions 3–4 and the courgettes only 2.

Take about 1 pt/600 ml of the steaming water (if there is not enough, make it up with plain water) and stir the tomato purée into it. Just before serving heat the liquid to nearly boiling point, stir in the vegetables and leave them for 2 minutes to heat through. Eat it immediately or the vegetables will cook further and loose their fresh taste and crispness.

Make the pesto by buzzing everything together in a food processor or blender; if you use a processor you may find that the small quantity means that you have to stop it once or twice to scrape it down. You can either stir some pesto into the soup just before serving it, or hand it round separately so that everybody can add as much or as little as they like.

Celeriac and Red Pepper Soup

This carrot-coloured soup has an interesting flavour and is really for eating hot in the winter. However, should you find celeriac still in the shops during a warm spell in May, it would be nice to eat it cold with a good swirl of yoghurt or sour cream.

1 celeriac, about 1 lb/500 g
1 medium potato
½ small red pepper
1 clove garlic
salt and pepper
yoghurt or sour cream

Peel the celeriac and the potato and cut them into cubes. Cut the red pepper into 3 or 4 strips. Put the celeriac, potato, red pepper and unpeeled garlic to steam for about 10 minutes or until the celeriac and potato are soft.

Remove the skin from the red pepper (it should come away quite easily) and peel the garlic. Purée all the vegetables together with a little of the steaming water in a food processor or blender, then rub them through a fine sieve. Add more of the steaming water and, if necessary, plain water, to make the volume up to about 1¾ pt/1 litre and season with salt and pepper.

The soup should be served piping hot with a swirl of yoghurt or sour cream.

Sorrel (or Watercress) and Yoghurt Soup

Sorrel soup is one of the joys of the herb gardener, for unfortunately it never seems to be grown and sold commercially. However, a very good soup can be made using watercress as a substitute.

The yoghurt will need to be stabilized, which is not difficult, to prevent it curdling when heated in the soup.

½ pt/300 ml natural yoghurt
2 teaspoons cornflour
6 oz/175 g fresh sorrel or watercress, picked over
1 medium potato, peeled and cubed
2 teaspoons sugar
salt and pepper
2 egg yolks
1 tablespoon milk

Stabilize the yoghurt by beating the cornflour into it and heating it slowly to boiling point stirring constantly. Simmer it, still stirring frequently, for 5 minutes, then remove from the heat and let it cool.

Steam the sorrel or watercress and the potato for 10 minutes, then purée in a food processor or blender with a little of the steaming water, the sugar, and salt and pepper.

In a saucepan whisk the egg yolks and the milk together and add the sorrel or watercress purée, together with a further ¾ pt/450 ml of the steaming water. Heat the soup, stirring all the time, until the egg yolks have cooked and slightly thickened it. Remove the pan from the heat, stir in the stabilized yoghurt, adjust the seasoning and bring the soup back to just below boiling point before serving.

Lightly Spiced Spinach and Lentil Soup

Spinach and lentils are a combination that is much used in Indian cookery and one that lends itself well to spices. You can spice this soup as much as you like or you could leave them out altogether. The amount of spices given doesn't make a very hot soup but if you are worried, add the spiced onion to the food processor or blender a teaspoon at a time, tasting as you go and stopping when you feel the soup is hot enough.

4 oz/125 g lentils
1 lb/500 g spinach
salt and pepper
5 cardamom pods
2 tablespoons sunflower or peanut oil
1 clove garlic, crushed
½ teaspoon ground cumin
½ teaspoon turmeric
⅛ teaspoon chilli powder
1 onion, chopped

Wash the lentils well and leave them to soak for about an hour. Meanwhile, wash and pick over the spinach—you can use frozen spinach which, like the fresh spinach, can be steamed in a top basket while the lentils are cooking. Drain the lentils, put them into a dish that will fit into your steamer basket, salt them and pour over about half their volume of water.

Put the lentils on to steam and, if you have second basket, wait for 10 minutes and then put the spinach, sprinkled with salt, on the top layer. The lentils will take about 30 minutes and the spinach 20.

While they are steaming you can make the onion and spice mixture. Crush the cardamom pods to open them, take out the seeds and crush. Heat the oil in a small frying pan, add the garlic and all the spices and let them sizzle for a few moments before stirring in the onion. Leave it to cook for 10 minutes or so until the onion is cooked and very soft.

Turn the cooked lentils and spinach and the onion mixture into a food processor or blender (you will probably need to process it in two batches) and process until they are smooth. Turn it into a bowl and stir in enough of the steaming water to bring the volume up to about 2 pt/1.2 litres. Check the seasoning and either serve immediately or reheat when needed.

Jerusalem Artichoke Soup

A simple soup made in a simple way, but one that seems to preserve the flavour. It is both warming and filling if served with some freshly fried croûtons.

1 lb/500 g Jerusalem artichokes
1 pt/600 ml light chicken stock, or mixed stock and steaming water, or milk
2–3 tablespoons chopped parsley
salt and pepper

Prepare the artichokes and steam them, using whichever method you prefer (p. 124).

In a food processor or blender purée the artichokes with a little stock or steaming water. If it is necessary to eliminate any pieces of skin, sieve the purée. Pour the purée into a bowl and stir in the remaining liquid and the parsley and finally season it with salt and a good grinding of black pepper. Cover the bowl and reheat when needed.

EGGS

Eggs, particularly when served as a separate course, need to be cooked very carefully and very gently. A bain marie in the oven has been the usual way of cooking most of these dishes, but I think that a steamer does an even better job. The temperature of steam seems to be correct, the cooking is even, it is easy to look and check on progress and, of course, there is no need to heat up the oven. Oeufs en cocotte when cooked *au point* are quite delicious and I give instructions for cooking them in a steamer followed by three variations.

A custard also steams beautifully and remains very light. As well as the recipe for Petits Pots aux Courgettes and the Japanese mushi or steamed savoury custards given here, there are several sweet custards in the chapter on puddings (p. 187–203) and a savoury tomato one in the vegetable section on p. 166.

Eggs can easily be either soft or hard 'boiled' in a steamer and they take a little bit longer than in a saucepan of fast bubbling water. This means that the timing is not quite so crucial and makes it easier to obtain the perfect runny yolked egg which can be used for oeufs mollets or eaten from an eggcup for breakfast.

Oeufs en Cocotte

A great standby for a first course, but it is essential to get the cooking time right; the white should be set and the yolk runny. There are endless variations on this dish and you can put practically anything in the bottom of the ramekin before breaking the egg over it: leftover fish, minced chicken, tomato sauce, Danish lumpfish roe or, once in a lifetime, caviar.

I like the eggs plain and simple, as given here, or with perhaps a few chives snipped over the top just before serving them. If you have hungry people, large ramekins or small eggs, you may want to cook 2 each but if you do that remember to increase the steaming time slightly.

½ oz/15 g butter
4 eggs
salt and pepper
4 tablespoons double cream

Use the butter to grease 4 ramekins. Break an egg into each one and sprinkle salt and pepper over the top. Place the ramekins in your steamer (you may need to use 2 layers) and steam them for 3 minutes. Remove the lid and spoon a tablespoon of double cream over the top of each one, then steam for a further 3 minutes. However, if they seem to be cooking fast when you pour over the cream, check again after 2 minutes, or, if slowly, leave them for a further 4 rather than 3 minutes. Serve them immediately with lots of hot crusty bread and butter.

Oeufs en Cocotte Soubise

In this version I have cut down on the cholesterol by eliminating the butter and cream and replacing it with olive oil and using margarine to grease the ramekins.

a little sunflower margarine
1 Spanish onion
1 tablespoon olive oil
salt and pepper
4 large eggs

Use the margarine to grease the ramekins.

Peel and chop the onion and put it to sweat in a non-stick frying pan in which you have warmed the olive oil. Cook, over a medium heat, for about 10 minutes or until the onion is soft and yellowing, then season with salt and pepper. While it is cooking stir constantly to stop the onion burning and if really necessary drizzle on a little more oil, but try and keep the amount you use to a minimum.

Break an egg into each ramekin and sprinkle it with salt and pepper. Spoon a quarter of the onion mixture onto each egg and cover the ramekins with a piece of foil or cling film. Put them to steam, and check after about 5 minutes, pulling back the onion with a fork to see if the white has set and leaving them for a further minute or two if necessary.

Oeufs Fiesole

The rather fanciful name for this dish comes from the fact that it is really oeufs Florentine without the sauce. It makes a good light first course, which can be served either warm or cold, and is surprisingly quick and easy to make. It is cooked in spinach-lined ramekins and, if you only have a small steamer, they can easily be cooked one after another and then eaten cold.

Serve the spinach parcels just as they are, or decorate with a little peeled tomato, more spinach, a colourful nasturtium flower or some herbs.

20 small to medium spinach leaves
butter
4 eggs
nutmeg
salt and pepper
4 slices of brown bread

Wash the spinach leaves, steam them for 3 minutes and spread them out to dry on kitchen paper or a tea towel. Butter 4 ramekins well, then arrange 5 spinach leaves in each one so that the bases and sides are covered, and the ends of the leaves are hanging over the edges.

Break an egg into each ramekin, sprinkle it with a scraping of nutmeg, salt and pepper and fold the ends of the spinach leaves neatly over the top. Cover each ramekin with a piece of cling film or foil and steam them for 10 minutes. Cool the ramekins slightly and if the spinach has given off a lot of water use a piece of kitchen paper to mop it up.

Cut a round, slightly bigger than the ramekins, from the middle of each slice of bread, butter it and place it in the centre of the plate. Slip a knife round the inside of the ramekins and turn a spinach parcel out onto each round of bread.

Eggs Pasha

Another version of oeufs en cocotte, but this one is eaten cold. The lumpfish roe goes well with the eggs and makes a surprise as people dig into the ramekins—use either the black or the red variety. It also looks very fresh, the eggs being covered with a jellied cream which is topped with snipped chives and a little paprika.

2 oz/50 g jar lumpfish roe
butter
4 eggs
salt and pepper
3 tablespoons chicken stock or water
1½ teaspoons gelatine
¼ pt/150 ml double cream
1 tablespoon sherry
snipped chives
paprika

Divide the roe between 4 well-buttered ramekins. Break an egg into each one and sprinkle pepper and a little salt over it; remember the roe is salty. Cover each ramekin with a piece of cling film or foil and steam for 6–8 minutes. The eggs will go on cooking as they cool down so remove the ramekins from the steamer while the whites are still slightly translucent.

Leave the ramekins on one side until they are completely cold. Put the chicken stock or water into a small bowl, sprinkle the gelatine over it and put it in the steamer for a few minutes to melt. Let the gelatine mixture cool, but don't let it set, then stir in the sherry and the cream. Spoon it over the cold eggs and immediately sprinkle the top with some snipped chives and a little paprika. Leave to set and serve cold.

Petits Pots Aux Courgettes

A simple dish that is at its best in late summer when the tiny, firm and sweet tasting courgettes are available. I once tried making a less rich version with yoghurt and milk which was good, but did miss out on the lovely velvety smoothness that the cream gives it. If you try the yoghurt version you must stabilize the yoghurt to stop it separating; this is easily done by beating a teaspoon of cornflour into the pot of yoghurt and heating, as for Sorrel Soup (p. 27).

I have given instructions for steaming the custards in individual ramekins, and if your basket will only hold a couple, you can steam the other 2 on a second layer, but remember that they will take an extra 2–3 minutes to cook. You could otherwise make it in a larger oval or soufflé dish.

4 oz/125 g courgettes
salt, pepper and nutmeg
butter
4 eggs
¼ pt/150 ml single cream

Cut the courgettes into small dice, put them into a sieve, sprinkle with salt and leave them for half an hour or so for the juices to drain out. Rinse them under a tap and then pat them dry with a piece of kitchen paper. Butter 4 ramekins well and divide the courgettes between them.

Beat the eggs and cream together, season with salt, pepper and a good scraping of nutmeg and pour the mixture into the ramekins. Cover each one tightly with a piece of cling film or foil and steam for 12 minutes or until the custard has just set.

Chawan Mushi
(Japanese Savoury Steamed Custards)

In their quest for perfection and elegance in everything the Japanese have in their cuisine a small but important range of steamed or mushimono dishes. Chawan Mushi is one of the best known. It is served in individual lidded soup cups and eaten, unusually for a Japanese dish, with a spoon. The little cups themselves are very attractive and the dish is served hot and covered; the lid being removed by the diner who, when he has eaten, politely replaces it to show that he has finished. Nice as tradition is, mugs, or large ramekins, covered with foil are easy western alternatives.

The eggs are mixed with dashi, the seaweed and dried bonito stock that is used throughout Japanese cookery. This mixture is then poured into the soup cups, which already contain prawns, marinated chicken breast and mushrooms, often some decoration is added, then the cups are covered and put to steam until the custard has set.

Chawan Mushi is not difficult to make and a visit to a Japanese or oriental food shop, or some health food shops, should yield the ingredients needed. Dashi can be bought in little instant packets, which are perfectly acceptable, but you can make it yourself and I give instructions below. Strictly vegetarian health food shops won't sell dashi and, if you are making it yourself, they will only sell the kombu seaweed and not the dried bonito flakes; but you can make a light vegetarian dashi, following the instructions below and just using the kombu. You can replace the dashi with a light chicken or vegetarian stock and, although it might not be authentic, you could, especially for the vegetable mushi that follows, use a packet of instant miso soup, which is something that you might find in a health food shop.

You will also see that most of the ingredients can be replaced by an everyday European alternative. If you do this, you won't finish up with a Japanese dish, but you will have one that is light and pleasant to eat.

The prawns for Chawan Mushi should be uncooked, of the same type used in Chinese cooking (see Prawn and Beansprout filled Egg Skins, p. 181), but, if necessary, you could use large cooked prawns, either fresh or frozen and defrosted.

4 dried shiitake mushrooms or 4 medium fresh shiitake or other mushrooms
1 small chicken breast, skinned and boned (3–4 oz/75–125 g)
1 teaspoon sake, dry sherry or dry vermouth
1 tablespoon light soy sauce
salt
4 uncooked prawns, shelled and de-veined, or 4 cooked fresh or defrosted prawns
4 eggs
1 pt/600 ml dashi (see below)

Garnish

julienne strips or curls of lime or lemon zest

Put the dried mushrooms into a bowl of warm water and leave them to soak for an hour. Drain them, and, if you keep the water, it will make a good base stock for the vegetable mushi that follows or a mushroom soup. Cut away and discard any tough stems and cut each mushroom into two or three pieces. If you are using fresh mushrooms just cut off the bottom of the stems, wipe them over and cut them into two or three pieces.

Cut the chicken into cubes. Put the cubes into a bowl, sprinkle them with the sake, sherry or vermouth, the soy sauce and a little salt and leave to marinate for a few minutes. Sprinkle a little salt over the prawns.

Divide the mushrooms, chicken and prawns between 4 cups or ramekins. Break the eggs into a bowl, mix them lightly together but do not let them become frothy. Stir in the dashi and about ½ teaspoon salt. Pour the egg mixture over the ingredients in the cups and garnish with some julienne strips or curls of lime or lemon zest. Cover each cup and steam for 15–20 minutes or until the custard has just set. The finished custard will not be very firm and, in fact, this dish is often eaten as soup.

Dashi

½ oz/15 g kombu seaweed
½ oz/15 g dried bonito flakes

Put 1½ pt/900 ml cold water into a saucepan. Add the kombu and heat slowly. Just before it boils remove the kombu. Leave the water to come to the boil then remove the pan from the heat and lower the water temperature by adding 2 fl oz/50 ml cold water. Add the bonito flakes, return the pan to the heat but remove it the moment it comes to the boil. Strain the stock and use as required.

The Japanese then re-use the kombu and bonito flakes to make a secondary dashi which is used for simmered dishes and miso soups.

Put 2 pt/1.2 litres cold water into a saucepan and add the kombu and bonito flakes. Bring to the boil and simmer for 20 minutes or until the stock has reduced by about a third. Add a further ¼ oz/10 g dried bonito flakes and immediately remove the saucepan from the heat. Leave until the flakes settle, then strain off the stock.

Mount Koya Mushi
(Japanese Steamed Custards with Tofu)

This vegetarian mushi takes its name from the fact that Mount Koya is the base for the largest Buddhist sect in Japan. There is a version of this dish that has chicken in it, but as the Buddhist monks always adhere to vegetarianism, this must have been added by less strict visitors. Make it with dashi, without the dried bonito flakes if you want to keep it as a vegetarian dish, or use a vegetable stock or the water from soaking the mushrooms.

4 dried or 4 large fresh shiitake mushrooms
6 oz/175 g tofu
1 teaspoon sake, dry sherry or dry vermouth
2 teaspoons light soy sauce
1 carrot
8 mange-touts
4 eggs
1 pt/600 ml dashi or stock
salt

Garnish
mustard and cress and grated fresh ginger, or 8
little sprigs of watercress and julienne strips of
lemon zest

Soak and prepare the mushrooms following the instructions given for Chawan Mushi (p. 35).

Cut the tofu into cubes, put it in a bowl and sprinkle with the sake, sherry or vermouth and 1 teaspoon of the soy sauce and leave for a few minutes to marinate.

Peel the carrot and cut it into slices—the Japanese would groove the edges and cut the carrot slices into flowers or 'plum blossoms', which is not necessary but is aesthetically pleasing.

Top and tail the mange-touts and soften them and the carrot slices by steaming or cooking them in boiling water for 3 minutes. Keep on one side.

Break the eggs into a bowl and mix lightly to break them up, but don't let them become frothy. Stir in the dashi or stock, 1 teaspoon soy sauce and ½ teaspoon salt.

Divide the tofu and the vegetables between the cups, pour over the egg mixture, cover the cups and steam for 15 minutes. Remove the covers and place a few stems of mustard and cress and a little freshly grated ginger or 2 sprigs of watercress and strips of lemon zest on each one. Cover again and steam for a further 5 minutes or until the custard has set.

STEAMED SOUFFLÉS AND
SAVOURY PUDDINGS

Steamed soufflés are, to me, the great surprise of this book. My research, especially into books of the 1930s, produced several recipes for them, so, heart in mouth, I cooked one and have been doing so ever since. A steamed soufflé rises like a puffball but, I must admit, behaves as if pricked with a pin almost the moment it comes from the steamer. However, this doesn't seem to matter as they remain light and moist and retain their delicate flavour. A lovely example of this is Ambrose Heath's steamed oyster soufflé from his 1934 book *Good Savouries*.

Oyster Soufflé

Pound the raw flesh from a couple of small whitings. Melt two ounces of butter and mix with it an ounce and a half of flour. Cook it a little, and then moisten with half a pint of milk and the liquor from six large oysters. Whip well and when it is quite smooth, pour in half a gill of cream, whipping and cooking a little longer. Add the oysters, which you have bearded and cut into small pieces, season with salt, pepper and, if you like it, a hint of grated nutmeg, and add the yolks of three eggs, one by one, a very little anchovy essence and the pounded fish. Whip the whites of the eggs well, and add them as the last. Pour the mixture into a soufflé case, and steam for three-quarters of an hour.

Steaming is also a good way to cook a soufflé if you are going to layer it: the layers will remain in position and will be heated slowly and gently without being overcooked. Nancy Shaw, in her wonderful slim volume of 1936 *Food for the Greedy*, gives a lovely sounding recipe for a steamed sole soufflé layered with slices of cooked lobster and button mushrooms. Perhaps not for everyday eating, but why not try it for something special?

As well as savoury and a couple of sweet soufflés I have included some recipes for the equally old fashioned steamed savoury puddings. These puddings are quick and easy to make, and being the perfect supper dish for a hungry family are also ready for revival.

Soufflé dishes

In the soufflé recipes I have suggested a size of soufflé dish, but obviously the dish you use will depend on what you own and on what will fit into your steamer. As long as it is straight-sided and you fill it no less than half and no more than two-thirds full you can use any soufflé dish, just adjust the cooking time and perhaps the amount of mixture you make.

Soufflé dishes differ from cake tins in that they are measured by liquid capacity and not by diameter. This is because they vary in height, and an 8 in/20 cm soufflé dish could have a capacity of 1½ pt/900 ml, 2 pt/1.2 litres or 2½ pt/1.5 litres. Whether you need a shallow or deep one will be dictated by the diameter and height of your steamer. An electric steamer will take quite a large soufflé dish, but a deep saucepan insert is probably better, as you must leave room for the soufflé to rise. If using Chinese baskets you will need the large 12 in/30 cm diameter ones, as the smaller ones do not have the necessary height between the layers or under the lid.

All the soufflé mixtures, as is suggested for the Swiss Soufflés and the Chocolate Soufflé, can be divided up and cooked in individual dishes: a good standard size, which holds nearly ¾ pt/450 ml, is 3¾ in/8.5 cm in diameter and 2½ in/6 cm high. Four dishes will fit into one or two of the larger metal steamers, an electric steamer, the large Chinese basket or a fish kettle. Otherwise use even smaller dishes, but you will need six or eight of them, as steamed soufflés rise well; however, if your steamer will only hold four of them it would be possible to whisk half the egg whites, use half the mixture and cook the soufflés in two batches, perhaps only practical if you plan to serve a cold soufflé.

You could always cook your soufflé in a large saucepan in much the same way as a steamed suet pudding. Place the soufflé dish on a trivet or upturned saucer in the bottom of the saucepan, with simmering water up to the bottom of the dish. If you do this, tie a piece of string around the dish and loop it across the top to make a handle, or you will have great trouble removing it when it is cooked.

When I am steaming soufflés I either cover each one with a very loose piece of greased cling film, which is not heavy, seems, if necessary, to expand with the soufflé and is also easy to peel off when the soufflé is served, or I put a tea towel over the top of the steamer or saucepan before fitting the lid. This catches the steam and stops the condensation dripping back into the soufflés, while enabling them to rise above the level of the dish.

Cheese Soufflé

I have not specified a variety of cheese in the list of ingredients, as this is very often dictated by what is in the house. You must, however, use a hard cheese and here are some suggestions. Cheddar, especially a strong one, can be very good, or use half Cheddar and half Double Gloucester to give the soufflé a lovely tawny colour. For a different and slightly dryer taste use two-thirds Cheddar and one-third Parmesan. Gruyère is nice, but best of all, I think, is a Gruyère/Parmesan mixture, especially for the little Swiss Soufflés given below.

Serve the soufflé plain, perhaps with a salad on the side, or turn it out and serve with a tomato sauce. Another way, which is especially nice for the individual soufflés, is to sauté some fresh spinach with butter, seasoning and garlic. It can then be arranged on individual plates in a circle round each soufflé.

2 oz/50 g butter plus extra for greasing the soufflé dishes
1½ oz/40 g flour
½ pt/300 ml milk
4 oz/125g cheese, grated
4 eggs, separated
salt, pepper and nutmeg

Well grease a 2 or 2½ pt/1.2 or 1.5 litre soufflé dish or some smaller ones.

Melt the butter in a saucepan, add the flour, mix well and cook it gently for 2 minutes without letting it brown. Turn the heat up a little and gradually add the milk. Whisk constantly and cook until the sauce is thick and smooth. Take the saucepan off the heat, stir in the cheese and season with salt, pepper and some freshly grated nutmeg. Leave to cool slightly before adding the egg yolks. Whisk the egg whites until they are stiff, but not dry, and using a metal spoon fold them into the cheese mixture.

Pour the mixture into the prepared dish or divide it between the smaller dishes, cover with a loose piece of greased cling film, or put a tea towel over the top of the basket, and steam for 35–40 minutes for a large soufflé or 20–25 minutes for smaller ones.

Swiss Soufflés

These little soufflés make a delicious luncheon dish or first course for a winter dinner. The quantities given are enough for six. As the soufflés are turned out you may find it easiest to line each dish with cling film and then brush the inside with a little oil.

You can make the soufflés ahead of time, turn out when cold and cover with the cream. They may take a minute or two longer under the grill, but the result is equally good.

Cheese Soufflés as above, cooked in 6 small dishes.

Sauce

beurre manié made with 1 oz/25 g butter and ½ oz/15 g flour
½ pt/300 ml crème fraîche (p. 126) or double cream
1 oz/25 g Gruyère cheese, grated
salt and pepper

Make the Cheese Soufflés following the recipe above. While the soufflés are steaming, make the beurre manié by softening the butter with a wooden spoon, then working in the flour to obtain a paste. Make the sauce by heating the cream and whisking in, bit by bit, the beurre manié; continue to cook and stir until the sauce is thick and smooth. Season to taste.

Turn the cooked soufflés out into a well greased ovenproof dish, pour over the sauce and sprinkle the cheese over the top. Put it under a grill for 5 minutes. Serve the soufflés immediately while the golden brown top is still bubbling.

Jerusalem Artichoke Soufflé

When I revised Marika Hanbury Tenison's book *Magimix Cookery*, I added a recipe for a Jerusalem Artichoke Soufflé which I thought was very good and very subtle. Steamed, it is even better, as the artichokes give a wonderful flavour to this moist and light soufflé.

12 oz/375 g Jerusalem artichokes
2 oz/50 g butter plus extra for greasing the dish
1½ oz/40 g flour
7 fl oz/200 ml milk
4 eggs, separated
salt and pepper

Peel the artichokes and steam them for 15–20 minutes (p. 124) or until they are soft. Purée them in a food processor or blender or push them through a sieve.

Well grease a 2½ pt/1.5 litre soufflé dish.

Melt the butter, stir in the flour and cook for a minute or two before slowly adding the milk, stirring constantly. When it is thick and smooth take it from the heat and stir in the artichoke purée followed by the egg yolks. Season with salt and pepper. Whisk the egg whites until stiff and using a metal spoon fold them into the artichoke mixture.

Pour the mixture into the prepared soufflé dish and steam, either covered with a loose piece of cling film or with a tea towel under the lid, for 35–40 minutes. Serve immediately.

Cold Gruyère Soufflé

When I first made this I watched in dismay as it slowly sank back into the dish from the immense heights it had achieved while steaming. I firmly decided that it would be like a piece of lead and only fit for the dustbin, but then, having nothing else in the house, I had to be brave and give it to a friend for lunch. She promptly asked for the recipe!

Served with salad it makes a good lunch dish or it would happily replace the cheese course at a dinner party. Some people would like it with a tomato sauce, but I am never very keen on adding a strong flavour to what is essentially a delicate one and prefer it as given, dusted with Parmesan and parsley.

6 fl oz/175 ml milk
1 bay leaf
5 black peppercorns
1½ oz/40 g butter
1 oz/25g flour
3 eggs, separated
3 oz/75 g Gruyère cheese, grated
salt and a pinch of cayenne pepper
Garnish
1 teaspoon grated Parmesan cheese
1 teaspoon finely chopped parsley

Pour the milk into a small saucepan, add the bayleaf and peppercorns, bring it to boiling point, then remove it from the heat and leave it to infuse for 15 minutes or until needed. Well grease a 2½ pt/1.5 litre soufflé dish.

In another pan, melt the butter, stir in the flour and cook it, but don't let it colour, for a couple of minutes. Slowly add the strained milk and keep stirring until it is smooth and thick. Take it off the heat and quickly and thoroughly beat in 1 egg white; added like this it acts as an additional stabilizer. Stir in the grated Gruyère followed by the egg yolks and season with salt and a pinch of cayenne.

Whisk the remaining egg whites until they are stiff and fold them into the cheese mixture. Pour it all into the prepared soufflé dish, cover with a very loose piece of cling film, or use a tea towel under the lid, and steam for 25 minutes.

Leave the soufflé until cold, then refrigerate until just before you are going to serve it. Turn it out and sprinkle the Parmesan and parsley, which have been mixed together, over the top.

Soufflé filled with Shrimps in Rouille

This soufflé has what can only be described as a choux pastry base, the difference being that two of the egg whites are whipped and folded in just before cooking.

I have given instructions for making a mild rouille, but if you like it stronger, you can always add more garlic, replace some of the red pepper with a chilli, or add some chilli powder.

soufflé

¼ pt/150 ml milk
½ oz/15 g butter
scant 2 oz/50 g plain flour, sifted
2 oz/50g strong Cheddar cheese, grated
3 eggs (2 separated)
salt and pepper

filling

1 small red pepper
½ slice of bread
1 large clove garlic, crushed with a little salt
3 tablespoons olive oil
4 oz/125 g shrimps, cooked and peeled

First make the filling: cut the pepper into quarters, discard the stalk and any seeds and steam it for 5–10 minutes. Leave to cool slightly then pull off the skin and roughly chop the flesh. Soak the bread in water, squeeze it out and put it together with the pepper pieces, the garlic and 1 tablespoon olive oil into the bowl of a food processor or blender. Process until everything is very finely chopped, then add the rest of the oil, more salt if necessary, and process again briefly to amalgamate the rouille. Spoon the rouille into a bowl, add the shrimps and stir to mix.

To make the soufflé: put a small saucepan containing the milk and butter onto the stove. Slowly melt the butter, then raise the heat and bring the mixture to the boil. Remove the pan from the stove, quickly add all the flour and beat until the mixture forms a smooth ball and leaves the sides of the pan.

Put the pan on one side to cool, then beat in the cheese, the whole egg and 2 egg yolks and season with salt and pepper. Whisk the remaining 2 egg whites until they are stiff, and fold them in. Transfer half the mixture to a well greased 2 pt/1.2 litre soufflé dish. Spoon the shrimps in rouille into the middle—leave ½ in/1 cm round the edge and cover with the remaining soufflé mixture. Alternatively, you could divide it between smaller soufflé dishes.

Place the soufflé dish, covered with a loose piece of greased cling film, in the basket of your steamer, or cover the basket with a clean tea towel, put on the lid and steam for 25–30 minutes.

Spinach Pudding

This is more substantial than a soufflé but still very light. Test it carefully when the steaming time is up: the centre should be moist but not too runny.

1 lb/500 g fresh spinach or 8 oz/250 g cooked frozen spinach
2 shallots or 1 small onion, chopped
1 clove garlic, crushed
½ oz/15 g butter plus extra for greasing the dish
3 oz/75 g bread
3 eggs, separated
½ pt/300 ml milk
salt, pepper and nutmeg

If using fresh spinach, wash it and steam it for 10–12 minutes, turning it every 2 or 3 minutes. Drain it and, protecting your hand from the heat by wearing a rubber glove, squeeze it dry with either a 'J' cloth or about 3 thicknesses of kitchen paper.

Fry the shallots or onion, with the garlic, in the butter until they are soft and transparent. Put the bread into a food processor or blender and reduce it to crumbs. Add the spinach, egg yolks, milk, onion and garlic, season with salt, pepper and grated nutmeg and process until the spinach is chopped. (If you are using a blender you may find you have to remove the breadcrumbs, chop the spinach on its own and finally mix everything by hand.)

Whisk the egg whites until they are stiff, then fold in the spinach mixture using a metal spoon. Transfer it all to a well greased 2½ pt/1.5 litre pudding basin and either cover it with a loose piece of greased cling film or put it in the steamer basket and cover that with a clean tea towel before putting on the lid. Steam it for 50 minutes.

Sweetcorn Pudding

A quick to make family dish using store cupboard ingredients. It is filling and the only accompaniment it needs is a mixed salad.

1 can sweetcorn (12 oz/375 g)
3 tablespoons milk
3 oz/75 g white bread
5 eggs
2 tablespoons double cream
1 medium onion, chopped
2 oz/50 g butter
1 tablespoon chopped parsley
salt and pepper

Drain the sweetcorn and mix the juice from the tin with the milk. Tear the bread into pieces, soak it for 10 minutes in the juice and milk, then mash with a fork or purée it in a food processor.

In a bowl beat together 3 of the eggs and the cream and keep on one side. Cook the onion in the butter, in a small frying pan. When the onion has softened, pour in the eggs and cream and cook, stirring continuously, until they are lightly scrambled. Take the pan from the heat and stir in the sweetcorn, the bread, the 2 remaining eggs and the parsley; season with salt and pepper.

Pour it all into a well greased 2½ pt/1.5 litre basin, cover with greased foil and steam for 50–60 minutes; the pudding should be set round the edge but still moist in the centre. You can serve it from the bowl or turn it out onto a plate.

Hot Chocolate Soufflé

A simple, rich and gooey chocolate soufflé which rises wonderfully and makes a dramatic end to a meal. If you like you can make it ahead, refrigerate it and serve it cold. It will have dropped from its risen height but will remain very light and taste like an especially good chocolate mousse. For a party you could, at the same time as the egg yolks, add a drop of brandy and/or a few brandy soaked raisins.

4 oz/125 g chocolate
2 oz/50 g caster sugar
4 eggs, separated
1 extra egg white
butter for greasing the soufflé dish

Well grease a 2½ pt/1.5 litre soufflé dish or four ¾ pt/450 ml soufflé dishes.

In a bowl over the steamer melt the chocolate, remove from the heat and add the sugar. Stir until the sugar has dissolved, then add the egg yolks, stirring gently to incorporate them into the mixture.

Whisk the egg whites until stiff, stir a third of them into the chocolate mixture and then very lightly fold in the rest. Pour the mixture into the prepared dish or dishes and cover loosely with a piece of cling film or foil. Steam for 15–18 minutes for small dishes and 20–25 minutes for one large dish.

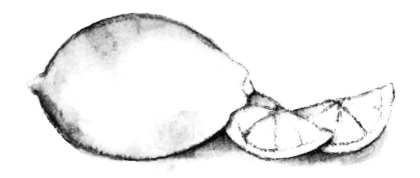

Soufflé aux Fruits

A delicious dinner party dish, but one that will take a minute or two in the kitchen between the first and main course. You can, of course, prepare the basic mixture ahead, but it will then need reheating, perhaps over the steamer, while you are whisking the egg whites, as they should be folded into a warm mixture.

4 sponge fingers
2 slices fresh pineapple, about 4 oz/125 g
2–3 tablespoons Kirsch
1½ oz/40 g butter plus extra for greasing the soufflé dish
1½ oz/40 g flour
8 fl oz/250 ml milk
3 eggs, separated
1 teaspoon vanilla essence
3 oz/75 g sugar

Well grease a 2½ pt/1.5 litre soufflé dish. Cut the sponge fingers into pieces about ¼ in/5mm long and put them in the bottom of the dish. Cut the core and peel from the pineapple, chop the fruit into cubes and put them in the dish. Sprinkle the Kirsch over the top and leave it to soak.

In a small saucepan melt the butter, stir in the flour and cook for 2–3 minutes before gradually whisking in the milk. Bring to the boil and continue to cook, stirring constantly, for a further 2 minutes. Take from the heat and leave to cool a little before adding the egg yolks and vanilla essence. Add the sugar to the egg whites and whisk them together until stiff. The whites will not come up quite as much as they would on their own; you will get a thicker mixture rather like an Italian meringue. Fold the mixtures together and steam, covered with a tea towel or loose piece of cling film, for 25–30 minutes.

Variations

This soufflé can be made with different fruits depending on the season; just remember to match the liqueur and the basic soufflé flavouring with the fruit that you choose: try fresh, stoned cherries and Maraschino, or an orange soufflé using skinned orange segments with an orange based liqueur such as Cointreau or Grand Marnier and the vanilla essence replaced with fresh orange zest.

For something more exotic, that would make a lovely change at Christmas time, use a mixture of thin slices of fresh mango and papaya. For this you will need a fresh tasting liqueur, perhaps a light orange flavoured one or Kirsch.

A ginger soufflé is also good. Add 2 or 3 chopped knobs of stem ginger to the sponge fingers, sprinkle over some ginger syrup and ginger wine. Add another finely chopped knob of stem ginger to the soufflé mixture and replace the vanilla essence with a teaspoon of the syrup from the jar.

FISH

Although nobody would deny that a fish kettle, which can be used to steam as well as poach fish, is the classic way to cook a salmon, the thought of steamed fish brings a grimace to many people's faces. As a method it is often inextricably linked in their minds with a plate of watery, overcooked cod which was at one time an inevitable part of school or hospital food. Things are improving, and many recipes are now being published for steamed fish, for it is cooked at what seems to be the ideal temperature, giving a lovely result which is moist, full of flavour and flakes perfectly.

A fish kettle, if you are lucky enough to own one, is the best utensil for any large fish, but it is not essential and a little bit of ingenuity will often solve the problem. There is a good story of

Brillat-Savarin who in 1822 went to dine with some friends in the country. They produced a large turbot but they had no turbotière (a fish kettle made exclusively for turbot in the diamond shape of the fish), and were worried about how to cook it. Brillat-Savarin refused to let them cut the fish in two, saying firmly that the turbot would stay whole until its presentation at the table, and he then went on to solve the problem. He cut a flat tray from a wine basket that had been made to hold 50 bottles, and then put a bed of onions and herbs onto it, placed on this the washed and seasoned fish and covered it with more onions and herbs. A lid was placed on the top and the whole thing was put over the copper in the laundry. The steam is said to have cooked the large fish gently and evenly and after 30 minutes it was 'à point et bien blanc'.

Now that a 'copper' as such hardly exists I am not going to suggest that you should swirl a fish round in your washing machine. However, you could, if you like, follow Prue Leith and cook one in the dishwasher, for she says that the hot water and steamy drying provide perfect fish-cooking conditions. But there are easier ways of cooking a fish and, if your utensil is small, you can cook it cut it in half, or even three, and then put it back together on the serving dish. Personally I agree with Brillat-Savarin and try to keep the fish whole; chiefly, perhaps, because I like the drama of producing it complete and beautiful on its dish. Wrapping the fish in 'J' cloth, as for the salmon or trout on p. 63, and then curling it round in the top of a large steaming tray or Chinese basket works well and a 5 lb/2.5 kg fish will easily fit into a 12 in/30 cm diameter basket.

If your fish is too big for any utensil you own you will have to wrap it in foil and cook it in the oven. Make sure that it has plenty of juice and butter with it and set the oven on a very cool temperature gas 2/150° C/300° F. Allow 12 minutes per lb/500 g for a fish of 5 lb/2.5 kg or over.

How to cook a large fish is, in most households, an infrequent problem and ways and means of cooking fish fillets, fish steaks or the smaller trout are more likely to exercise the cook's brain. Fish is one of the most versatile of foods and is nowadays treated with the respect it deserves, having re-established itself as food to be bought fresh, rather than in breadcrumbed rectangles. In this chapter I give a variety of recipes and ideas but it is worth remembering that very often there is nothing better than a really fresh piece of fish, perfectly cooked and served with melted butter sharpened up with a squeeze of lemon juice.

However, everybody likes a change and nouvelle cuisine is responsible for many of the exciting and different dishes that you will meet in restaurants or cookery books. The best of these are rather like a dress from Dior in that they have a perfect but simple base that has then been added to with thought, care and sophistication. Wonderful light mousselines in pretty colours spotted with herbs or green peppercorns are layered in terrines, wrapped in fillets or piped onto salmon steaks. Or the fish is accompanied by a sauce with a perfect texture and a subtle taste, being made with the addition of some unusual herb, fruit vinegar, nut oil or rice wine. But the simple, often steamed, base is rather like the little black dress, for it is the essential, never to be forgotten part of the whole, which keeps the delight and surprise of the dish without letting it go over the top.

Fish steaming times

These are suggested timings for fish or fish pieces that are put directly in the bottom layer of the steaming basket over simmering water. The steaming time is dictated more by the thickness than by the weight of the fish and firm fish such as salmon or sea bass will take longer to cook than delicate fish such as plaice. It is impossible to give totally accurate timings so before removing the fish from the steaming basket always check, using a fork, to make sure it is flaking and coming away from the bone. If the fish is placed in any sort of container, wrapped in foil, or if it is stuffed, laid on a bed of vegetables or steamed on a second layer, the cooking times will need to be increased. If you are steaming a large piece of fish or a whole fish it is a good idea to lay it on a piece of muslin or a 'J' cloth so that it can easily be removed from the basket in one piece.

Whole fish

Trout or whole fish (up to 10 oz/300 g)	
– to be eaten hot	1 minute per oz/25 g plus 2 minutes
– to be eaten cold (leave in turned off steamer until cool)	45 seconds per oz/25 g plus 2 minutes
Whole fish (11 oz-1 lb/350-500g)	1 minute per oz/25 g
Whole fish (1-4 lb/500 g-2 kg)	12 minutes plus 3 minutes per lb/500g
Salmon or large whole fish (4-7 lb/2-3.25 kg)	
– to be eaten hot	6 minutes per lb/500 g
– to be eaten cold (leave in turned off steamer until cool)	5 minutes per lb/500 g

Flat fish

Whole sole or plaice (10-12 oz/330-375g)	8-10 minutes

Fillets or steaks

(up to 8 oz/250 g)	1 minute per oz/25 g plus 2 minutes

Shrimp and Courgette Salad

An excellent salad which is quick and easy to make. The colours are very pretty and fresh looking, making it a perfect first course or lunch dish for a hot summer's day. Make the dressing with the best quality olive oil you can find and serve the salad with wedges of fresh bread which can then be used to mop up the juices.

8 oz/250 g fresh or frozen shrimps
8 oz/250 g small courgettes
salt and pepper
1 crisp lettuce heart
8 oz/250 g tomatoes
dressing
1 clove garlic
1 tablespoon lemon juice
1 dessertspoon wine vinegar
3 tablespoons olive oil
Garnish
2 tablespoons chopped parsley

If you are using frozen shrimps put them into a sieve and leave them over a bowl, for at least an hour, to defrost and drain. Cut the courgettes into strips about the size of a potato chip, put them into another sieve, sprinkle them with salt and leave them for 20–30 minutes to sweat out the juices.

Set the steamer to heat up and use it first to skin the tomatoes. Keep the water at a slow simmer; rinse the salt off the courgettes under a cold tap, steam them for 3 minutes, then rinse them again under cold running water to set the colour.

To make the dressing: crush the garlic into a bowl, stir in the lemon juice, vinegar, and oil; season, remembering that the courgettes will already be adequately salted. Halve the tomatoes, deseed them and discard any hard core. Cut each half into 6–8 pieces.

Add the shrimps, courgettes and tomatoes to the dressing and gently toss them all together. Arrange 2 or 3 lettuce leaves on each plate, divide the shrimp mixture between them and garnish with chopped parsley.

For a change you could arrange 3 lettuce leaves on each plate, placing separate piles of shrimps, courgettes and tomatoes on each one. Just before serving, drizzle the dressing over the top.

Fish and Vegetable Terrine

This terrine, with its rich mosaic of colours, makes an ideal dish for a buffet party. It also has the advantage of having no added butter or cream. The vegetables and fish are all steamed separately and then assembled and held together with a well flavoured fish jelly.

I have sometimes made it with the leeks quartered lengthwise and then laid down the terrine, but this makes it very difficult to cut into neat slices. The instructions therefore tell you to chop the leeks before assembly. Even so it can fall to pieces and the easiest way to cut it is to hold a cling film covered board firmly against the end of the terrine and to cut, using a sawing action, with a very sharp knife. You can then lift the board with the cut slice on it and slide it onto a plate.

serves 8–10

1 lb/500 g monkfish tail
12 oz/375 g salmon tail
1 lb/500 g fresh spinach
2 medium carrots, about 4 oz/125 g
2 leeks, about 8 oz/250 g
4 oz/125 g mange-touts
¼ pt/150 ml white wine
zest and juice of ½ lemon
1 shallot
salt and pepper
2 teaspoons gelatine
2 tablespoons dry vermouth or sherry
oil for greasing the terrine

Cutting lengthwise down the monkfish, remove the flesh in 4 fillets. Remove any grey membrane and keep the fillets on a plate covered with cling film. Skin the salmon, remove the flesh in fillets and, using a very sharp knife, slice them lengthwise to give you 8 thin pieces. Reserve them with the monkfish.

Prepare the vegetables: wash and pick over the spinach, discarding any tough stalks. Top and tail and peel the carrots. Wash the leeks well and cut off any tough outside leaves. Top and tail the mange-touts and destring if necessary.

Put the monkfish and salmon bones in the steamer bottom and add ¾ pt/450 ml water, the white wine, the lemon zest and juice and the shallot. Bring to the boil and simmer, very slowly for about 35 minutes, cooking in turn the vegetables and the fish over it.

Steam the spinach, sprinkled lightly with salt, for 12 minutes, turning it 2 or 3 times, then leave it to cool. Steam the carrots and leeks for 6 minutes, add the mange-touts, sprinkle them all with salt and steam for a further 12 minutes—the vegetables need to be well cooked. Remove the vegetables and leave to cool.

Squeeze the spinach dry and chop it roughly. Chop the leeks and cut the carrots lengthwise into strips.

Put the monkfish in the basket and steam it for 3 minutes. Add the salmon, keeping the fillets as flat as possible, and steam for a further 3 minutes. Remove the fish, which should be just cooked, return to the plate and cover with cling film. Strain the fish fumet from the steamer and keep on one side.

Measure out the fish fumet: you will need ½ pt/300 ml and if you do not have enough make it up with water. Put 2 tablespoons of the fumet into a bowl, sprinkle over the gelatine, set it either over your steamer or in a saucepan of nearly boiling water and stir until it has dissolved. Add the remaining fumet and the vermouth or sherry, leaving the bowl in the cooling water to keep if from setting.

Well grease a 2 pt/1.2 litre terrine or loaf tin, or use a non-stick one. Pour about a third of the fish jelly into the terrine or tin, put it in the freezer for about 20 minutes or until it has set solid. You can now assemble the terrine. The order I give here is just a suggestion, and you may well prefer to do it differently, thus obtaining a different juxtaposition of colours.

Lay half the salmon on the jelly and cover it with half the spinach. Follow this with a layer of leek interspersed with strips of carrot. Lay the monkfish fillets on top of this, with two thick ends to the middle and one to each end. Fill the gaps between the fillets with the mange-touts, then put in another layer of leek and carrot, followed by the spinach and on top the remaining salmon fillets.

Pour the remaining fish jelly over the terrine, cover it with a double layer of cling film and refrigerate for several hours or overnight. Turn it out by dipping it briefly in hot water and using a spatula to loosen it round the edges. Serve in slices.

An Italian Fish Salad

Italian restaurants often have a table, frequently placed strategically near an open door, on which there is a colourful array of *antipasti*. Dishes of crudités, marinated red peppers, Parma ham wrapped round little slices of melon and a seafood salad with squid, prawns and mussels glistening in a lemon and oil dressing.

The exact mix of fish will depend on what is in season or what your fishmonger has, but squid and a shellfish of some kind are considered essential. Serve it as a first course for 4 or alongside other *antipasti* at a party for more people.

1 lb/500 g mussels
12 oz/375 g squid
8 oz/250 g monkfish
4 oz/125 g prawns, cooked and peeled
3 tablespoons olive oil
1 tablespoon lemon juice
1 tablespoon chopped parsley and (if possible) summer savory or chervil
salt and pepper

Thoroughly scrub the mussels, pulling out any beard and discarding any that are broken or open. If your fishmonger has not prepared the squid, clean it and remove the transparent bone and cut off the head (p. 72). Keep the body whole and the tentacles in bunches. Leave the monkfish in one piece.

Steam the mussels for 5-7 minutes or until they open. Discard any that remain shut and leave the rest to cool.

Put the squid, including the tentacles, and monkfish to steam. Small squid will take 5 minutes and large ones a little longer so remove them with a slotted spoon when they are cooked. The monkfish will take 8–10 minutes, depending on how thick the piece is.

Cut the bodies of the squid into rings. Take the monkfish from the bone and cut the flesh into chunks and remove the mussels from their shells. Mix all the fish together and dress with the oil, lemon juice, herbs and lots of salt and pepper.

Scallop, Sole and Artichoke Salad

Scallops are always a treat and they steam very successfully. They are good served hot with a sauce such as beurre blanc (p. 60), but they are also satisfying to eat cold and make a good addition to a salad. The amounts given are enough for a first course, but, if you doubled the quantities, you could easily serve this as a light main course.

Fresh arthichoke hearts are, unless you have a kitchen garden, a once in a while extravagance, but tinned ones are acceptable and improve if they are soaked for an hour or so in vinaigrette. This salad should have at least 3 different sorts of greenery, and preferably ones with contrasting textures and colours; Little Gem lettuce, rocket and one of the leaves with a pink tinge are a good combination.

13 oz/400 g can artichoke hearts
selection of salad leaves
2 Dover or lemon sole fillets
4 large scallops with their corals
vinaigrette
2 tablespoons lemon juice
4 tablespoons olive oil
4 tablespoons sunflower or grapeseed oil
salt and pepper

Make a vinaigrette by combining the lemon juice with the oils and seasoning it with salt and pepper. Open the can of artichoke hearts (there will probably be 6 of them), drain them and put them in a dish. Pour the vinaigrette over the hearts and leave them to soak for an hour or so.

Arrange the salad leaves on 4 plates, leaving places for the fish and artichokes.

Skin the fish fillets and cut them down the centre, then cut each half into three. Wash the scallops, removing any muscle or black bits, and cut each one in half. Heat the steaming water to a very gentle simmer, and the steam the scallops and pieces of sole for 2½ minutes (check that they are cooked before removing) and the corals for 2 minutes.

While the fish is steaming take the artichoke hearts from the bowl, cut them in half and put 3 halves on each plate. Very carefully (you will probably need a flat fish slice) remove the fillets, scallops and corals from the steaming basket and arrange them on the lettuce and artichokes. Finally, spoon the vinaigrette over the salads.

Striped Fish Mousseline

It has almost become a requisite of any restaurant serving nouvelle cuisine to have striped fish terrine listed among its first courses and as a result it is a dish that is becoming both hackneyed and gimmicky. I find this sad for if it is properly made and simply served, with one sauce, and with no additions such as various feathery greens or citrus fruit slices, it can be one of the triumphs of modern food and food processor cooking.

The recipe I give below is simple, but it is not a dish to be hurried. To make a really light mousseline you need a mixture that binds properly and quickly and this will only happen if everything is properly chilled before you start. I find it worthwhile putting my food processor bowl and blade in the deep freeze for half an hour before I need it.

Eat the terrine in slices either warm with a beurre blanc (p. 60 but double the quantity) or cold when the slices can be arranged with one or two lettuce leaves dressed with a light sunflower oil vinaigrette.

serves 8–10

6 oz/175 g fresh spinach
8 oz/250 g skinned lemon sole fillets or a mixture of lemon sole and whiting
2 egg whites
salt and pepper
4 oz/125 g boned and skinned salmon
1 whole egg
¾ pt/450 ml double cream
oil for greasing the terrine
1 teaspoon green peppercorns (optional)

Wash and pick over the spinach, cook it (p. 162), squeeze it dry and refrigerate. Cut the white fish into cubes, put it in a bowl with the 2 egg whites, season with salt and pepper and refrigerate. Cut the salmon into cubes, put it in a bowl with the whole egg, seasonings and refrigerate. Refrigerate the cream.

Well grease a 1¾–2 pt/1–1.2 litre terrine or non-stick loaf tin.

Put the salmon and egg in the food processor and process for a minute or until completely smooth, then, with the motor running, slowly pour in ¼ pt/150 ml cream. The moment it has thickened stop the motor. Return the mixture to the bowl and refrigerate.

Put the white fish and egg whites in the processor and process for a minute or until completely smooth. Take out half the mixture and reserve. Turn on the motor and slowly pour in ¼ pt/150 ml cream and stop the machine when it has thickened. If you are using peppercorns, add them now and briefly pulse them in. Spoon the mixture into a bowl and refrigerate.

Make the green stripe by returning the remaining white mixture to the processor together with the spinach. Process until smooth, then add the final ¼ pt/150 ml cream. When it has thickened spoon it into the bottom of your terrine and smooth it over.

Spoon the white stripe over the green one, smooth the top and finish by adding the pink salmon stripe. Cover the terrine with a piece of greased foil and steam for 45 minutes.

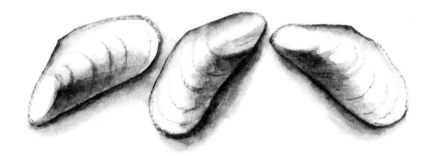

Scallop Mousselines with a Ginger Sauce

The delicate taste of scallops needs treating with respect for it can all too easily be overpowered and lost. However, the addition of a little bread adds some body and volume without disturbing the flavour of the dish. I have kept the cream content to a minimum, and the meal will need no more; the mousselines are best followed by something simple and straightforward such as Chicken and Tarragon (p. 89).

Ginger makes a nice addition to the sauce, but the flavour should remain in the background, so taste as you go; you can always add more with the cream and the egg yolk if you think it needs it. If you only have small ramekins the mousselines will cook very satisfactorily in well greased or cling film lined tea cups.

Before you start to make the mousselines, make sure that everything is very cold. If the weather is warm it is a good idea to put the food processor bowl and blade in the deep freeze for half an hour or so to cool it off before you start.

It is best to make the sauce while the mousselines are steaming, but it can be made first and then kept for a time in a bowl over hot, but not boiling, water.

4 large scallops, fresh or frozen and defrosted
2 oz/50 g crustless white bread
1 egg white
¼ pt/150 ml double cream
3 or 4 blades chives, finely snipped
salt and pepper
sauce
1 carrot
1 small leek or 3 spring onions
1 oz/25 g butter
1 heaped teaspoon finely chopped fresh ginger root
¼ pt/150 ml light chicken stock
3 tablespoons double cream
1 egg yolk

Trim the scallops and reserve the corals on one side. In your food processor, process the bread until it is in fine crumbs. Add the scallops and egg white and process until you have a smooth purée. Through the feed tube, slowly add the cream, stopping the machine when the mixture starts to thicken. Add the chives, season with salt and pepper and process briefly to mix them in.

Divide the mixture between 4 well greased or cling film lined ramekins or tea cups, cover with foil or cling film and steam them for 18 minutes. Put the corals in to steam for the final 2 minutes or steam them alone when the mousselines are cooked and while you are turning them out.

While the mousselines are steaming, make the sauce. Peel the carrot and cut it into thin strips or use the julienne disc on a food processor. Trim the outside leaves from the leek or spring onions, then wash and cut into julienne strips.

In a small pan melt the butter and sauté the carrot, leek or onion, and the ginger for a minute. Add the stock (if you make it with a cube keep the stock light and only use a little), season with salt and pepper, bring it to the boil and let it bubble for 3 minutes or until the vegetables are just cooked.

Mix the cream and egg yolk together and off the heat add them to the vegetables. Reheat, stirring constantly, until the sauce starts to thicken but do not let it boil or it will separate.

Spoon the sauce onto 4 warmed plates and turn a mousseline out into the centre of each. Put a coral on the top and serve.

Salmon Filled Watercress Cake

This dish is loosely based on a filled roulade that used to be made as a lunch dish by Joanna Benson when we worked together for Magimix.

The watercress mixture is steamed in a cake tin, so check that you have one to fit your basket. A 7 in/18 cm tin will just fit into the middle sized bamboo basket or an 8 in/20 cm tin into an electric steamer. I give instructions for a cake to serve 8 people, with the watercress base being cooked simultaneously in 2 tins in 2 layers or, in 1 tin, half the mixture at a time; keep the second half cool and covered while the first half is cooking. You can, of course, cut the ingredients in half and make a one layered cake for 4 people, but if you do so I suggest that you use 3 small eggs or 2 very large ones.

serves 8

watercress cake

2 oz/50 g watercress, picked over

5 eggs, separated

salt and pepper

2 oz/50 g fresh breadcrumbs

salmon filling

1 onion, roughly chopped

1 carrot, roughly chopped

6 black peppercorns

12 oz/375 g salmon tail

1 sachet gelatine

½ fennel bulb

4 tablespoons sour cream

4 tablespoons light vegetable oil mayonnaise

4 tablespoons white wine

butter for greasing tins

Prepare 2 cake tins by greasing them well and lining the bottoms with silicone paper.

Chop the watercress finely, mix it into the egg yolks and season with salt and pepper. Whisk the egg whites until stiff, then gently fold them and the breadcrumbs into the watercress. Divide the mixture between the 2 prepared cake tins and steam for 10 minutes. Cool slightly, then turn them out onto a clean damp tea towel, cover with another one and leave until you are ready to assemble the cake.

To make the filling: take about 1 pint/600 ml of water for your steaming liquid and add to it the chopped onion and carrot and the peppercorns.

Steam the salmon tail for 18 minutes, or until it is just cooked and will come away from the bone. Remove the skin and flake the flesh. Put the bones and skin into the steaming liquid and simmer for a further 15 minutes.

Take ¼ pt/150 ml of the fish stock, sprinkle on the gelatine, stir to dissolve and leave on one side to cool, but don't let it set.

Reserve any feathery leaves from the fennel, then remove any tough outside leaves and dice the rest. Mix the sour cream, mayonnaise and white wine together, add the salmon and fennel and season with salt and pepper. Just as the gelatine mixture is about to set stir it into the salmon mixture, then quickly spread half onto one watercress cake, top with the other one and 'ice' it with the remaining mixture. Leave in a cool place and just before serving decorate the top with the reserved leaves.

Sole Fillets
with a Salmon Mousseline Stuffing

A frankly extravagant dish, but if you don't want to push out the boat too much it can be made with lemon rather than Dover sole fillets. The stuffing only uses a little salmon and it is worth looking out for a tail piece, which most fishmongers sell off comparatively cheaply and will also very often bone and skin for you.

4 small Dover or lemon sole fillets, skinned
4 oz/125 g salmon
1 large egg white
¼ pt/150 ml double cream
salt and pepper
lemon juice
beurre blanc
4 tablespoons dry white wine
4 tablespoons white wine vinegar
2 shallots, peeled and very finely chopped
8 oz/250 g very cold butter

Cut the salmon into chunks, put it into a bowl with the egg white and refrigerate until it is very cold. At the same time make sure that the cream is also in the coldest part of the refrigerator.

Turn the salmon and egg white into a food processor, season well with salt and pepper and a squeeze of lemon juice and process until smooth. With the machine running slowly pour the cream in through the feed tube and continue processing until the mixture thickens. Return the mousseline to the refrigerator and leave until needed. If it has not thickened enough to hold together, put it into the freezer for 10 minutes or so, (do not let it actually freeze) then process it again, when it should thicken properly.

Wash the fish fillets, pat them dry with kitchen paper and spoon a quarter of the mousseline onto each one. Carefully roll each fillet up and secure with a cocktail stick. Steam for 12–15 minutes, depending on the size of the fillets. Test by checking that a skewer inserted into the centre of the mousseline comes out clean.

Serve on individual plates and show up the colours by cutting each fillet into slices before spooning the sauce onto the side.

Beurre blanc

Put the wine, vinegar and shallots into a small, heavy and preferably copper saucepan. Bring to the boil, then, keeping the liquid at simmering point, no hotter, reduce it until you have about a tablespoon left. At this stage you can, if you wish, strain out the shallots, but if you do so, push very hard with a wooden spoon to squash out the liquid. Cut the butter into cubes and, over a very low heat, whisk them in one by one, watching to make sure that the sauce homogenizes and becomes thick and creamy. If it does start to become oily, plunge the bottom of the pan into a bowl of cold water and whisk hard to make it re-emulsify. Check for seasoning and serve.

Salmon steaks
with a Dill and Mustard Sauce

Gravad lax, or marinated salmon, with a slightly sweet dill and mustard sauce has become fashionable and is now easily available in many supermarkets. Hot fresh salmon steaks served with a sauce based on the same flavourings are very good or you can steam the steaks and serve them cold with the mayonnaise-based sauce; I give recipes for both sauces, the hot one with yoghurt being very simple. If you prefer something richer you could make a beurre blanc (p. 60), sweeten it with honey and flavour it with dill and mustard. You can, at a pinch, use dried dill weed, but fresh or frozen dill is just that much better.

New potatoes go beautifully with this dish and help to mop up the sauce. Steam them first and keep them covered in a low oven or steam them at the same time in a top basket.

4 salmon steaks
several sprigs of dill
salt and pepper
hot dill and mustard sauce
1 tablespoon Dijon or mild French Mustard
1 tablespoon sherry or port
1 tablespoon honey
small bunch dill
¼ pt/150 ml thick natural yoghurt
cold dill and mustard sauce
1 egg yolk
1 tablespoon Dijon mustard
2 tablespoons white wine vinegar
7 fl oz/200 ml light oil (sunflower or grapeseed)
1 tablespoon honey
small bunch dill

Lay 1 or 2 sprigs of dill in the steaming basket. Sprinkle the salmon with salt and pepper, place it in the basket and cover with the remaining dill. Follow the timings on p. 51 to steam it. Remove the cooked salmon and serve immediately (skinned and boned if you wish) or keep it covered and refrigerated until needed, then remove the skin and bones. Decorate with a sprig of dill.

Hot dill and mustard sauce

Mix together the mustard, sherry or port and honey and warm them in a small saucepan. Reserving 4 sprigs for decoration, chop the dill and stir it and the yoghurt into the saucepan. Season with salt and pepper and heat until warm, stirring constantly; do not let it get too hot or the yoghurt will separate. If you want more sauce, or a thinner sauce, you can stir in a little of the steaming liquid.

Cold dill and mustard sauce

Cream the egg yolk together with the mustard and vinegar, then slowly, as if making mayonnaise, drip and whisk in the oil. Reserving 4 sprigs for decoration, chop the dill and add it, the honey and salt and pepper to the sauce.

Turbot with Saffron, Tomato and Basil

A dish full of colour and flavour, especially if you use the tiny, sweet tasting 'Gardener's Delight' or cherry tomatoes: if they are unavailable you can use large tomatoes but they will need peeling, deseeding and cutting into cubes.

Saffron is expensive but you only need ½ teaspoon of the shreds. Powdered saffron is to be looked on with caution as it is very often made from the stamens of marigold rather than those of the crocus, but you can, and they are well worth buying, sometimes find Italian packets of 125 mg of powdered zafferano puro.

In the last few years basil has become *the* fashionable herb and this has led to the welcome spin off of it being available for a large part of the year. In the summer many garden centres sell plants in pots, and it is not that difficult and well worth the effort to grow from seed yourself. Keep it in a sunny window or a sheltered spot outside. I have several pots of it just outside my kitchen door, where it not only smells good but deters the flies. Basil is essentially a herb of the summer and the sun and does not dry well, but it does freeze and if you should happen to have a surplus it is well worth wrapping it carefully and putting it into the freezer.

four 4 oz/125 g turbot fillets or 4 turbot steaks
1 shallot, peeled and finely chopped
small clove garlic, crushed
½ oz/15 g butter
salt and pepper
lemon juice
1 onion
¼ pt/150 ml white wine
½ teaspoon saffron shreds or 125 mg packet powdered saffron
¼ pt/150 ml double cream
8 oz/250 g Gardener's Delight tomatoes, peeled
handful of basil leaves

Fry the shallot and garlic gently in the butter until they are yellow and soft. Season with salt and pepper and stir in a good squeeze of lemon juice. Wipe the fish clean and, if you are using fillets, make sure that as many bones as possible have been removed. Lay the fish in the steamer basket and spoon the shallot mixture over them. If you are using a steamer with a small basket and fillets of fish you can always cut the fish into cubes, mix in the fried shallot and spoon it into your basket.

Quarter the onion and add it with any fish bones that you may have to the steamer base. Pour in a minimum amount of water, no more than ½ pt/300 ml; you aim to end up with ¼ pt/150 ml of stock that is as concentrated as possible. Bring the water to the boil and let it simmer for a few minutes before cooking the fish, but be careful not to let it boil dry.

Bring the wine to the boil in a small saucepan, reduce it by half and keep it warm on the side until needed. If using saffron shreds, crush them to a powder. Stir the saffron into the cream and leave it for a few minutes to release its flavours.

Follow the timings on p. 51 to steam the fish but remember that if it has been cut into cubes it will cook more quickly so test it after 3 minutes. Remove the fish to a dish, cover and keep warm.

Add ¼ pt/150 ml of the steaming stock to the reduced wine, bring it back to the boil and reduce it by half again. Add the cream and saffron and boil until it thickens. A minute before serving add the tomatoes (they should be warm but not cooked) and the basil, tearing it into shreds as you do so. Place the fish on individual plates and spoon the sauce around it.

Trout Stuffed with Cucumber & Dill

With its fresh tasting stuffing, the fish is equally good eaten hot or cold. Ask your fishmonger to bone the fish from the back or do it yourself. You can start by cleaning the fish through the gills, but I find that the way I give below, which I learnt from my local fishmonger, is easier and works well. Cut off the fins then, using a sharp knife, cut the fish all the way down the backbone. Cut the flesh away from the bone on one side and then pull out all the innards. Use the knife to scrape the inside clean, and use a pair of strong scissors to cut the backbone behind the head and at the tail. The fish will lie flat if you now cut along the back of the head, but this is not absolutely necessary. Continue by cutting down the other side of the backbone and then lift if out. Lay the fish out and run your fingers over the flesh to detect any bones that are left, removing them with your fingertips or a pair of tweezers.

You can then stuff the fish, steam it and cut it across in slices to serve it. It seems to go a long way and I found that a large 5½ lb/2.75 kg pink trout easily fed 8 people. You could otherwise use a salmon trout or a salmon.

Wrap the fish in muslin or a 'J' cloth. The cloth will hold the stuffing in place and make it easy to transfer the cooked fish from the steamer or fish kettle to the serving dish. If you plan to eat the fish cold, leave it in the cloth, which will keep it beautifully moist.

serves 8

1 trout, about 5½ lb/2.75 kg, gutted and boned (see above)
½ pt/300 ml fromage frais or thick yoghurt
½ teaspoon cornflour (optional)
½ an egg white (optional)
1 cucumber
salt and pepper
several sprigs of dill, snipped, or 1½ teaspoons dried dill weed

If you are using yoghurt it is best to stabilize it first. Mix it with ½ teaspoon cornflour and ½ an egg white, heat it slowly and then leave it to cool before use.

Peel the cucumber, discard the seeds and cut it into cubes. Put it in a sieve, sprinkle it with salt and leave it to drain for 20 minutes. Heat your steamer and steam the cucumber for 3 minutes or until it starts to soften. Drain it and mix it with the fromage frais or yoghurt and the snipped dill. Give a good grinding of black pepper and taste to see if it needs any more salt.

Lay the prepared fish out onto a 'J' cloth or piece of muslin. Spoon the stuffing into the fish, fold it over, and wrap the 'J' cloth or muslin round it. If you are not going to cook it immediately sprinkle some water over it.

The fish can be cooked curled round in a large steamer basket or stretched out in a fish kettle. A 5½ lb/2.75 kg fish (weight before gutting and boning) will take 30 minutes to cook, but adjust the time according to the size.

Transfer the cooked fish to a large dish or plate, unwrap it and very carefully pull the cloth from underneath it. If you wish, remove the skin. Cut the fish into slices and serve.

Lemon Sole and Salmon with Spinach

Another good but simple fish dish; a piece of salmon wrapped in spinach and then rolled up in a lemon sole fillet. The spinach leaves, after any stalk has been cut off, should be about the same size as the lemon sole fillets.

18 spinach leaves
3–4 oz/75–125 g salmon fillet, skinned
4 small lemon sole fillets, skinned
salt and pepper
sauce
1 shallot, peeled and finely chopped
1 oz/25 g butter
1 oz/25 g flour
2 tablespoons wine
¼ pt/150 ml fish or light vegetable stock
¼ pt/150 ml single cream
lemon juice

Wash the spinach, lay the leaves in your steamer basket and blanch them by steaming for 3 minutes. Remove the basket from the steamer and leave the spinach to cool.

Cut the salmon into 4 pieces.

To make the parcels: lay out the lemon sole fillets, sprinkle lightly with salt and pepper, then cover each fillet with 2 leaves of spinach. Lay out a further 4 spinach leaves, sprinkle with salt and pepper, put a piece of salmon in the centre and wrap the spinach round it. Place the salmon packet on the spinach covered lemon sole, roll it up and secure it with a cocktail stick. Put them into your basket and steam for 8–10 minutes.

To make the sauce, sweat the shallot in the butter. When the shallot has softened stir in the flour. Add the wine, let it bubble for a second and then stir in the stock and the cream. Bring it slowly to the boil and, stirring frequently, let it simmer gently for about 5 minutes. Chop the remaining spinach leaves, add them to the sauce and finally season with salt and pepper and lemon juice to taste.

Plaice with an Oyster or Prawn Stuffing

Flat fish, such as plaice, can be boned or pocketed, as it is often called, then stuffed. The pocket, being of a good size, can take a generous amount of stuffing and here, I suggest filling it with the simplest mixture of tinned oysters, (or, if you are in the mood, half a dozen fresh ones) or fresh or frozen prawns. Both of these have, I think, an affinity with plaice. However, the fish is also good stuffed with mushrooms that have been chopped and sautéed in butter.

If possible, buy 2 large plaice rather than 4 small ones; they are easier to bone and stuff and they can be cut in half to serve. You will need two large steaming baskets, one on top of another, or otherwise a fish kettle, to hold the whole fish.

Most fishmongers will bone the plaice for you, but it should not be done too long before cooking, so I give instructions for doing it yourself.

Put the plaice on a board, dark side upwards, and using a very sharp knife cut all the way down the centre of the backbone. Scrape the fillet on one side and then the other away from the bones, but stop just before you reach the edge of the fish. Take a stout pair of kitchen scissors and cut the backbone at intervals all down the fish then, pulling with your fingers and scraping, where necessary, with the knife, remove the bone piece by piece. Once you have removed the first piece it will be quite easy to scrape under the rib bones with the knife and remove the rest. Wash the fish before stuffing it.

2 large plaice
8 oz/227 g tin oysters or 4 oz/125 g shelled fresh or frozen prawns
lemon juice
salt and pepper
cayenne pepper (optional)

Prepare the fish as described above. If using oysters or defrosted prawns, drain them. Open the flaps of the fish and squeeze a generous amount of lemon juice over the flesh, then sprinkle it with salt and pepper. Stuff the oysters or prawns into the sides of the fish, and squeeze over some more lemon juice. Season with salt, pepper and a little cayenne, if you wish, then bring the flaps together over the top of them. You may find that it helps to fasten the flaps together with a couple of cocktail sticks.

Steam the fish for 7–8 minutes. Remove it to a serving dish and, just before serving, carefully peel off the dark skin.

Poisson au Crème Fraîche

I have been deliberately vague in naming this recipe, as you can use fillets or steaks from any kind of white fish, depending on your mood, your purse and its availability: halibut, turbot or cod would all be suitable. Do try and use raspberry vinegar, for it adds a delicious and unusual sweetness to the finished sauce.

Crème fraîche is becoming much more widely available but it is easy to make. Hannah Wright gives very simple instructions in her book *Soups*: mix ¼ pt/150 ml double cream and 1 tablespoon sour cream together, cover and leave overnight in a warm place, or until it is semi-set.

This dish is good if it is accompanied by small carrots and inside stalks of celery, both of which can be steamed in the top layer of the steamer.

4 white fish steaks or fillets
3 tablespoons raspberry vinegar
½ teaspoon Dijon mustard

¼ pt/150 ml crème fraîche
salt and pepper
vegetables for steaming stock   1 large carrot, roughly chopped
2 sticks celery, roughly chopped
3 or 4 parsley stalks
4 peppercorns

Put the vegetables for the stock together with the peppercorns into the base of the steamer, add 1 pt/600 ml water, bring to the boil and simmer for about 20 minutes. Over the simmering stock steam the fish, following the timings on p. 51, until just cooked, then keep it warm, covered, in a very low oven while you make the sauce.

Put ¼ pt/150 ml of the strained stock and in a small saucepan, add the raspberry vinegar boil fast to reduce by two thirds. Lower the heat slightly, stir in the mustard and the cream, adjust the seasoning and cook, stirring frequently, until it has come to the boil and thickened slightly. Serve the sauce separately in a bowl or spooned beside the fish on individual plates.

Trout with a Citrus and Ginger Sauce

Plain steamed trout with an interesting and entirely fat free sauce. Accompany it with vegetables that will be enhanced by the citrus flavoured sauce such as calabrese and carrots.

4 small trout
1 medium onion, quartered
1 small carrot, halved
¾ in/1.5 cm fresh ginger root, peeled
1 lemon
1 large or 2 small oranges
3 teaspoons cornflour
2 tablespoons milk
salt and pepper

Fill the base of your steamer two thirds full of water and put it to heat up. Add the onion and carrot together with half the ginger root and a large piece each of lemon and orange zest to the steaming water. Bring to the boil and simmer for 10–15 minutes to obtain the maximum flavour before cooking the fish.

Cut all the remaining peel and pith from the lemon and orange and, using a sharp knife, cut out and reserve the individual segments, discarding all of the outside membrane but keeping any juice that runs out. Stir the cornflour into the milk and keep it on one side.

Wash the trout and steam them following the timings on p. 51 or until they are cooked. Remove them to a board, skin them and remove the heads and tails. Gently, using a fish slice, remove the 2 top fillets to a dish; it is probably easiest to remove 1 fillet at a time rather than to try to take the whole top half of the fish. Pull out the backbone, discard it and any other bones that you see, then, again using the fish slice, transfer the remaining 2 fillets to the dish. Cover the fish with foil and put the dish in a low oven to keep warm while you make the sauce.

Strain ½ pt/300 ml of the steaming liquid into a saucepan, add the reserved citrus juices, then boil it fast to reduce it to about ¼ pt/150 ml. Stir in the citrus fruit segments, the rest of the ginger root, finely grated, and season with salt and pepper. Add the cornflour mixture, ½ teaspoon at a time, bubbling it up to thicken the sauce between additions. Watch the consistency carefully, and once you have achieved a good pouring sauce, stop, or the sauce will go thick and glue-like. Check the seasoning, then pour the sauce onto 4 heated plates, gently placing the fish fillets in the centre of each pool of sauce.

Red Mullet with Fennel and Anchovies

Red Mullet, although the ones we buy are most likely to be caught off our shores, always make me think of the Mediterranean. They somehow have the look and taste of a fish from sunny waters and they are at their best if cooked with tomatoes and olives or with fennel and anchovies as given here. The liver of a red mullet is considered a delicacy so try to make sure that it is left in when the fish is gutted.

4 whole red mullet, about 8–10 oz/250–300 g each
salt and pepper
8 anchovies
1 large bulb fennel
4 teaspoons olive oil
1 clove garlic, crushed

Wash the mullet, make sure that they are thoroughly descaled and sprinkle the inside with salt and pepper. Make two crosswise slashes in the side of each fish and lay an anchovy into each cut. Cover and refrigerate the fish until you are ready to cook them.

Wash the fennel, cut it into strips, lay them out to make a bed on the bottom of your steamer basket and sprinkle them with salt and pepper. Steam the fennel for 8 minutes, or until it is just softening, then lay the mullet on top of it. If you have a small basket it will not matter if the fish are laid on top of each other, but you could spoon a little of the fennel between them to make a steam passage. Steam the mullet for 10 minutes and while they are steaming heat up the olive oil and cook the garlic gently in it. Remove the mullet to a serving dish or separate plates, spoon the fennel onto the side and pour the hot oil over them.

Poisson Provençale

A friend of mine voted this one of the best fish dishes she had had for a long time and it is unusual as the fish is served on a bed of steamed ratatouille. I use lemon sole but fillets of other white fish, such as plaice or Dover sole, could be used instead.

The aubergine base is exactly the same as for Stuffed Aubergines (p. 128). I have repeated the ingredients here to enable you to see what is needed for the complete dish without having to shuffle round the book.

4 large fillets of lemon sole, skinned
stuffed aubergines
2 medium, long shaped aubergines
salt and pepper
1 tablespoon olive oil
3 shallots or 1 small onion, peeled and chopped
2 cloves garlic, crushed
8 oz/250 g tomatoes, peeled, deseeded and roughly chopped
medium bunch basil, chopped, or 1 teaspoon dried oregano
juice of 1 lemon

Make the ratatouille mixture by following the recipe on p. 128, using ½ the herbs and ½ the lemon juice to flavour it, then spoon it into the empty aubergine shells and lay them flat in your steamer basket. If you are using a small steamer or Chinese baskets, put them in 2 layers, swop them round half way through cooking and slightly increase the time.

Place a fish fillet on top of each aubergine half. Lightly sprinkle each one with salt, pepper and the remaining herbs and lemon juice. Steam for 15–18 minutes to cook the fish and reheat the ratatouille bases. Serve immediately with plenty of crusty bread and butter.

Boned Trout
with a Julienne of Vegetables

It is easy to bone a whole trout and very useful if you are then going to stuff it or, as suggested here, lay vegetables on top of it. It also makes it so much easier to eat.

The sauce is undeniably rich, but the quantities given only provide for a spoonful each, which I find to be enough. You could slightly alter the flavour by cutting down on the lemon juice and adding several sprigs of fresh tarragon to the stock when reducing it. The tarragon would then be strained out with the shallots but you could stir in a teaspoon of the finely chopped herb at the last minute.

2 trout, 12–14 oz/375–450 g each (or 4 small ones, about 8 oz/250 g each)
1 oz/25 g turnip
3 oz/75g carrot
3 oz/75 g celery
6 small spring onions
zest and juice of 1 lemon
salt and pepper
2 shallots or 1 small onion, roughly chopped
¼ pt/150 ml double cream
1 oz/25 g cold butter, diced

Most fishmongers will gut and possibly bone the fish, but it is much better if it is done at the last minute and it is not difficult to do. Use kitchen scissors to cut all the way down the fish's belly; remove and throw away all the innards and then wash the fish under running cold water to clean it. To bone the fish: continue the cut right up to the tail, then lay the fish, backbone up, on a board and loosen the backbone by pressing down on it with the palm of the hand. Turn the fish over and use a knife to remove the backbone – it should bring all the other little bones with it. Keep the bones to add to the liquid in the steamer.

Peel the turnip and carrot and remove any stringy pieces from the celery and spring onions, then cut all the vegetables into thin julienne strips or put them through the julienne or coarse grating disc on a food processor.

Prepare the steamer liquid by adding the fish bones and a slice of lemon zest to the water. Lightly sprinkle the vegetables with salt and pepper, then steam them for 4 minutes. Remove them with a slotted spoon and place them on the inside of the fish. Put the fish into the steamer basket, either flat or folded over so that the vegetables are enclosed, and steam for 5–6 minutes if flat and 8–10 minutes if folded over. Carefully remove the fish and vegetables and keep warm in a covered dish in a very low oven.

Make the sauce by putting into a saucepan ½ pt/300 ml of the strained steaming liquid. Add the remaining zest and the juice of the lemon, the shallots or onion, and a little salt and pepper. Boil very hard for 10 minutes or so, or until the liquid is reduced to 2–3 tablespoons. Strain it and return to the saucepan. Stir in the cream and bring to the boil, stirring frequently. Bubble fast for about 4 minutes to thicken the sauce, then, piece by piece, stir in the butter. Test for seasoning and serve with the fish.

Fish with Lemon, Capers and Croûtons

Any type of white fish fillet goes well with this sauce, as do the more chunky pieces of haddock or cod.

4 white fish fillets
1 slice of stale bread
2 oz/50 g butter
1 large or 2 small lemons
salt and pepper
1 shallot, finely chopped
1 teaspoon flour
2 teaspoons drained capers
small bunch parsley, finely chopped

Cut the bread into small cubes and if it is crumbly put it in the oven for a few minutes to dry out. Melt half the butter in a small frying pan, fry the bread until crisp, transfer the croûtons to a bowl and keep them warm in a low oven.

Cut the lemons into slices, reserving about a tablespoon of juice, and lay them on the bottom of your steaming basket. Place the fish on top of the lemon, sprinkle it lightly with salt and pepper and steam it following the timings on p. 51.

While it is steaming, sauté the shallot in the remaining butter and, when soft, stir in the flour followed by the reserved lemon juice and some of the steaming liquid (enough to thin the sauce to a pouring consistency). Stir in the capers and half the parsley, season with salt and pepper and finally, just before serving, add the croûtons.

Serve the fillets on individual plates with the remaining parsley sprinkled over the top and the sauce on the side.

Haddock Fillets Marinated in Yoghurt

Another dish with many possible variations. I give a tomato flavoured yoghurt marinade and a variation which is based on the Indian tandoori mix. If, when making the tandoori version, you only like a hint of cumin, just use about half the amount given.

Wash and steam some rice (p. 172), cover with a damp tea towel to keep warm or finish cooking it in the top layer of your steamer while you cook the fish.

4 pieces haddock or cod fillet, 1¼–1½ lb/600–750 g
juice of ½ a lemon
marinade
4 tablespoons thick natural yoghurt
1 tablespoon tomato purée
1 shallot, very finely chopped
½ clove garlic, crushed
¼ teaspoon cayenne pepper
salt

Make the marinade by mixing all the ingredients together and tasting to check on the seasoning. Refrigerate until needed.

Put the fish in the steamer basket and sprinkle it with a little salt and the lemon juice. Place the basket over a plate or draining board so that any excess juice can drain away. Cover and leave for 20 minutes, spoon over the marinade, cover again, and leave at room temperature for about 4 hours.

Steam the fish, without disturbing the yoghurt on top of it, for about 8 minutes, depending on the size and thickness of the individual fillets.

Variation

Mix the following ingredients together for the marinade.

4 tablespoons thick natural yoghurt
½ teaspoon ground cumin
¼ teaspoon ground cardamom
1 desertspoon finely chopped fresh ginger
1 clove garlic
1 teaspoon paprika
salt

Stuffed Squid

Your fishmonger will probably prepare the squid for you, but it is not difficult to do yourself and I give instructions below.

Serve the squid on their own, with a light tomato sauce or drizzled with some hot olive oil with garlic crushed into it.

1½ lb/750 g squid
1 Spanish onion, finely chopped
3 cloves garlic, finely chopped
2 tablespoons olive oil
1 oz/25 g blanched split almonds
small bunch parsley, finely chopped
few sprigs fresh oregano, chopped or ½ teaspoon dried oregano
2 oz/50 g fresh white breadcrumbs
1 hard-boiled egg, chopped
1 egg
salt and pepper

Take each squid separately and grasp the head, just below the tentacles; pull gently and the head will come away from the body with the innards attached to it. Cut off the tentacles and remove the mouth or beak of the squid from the centre of each one. Keep the tentacles, but discard the head and innards.

Wash the body under running water and pull out and discard the transparent bone. Pull off the mottled skin of the body, cut off the 2 triangular fins and reserve them with the tentacles. Wash the squid again, pat dry and keep, covered in the refrigerator until you are ready to stuff them.

To make the stuffing, fry the onion and garlic gently in the oil until soft. Add the almonds and fry until they start to look transparent, then mix in the herbs and remove the pan from the heat. Stir in the breadcrumbs and hard-boiled egg together with the chopped reserved fins and tentacles. Bind together with the raw egg and season. Use a teaspoon to stuff the squid; don't fill them more than two-thirds full as the squid will shrink while cooking and if overfilled could burst. Use a cocktail stick to close the sac. Steam for 20 minutes.

Marinated Cod
Wrapped in Chinese Leaves

Chinese leaves go particularly well with the Chinese flavourings of this dish and make excellent wrappers for the parcels.

I have given instructions using cod steaks, and then skinning and boning them, because I think the pieces of cod are nicer if they are chunky. If you buy a piece of fillet and then skin it and cube it the resulting pieces will be much thinner and will also be likely to flake up in the marinade.

4 cod steaks, 6–7 oz/175–225 g each
2 tablespoons dry sherry or rice wine
2 tablespoons soy sauce
2 teaspoons sesame oil or vegetable oil
½ in/1 cm fresh ginger root, peeled and finely chopped
1 teaspoon sugar
1 teaspoon salt
1 head Chinese leaves
16 small button mushrooms
4 spring onions

Skin the cod steaks, then, using a sharp knife, divide each steak into four, discarding the bone.

Mix together the sherry or rice wine, the soy sauce, oil, ginger, sugar and salt. Put the cod pieces to marinate in this mixture for about 15 minutes.

Separate the Chinese leaves. You will need 16 altogether, each of which should be 6–8 in/15–20 cm long and as wide as possible. Blanch the leaves by steaming them for 3 minutes, then leave them to drain and cool down.

Wipe the mushrooms and cut off the bottom of the stalks. Trim away the roots and most of the green part of the spring onions, then slice lengthways into fine strips.

To make the parcels, lay out a Chinese leaf and place on it a mushroom and a piece of cod (try to make sure this still has a few scrapings of ginger adhering to it), and top with a few strips of spring onion. Fold over the leaf, wrap it into a neat parcel and secure it with a cocktail stick.

When you are ready, steam the parcels for 5–8 minutes. Remove the cocktail sticks as you transfer them to the plates.

Clear Steamed Fish in the Chinese Style

Grey mullet is especially suited to this simple method and Chinese flavourings. Otherwise you could use trout or bream or, for a special treat, sea bass. Like most fish dishes, the fresher the fish the better and, if there is room in your steamer, leave the head on. This is supposed to prove to the eaters that the fish is indeed fresh.

You can, if necessary, cut the fish in two, for like most Chinese dishes it should be steamed on a dish or a plate with slightly raised edges to retain all the juices.

1 grey mullet, about 1½ lb/750 g, cleaned and scaled
salt
1 tablespoon finely chopped fresh ginger
6 medium spring onions
2 tablespoons vegetable oil plus 1 tablespoon sesame oil or 3 tablespoons vegetable oil
2 cloves garlic, peeled and finely sliced
1 tablespoon light soy sauce
1 tablespoon rice wine or dry sherry

Wash the fish, pat it dry with kitchen paper, then rub it all over with salt and leave to let the flesh firm up for about half an hour. Place it on a dish, put half the ginger inside the fish and sprinkle the rest over the top. Steam for 18–25 minutes (depending on the thickness of the fish) until it is just cooked. Meanwhile, neatly shred the spring onions and put the oils to heat in a small saucepan, add the garlic and cook until it just starts to brown.

Sprinkle the soy sauce and wine or sherry over the cooked fish and then cover it neatly with the spring onions. Finally pour the hot oil and garlic mixture over the top, letting it sizzle to just soften the onion and give the whole dish a lovely shine. Serve immediately.

Stuffed Herrings

Herrings, one of the cheapest foods available, should not be sneered at, for they make very good eating. They are a very oily fish, which the Scots cook in a coating of oatmeal, while the British frequently bake them in water spiked with vinegar or lemon juice. However, I find that they steam well and that the cooked flesh flakes away from the backbone (a great advantage with such a bony fish) and does not seem to be too rich and overpowering. You can bone them: turn the fish, slit side down, onto a board, press hard on the backbone to loosen it and then pick it out, but it does not seem to come away too easily and there are usually some bones left.

I give two stuffings, one using the soft roes (you will only need one for each fish, so its pair can be kept and served lightly fried on a piece of buttered toast), and a variation for those who don't like roes or for the many occasions that the fish come without them, simple but good and also suitable for mackerel.

Serve with potatoes and perhaps buttered chicory (p. 145).

4 herrings, cleaned
soft roe stuffing
1 shallot, finely chopped
½ oz/15 g butter
2 tablespoons fresh breadcrumbs
2 teaspoons chopped parsley
squeeze of lemon juice
salt and pepper
4 soft roes, chopped

To make the stuffing, fry the shallot gently, until transparent, in the butter. Add all the other ingredients, except for the roes, and fry for a further minute. Finally, add the roes, stir to mix them in, then remove the pan from the heat.

Spoon the mixture into the herrings and put them, stuffed side up, into your steamer basket. Steam for 15 minutes.

Variation

Make a breadcrumb stuffing using the following ingredients:

2 shallots, finely chopped
1 oz/25 g butter
4 tablespoons fresh breadcrumbs
1 teaspoon Dijon mustard
1 tablespoon chopped parsley
½ teaspoon chopped sage
salt and pepper

Moules Marinière

A wonderful dish which, except for the cleaning and scrubbing of the mussels, is exceptionally easy and quick to make. Mussels should be served piping hot with French bread and butter and a dry white wine. The 4 lb/2 kg of mussels given in the ingredients should feed 4 people for a main course; if you are serving them as a first course you will need about 2 lb/1 kg of mussels.

4 lb/2 kg mussels
½ pt/300 ml dry white wine
¼ pt/150 ml water
2 shallots or 1 small onion, chopped
1 carrot, chopped
6 peppercorns
parsley stalks
3 tablespoons chopped parsley
salt (optional)

Thoroughly wash and scrub the mussels, pulling out any beards and discarding any that are open, or stay open when you give them a sharp tap.

Put the wine, water, shallots or onion, carrot, peppercorns and parsley stalks into the base of the steamer and bring it to simmering point. Put the mussels in the basket; you may find that it is easier to steam them in two or even three batches, but if you do this you must keep the first batch covered in a warm oven. Steam the mussels for 5–7 minutes, take out all the opened ones and leave the rest to steam for a further 2 minutes. Throw out any that are still closed, then pile the mussels into a large bowl, or separate soup plates, and sprinkle them with the chopped parsley. Strain the liquid through muslin, add salt to taste and pour it over the mussels.

Moules Poulette

Another classic recipe for mussels. It is very rich and is, I think, best if eaten in comparatively small quantities as a first course, served with crusty bread and butter.

3 lbs/1.5 kg mussels
½ pt/300 ml dry white wine
¼ pt/150 ml water
2 shallots or 1 onion, chopped
1 carrot, chopped
6 peppercorns
2 oz/50 g butter
1 oz/25 g flour

2 egg yolks
juice of ½ a lemon
½ pt/300 ml cream
salt and pepper
parsley or fennel, chopped

Wash and scrub the mussels very thoroughly. Put the wine, water, shallots or onion, carrot and peppercorns to boil in the base of your steamer and in one, two or even three batches steam the mussels for 5–7 minutes. Take out all the opened mussels and steam the remainder for a further 2–3 minutes, then discard any that have not opened. Take each mussel from its shell, holding it over a dish to catch any liquid, and put them in a covered bowl to keep warm in a low oven. Strain the steaming liquid through muslin and add the mussel liquid.

Make the sauce by melting the butter, stirring in the flour and then slowly adding ½–¾ pt/300–450 ml of the strained steaming liquid and cooking until it thickens. Whisk the egg yolks and the lemon juice into the cream, add it to the sauce, let it bubble up and season it well.

Divide the warm mussels between 4 soup plates, pour the sauce over them and sprinkle some chopped parsley, or even better, fennel over the top.

Creamy Kedgeree

Kedgeree is one of those dishes that can be everyday or thoroughly extravagant. A little bit of leftover cod makes a perfectly acceptable kedgeree, but it is more usually made with smoked haddock and is good with salmon. Robin McDouall, who recommended kedgeree for breakfast, lunch or supper, said that made with lobster it becomes a dish for dinner – something I haven't tried!

The proportion of fish to rice can be varied: equal weights after cooking are a good rule of thumb, but you can use less fish and perhaps make it up with an extra egg or, as here, slightly more, but don't let the fish swamp the rice. If you like your kedgeree plain, leave out the addition of cream and egg at the end and simply serve it with a knob of butter.

6 oz/175 g fish
3 eggs
5 oz/150 g Basmati or long grain rice
salt and pepper
3 tablespoons cream
1 tablespoon chopped parsley

Steam the fish for 4–5 minutes and when cooked remove the skin and bones and flake the flesh. Steam 2 of the eggs for 12 minutes or until hard, cool them quickly in a bowl of cold water, then shell and chop them.

Wash the rice well and place it in a bowl with 7 fl oz/200 ml water and a little salt. Set the bowl in your steamer basket and steam for 25 minutes. If when the rice is cooked it still seems to be wet, drain off the water, cover it with a tea towel and steam if for a few more minutes to dry it out.

Add the skinned and flaked fish and the chopped egg to the rice and season with a little salt and a very good grinding of black pepper. Cover with a tea towel and leave in the steamer for a further 3 minutes for the fish and egg to heat through. Beat the remaining egg with the cream and stir them into the rice. Again cover the dish with the tea towel and steam for a further 2 minutes. Finally, fluff up the kedgeree with a fork, sprinkle it with parsley and serve.

Indian Kedgeree

The fish counter of my local supermarket has a lovely lady who is a dab hand at organising everybody's kedgeree. She won't let any of her customers leave with just a piece of smoked cod and always insists on picking out a nice mixture. The ingredients used for this dry, slightly curried kedgeree were chosen one day by her, though she gave me so much that I have left out the addition of a tin of tuna, and possibly one of sardines, that she also recommended.

I have used brown rice, but kedgeree is a dish of interchangeable ingredients, and Basmati rice, as long as it is dried out well after cooking, would do just as well. If you have a hungry family increase the amount of rice to 10 or even 12 oz/300–375 g.

serves 8

4 oz/125 g smoked mackerel fillet
4 oz/125 g boned kipper fillet
8 oz/250 g smoked Finnan haddock fillet
4 eggs
8 oz/250 g long grain brown rice
2 oz/50 g butter
1 tablespoon vegetable oil
½ teaspoon good quality curry powder plus ½ teaspoon turmeric or more or less, according to taste
1 large onion, chopped
salt and pepper

Steam the mackerel and kipper for 1 minute each, the haddock for 4 minutes, and the eggs until hard, about 12 minutes. Remove the skin and as many bones as possible from the fish and flake it into a bowl. Plunge the cooked eggs into a bowl of cold water, then peel and chop them and mix them with the fish.

Wash the rice, place it in a bowl with 12 fl oz/350 ml water and a little salt and steam it for 35–40 minutes or until soft. If necessary drain any remaining water from the rice and put it back in the steam for a couple of minutes to dry out.

Melt 1 oz/25 g of the butter with the oil in a frying pan, sprinkle on the curry powder and the turmeric and mix them in, add the onion and fry until it is well cooked. Remove the pan from the heat, add the remaining butter and season with salt and pepper.

Combine the fish and eggs with the rice, then mix in the onion and butter mixture. Transfer it to a dish, cover it until needed, then reheat in the top of the steamer or in a low oven.

POULTRY

A chicken can be steamed whole or, if your basket is not big enough or high enough, it can be cut into halves or quarters and then steamed. The steamed chicken is used in exactly the same way as a boiled chicken and can be eaten hot warm or cold, with or without a sauce.

It is usually advocated that chicken which is to be eaten cold is gently boiled and then left to cool in the stock, but this, more often than not, leads to a chicken that is falling to bits by the time it is removed from the pan. Steaming is much easier to control and there is very little difference in the result.

The chicken recipes that I give mostly use joints of chicken. These are now easy to buy and very practical and also obviate the problem of dividing up the white and dark meat. If you prefer, as I do, to buy corn-fed or free-range chickens, you can joint them yourself and then use the legs or wings separately from the breasts. I think probably the very best chicken dish possible is the breasts of a free-range chicken, seasoned, lightly steamed and served with butter, lemon juice and a sprinkling of the freshest of herbs.

I have a horror of frozen chickens, for I really do feel that they miss out on both taste and texture, and they are banned from my kitchen. If, however, you do steam a chicken that has been frozen you must be doubly sure that it is properly defrosted and then thoroughly cooked. Steaming does not bring the meat to a very high temperature and therefore would not kill off any traces of salmonella that might exist if any part of the chicken was still below room temperature when it was put on to steam.

As well as the chicken recipes I give two for duck. I have left out turkey, as it is rather large for most steamers, but separate joints could be steamed and served hot or cold with a favourite sauce. Game does not spring to mind in the context of steaming, as it is best either roast or slowly casseroled. You could, however, partly steam a young partridge, then put it in a nest in the centre of a cabbage, steam it until cooked and serve it sprinkled with fried breadcrumbs mixed with some bacon.

The table below gives you approximate timings for steaming whole chickens and joints, but before you remove the poultry from the steaming basket check that it is cooked by piercing the thickest part of the chicken with a skewer and making sure that the juices run out clear.

Chicken steaming times

Whole chickens		
Poussins	12–14 oz/375–450 g	30–35 minutes
Chickens	2½ lb/1.25 kg	45 minutes
	3 lb/1.5 kg	50–55 minutes
	4 lb/2 kg	1¼ hours
Halved chickens		
Small	1–1½ lb/500–750 g	30–35 minutes
Large	2 lb/1 kg	40–45 minutes
Chicken joints		
Breasts – off the bone		12–14 minutes
Breasts – on the bone or stuffed		15 minutes
Chicken quarters		20–25 minutes
Chicken legs		15–20 minutes
Chicken drumsticks		12–15 minutes

Mousseline of Chicken
with Avocado

Avocados are encased in a light chicken mousseline, steamed in a terrine and turned out to be eaten in slices. The slices with their bright green centres are ravishing to look at and, providing you stick to the mousseline making rules of keeping everything very cold, this is both an easy and a quick dish to make: however, as with all mousselines, a food processor is essential. Refrigerate the chicken, eggs and cream for several hours before making this dish and, if you have room, put your food processor bowl in the deep freeze.

The terrine can be eaten hot or warm, and is good with a beurre blanc (p. 60) or a hollandaise sauce. Add some new potatoes, also just warm, and it makes a very satisfactory light main course. It can also be eaten cold, served on a bed of crisp lettuce sprinkled with chives and accompanied by a vinaigrette sauce.

8 oz/250 g skinless chicken breast
1 or 2 sprigs of tarragon
2 eggs
salt and pepper
8 fl oz/250 ml double cream
2 small or 1 large ripe avocado
juice of 1 lemon
butter for greasing the terrine

Cut each chicken breast into about 6 pieces and put them and the tarragon in the food processor. Process for a minute, or until the chicken is totally smooth, then, through the feed tube, slowly add the eggs which have been whisked together with some salt and pepper.

I now stop and put it all back in the refrigerator to get really cold again, but if your cream is ice cold you can carry straight on. With the processor running, pour the cream in a steady stream through the feed tube and stop the machine the moment the mixture has amalgamated. If everything is cold you should have no trouble with the mixture separating and, if you don't overprocess the mousseline, it will be light and fluffy.

Well grease a 2 pt/1.2 litre terrine, or use a cake or bread tin or whatever will fit into your steamer basket. Use a sharp knife to peel the avocados, cut them in half, remove the stones and brush them all over with lemon juice.

Spoon about half of the mousseline mixture into the terrine, then press the avocados into it. They should be very close together but, if possible, not quite touching each other or the sides. Cover them with the remaining mousseline, using a spoon to fill up any gaps and the holes from the stones. Smooth over the top, loosely cover with foil or a double layer of cling film and steam for 30–35 minutes. Test that it is ready by plunging a skewer into the centre and checking that it comes out clean.

Turn it out onto a dish and serve hot, warm or cold.

Summer Chicken with Herbs

This dish illustrates that steaming is a good method of cooking a chicken that is to be eaten cold. The sauce uses the steaming stock which is strengthened by being boiled for a second time, with the addition of the carcass and bones of the chicken.

This is a good hot weather dish and one that can be made with many different flavourings. Use fresh herbs and choose ones that blend well together: try tarragon with parsley and chives combined with a couple of sorrel leaves or a little watercress; chervil with some dill, chives and parsley; or rather sharper, grated orange zest mixed with marjoram, lemon thyme, parsley and basil.

1 chicken 2–2½ lb/1–1.25 kg
1 onion, roughly chopped
1 carrot, roughly chopped
1½ teaspoons gelatine
¼ pt/150 ml double cream
handful of fresh herbs (see above), finely chopped
salt and pepper

If the chicken will fit into your steaming basket cook it whole, but if it is too big, cut it in half or joint it. Add the onion and carrot to the steaming water and steam the chicken until it is cooked, following the timings on p. 82. Remove the chicken from the steamer, skin it and cut off all the meat, chopping it into bite sized pieces. Keep it in a dish, covered and refrigerated. Return the carcass and bones to the steaming water, bring it back to the boil and simmer it for a further 15–20 minutes.

Put a tablespoon of the stock into a small bowl, sprinkle over the gelatine, put it over the steaming stock and stir until it melts. Remove the steamer from the heat, strain the stock, measure out ¼ pt/150 ml of it (the rest can be kept for some other use) and stir in the melted gelatine.

Leave it on one side until it is on the point of setting, then stir in cream and the finely chopped herbs and season with salt and pepper. Pour it over the chicken and either leave it in the dish to set or spoon it into a cling film lined bowl so that it can be turned out onto a plate before serving.

Garlic Chicken

Cookery books with a Mediterranean flavour often give a recipe for a chicken which is casseroled with up to 50 cloves of garlic. This chicken has a garlic and olive oil paste inserted under the skin and, as in the casseroled chicken, the garlic is well cooked, which leaves a subtle but not overpowering taste. You can, of course, add less, or perhaps even more, garlic according to your taste; just make sure that it is properly melted down and cooked before you start.

If your steamer basket is too small for a whole chicken, either cut it in half or quarters or use poussins or individual chicken breasts, stuffed with the garlic paste.

10 cloves garlic
1 tablespoon olive oil
1 teaspoon chopped fresh oregano or ½ teaspoon dried
salt and pepper
1 chicken about 3 lb/1.5 kg
1 oz/25 g butter and ½ oz/15 g flour amalgamated together for beurre manié

Peel the garlic cloves, cut each one into 3 or 4 slices and put them into a small saucepan with the oil—use a really fruity one—and 3 tablespoons water. Bring to the boil, then lower the heat and cook, with the oil just moving but not bubbling, for 30 minutes, by which time the water should have evaporated and the garlic be soft and cooked. Mash the garlic into the oil using a fork or a pestle and mortar. Stir in the oregano and season with salt.

Carefully work your index fingers under the skin of the chicken to lift it from the breast and the thighs. Spoon about half the garlic mixture into each side and with your fingers rub over the outside of the breast and thighs to distribute it as evenly as you can. Sprinkle the chicken with salt and pepper, place it in your steamer basket, over not too much water, and steam it for about 50 minutes, until cooked. Lift it out, draining any juices from the inside back into the steaming liquid, and put it, covered with foil, to keep warm in the oven.

Take about ½ pt/300 ml of the steaming liquid and, in a small saucepan, bring it to the boil and boil fast to reduce it by half. Thicken it slightly by whisking in the beurre manié and season to taste. Carve the chicken and serve the sauce separately.

Poussins A Ma Façon

Quick and easy but looks deceptively difficult. A perfect entertaining dish when you are in a hurry but have to produce something decent. I usually buy the smallest poussins I can find and serve everyone with a complete bird, but you can buy bigger ones and cut them in half after cooking.

Serve them with potatoes and a selection of vegetables; they will need no further sauce.

4 small or 2 large poussins
4 tablespoons chopped parsley
1 clove garlic, crushed
3 tablespoons fromage frais or thick yoghurt
zest and juice of 1 lemon
salt and pepper

Mix together the parsley, garlic, fromage frais or yoghurt, lemon zest and juice and salt and pepper to taste.

Gently push your index fingers between the skin and the breast of the birds, making as large a pocket as you can on each side of the breast bone, but take care not to puncture the skin. Spoon some stuffing into each pocket and steam the poussins for 30 minutes.

Galantine of Chicken

If you have a friendly butcher he may bone a chicken for you, but to do it yourself is not nearly as difficult as it sounds, and the instructions I give are, I hope, easy to follow. Steaming a stuffed chicken is an obvious way to cook it: with no water agitation the stuffing stays in place and the cooking temperature is ideal.

A chicken galantine makes a good party dish, as one chicken will feed quite a lot of people: the recipe below is enough for 6–8 but for more people you could easily use a large chicken and increase the amount of stuffing.

The chicken can be eaten hot or cold. If hot, you could serve it with a sauce made from the stock from the carcass and bones, thickened with a little beurre manié and flavoured with more fresh herbs. If cold; you could serve it just as it is or, for a special occasion, coated with aspic and decorated with a few thinly cut lemon slices and a sprig or two of a fresh herb.

1 chicken, 3–3½ lb/1.5–1.75 kg
1 tablespoon brandy
the chicken's liver
2 oz/50 g ham and 2 oz/50 g tongue or 4 oz/125 g ham
2 shallots or 1 medium onion, finely chopped
1 tablespoon butter
1 egg
12 oz/375 g pork belly, minced or finely chopped
1 oz/25 g pistachio nuts, shelled and halved (optional)
bunch of fresh herbs; a scrap of sage with some parsley, tarragon, chervil or whatever is available
salt and pepper

To bone the chicken: use a pair of scissors to cut off the wings at the centre joint and, if necessary, the legs at the ankle joint. Then, on a board, turn the chicken onto its breast and use a very sharp, narrow bladed knife to cut all the way down the centre of the back. With the point of the knife, and one side at a time, gently ease the flesh away from the bone. Use short sharp strokes and keep the blade of the knife as close to the bone as you can. When you reach the wings and the legs detach them from the carcass at the joint. Continue round, scraping the breast meat from the bone. When both sides are nearly complete, very carefully, so as not to pierce the skin, cut along the ridge of the breastbone and remove the carcass.

You now have a choice: you can leave both the leg and wing bones in, or take them both out, or, I think the best alternative, just leave the drumsticks to give the finished chicken some shape. Remove the wing bones by cutting through any tendons, then scrape down the bone and, remove it. Cut down the thigh bones, separating them from the drumstick, and removing them from the carcass, when you meet the joint. Boil up the bones to make a good rich stock and use it, if you wish, for a sauce for the finished dish.

To make the stuffing: pour the brandy over the chicken liver and leave to marinate for an hour or so. Cut the ham and tongue, if using, into matchstick sized pieces. Sauté the shallots or onion in the butter until soft and yellow.

Remove the chicken liver from the brandy and add the brandy, and the egg to the minced pork, then either process them together or beat well with a wooden spoon. Dice the chicken liver and stir it in (do not process as the meat should remain in small pieces), together with the ham and tongue, the shallots and their juices, the nuts, the herbs and a good amount of salt and pepper.

To stuff the chicken, lay it skin down on a board and season it well with salt and pepper. Heap the stuffing along the centre. Using a darning needle and preferably black thread (it is easier to see for removal), pull the sides together and sew it all the way up, oversewing or using blanket stitch. Keep it fairly loose so that the stuffing will not burst out half way through cooking.

Steam the chicken for 1¼ hours or until the juices run clear when the centre is pierced with a skewer. Remove the chicken from the steamer, place it breast side down and remove the stitches using scissors or a sharp knife, then turn it breast side up onto a serving dish. If you are eating it cold it is easier to leave it and take the stitches out just before serving.

To serve, cut it straight across in slices.

Boned Chicken
Stuffed with Rice

I like this rice-based stuffing for a boned chicken, but it is perhaps not quite such a good party dish as the Galantine on p. 86 as it doesn't slice so easily or go as far. The quantities below are enough for 4 people: for 6–8 you would need a 4 lb/2 kg chicken and half as much again of the stuffing.

You can eat it hot or cold: if hot, it is good served with the light avgolemono sauce on p. 114 (use the carcass and wings to make a good strong stock) and a casserole of Middle Eastern vegetables such as aubergines, courgettes, peppers and tomatoes. Otherwise serve it cold with a salad of mixed greens and avocado and another of tomato with basil or fresh herbs.

1 chicken, 2½–3 lb/1.25–1.5 kg
3 oz/75 g brown rice
1 tablespoon vegetable oil
1 oz/25 g slivered almonds
1 oz/25 g butter
1 medium onion, finely chopped
1 teaspoon tomato purée
1 oz/25 g dried apricots, chopped
zest and juice of ½ lemon
½ teaspoon ground cinnamon
salt and pepper
1 egg, beaten
small bunch of thyme or lemon thyme, finely chopped

Bone the chicken following the instructions for the Galantine on p. 86.

To make the stuffing: wash the rice well and put it in a bowl with 4 fl oz/125 ml or its own volume of water and steam it for 30 minutes or until cooked. In a small pan heat the oil and, in it, fry the almonds until they are golden brown. Remove the almonds from the pan, add the butter, let it melt, then sauté the onion until it is soft and golden. Take it from the heat and stir in the browned almonds together with tomato purée, apricots, lemon zest, cinnamon, salt and pepper. Stir the onion mixture into the rice and finally mix in the egg.

To stuff the chicken, lay it skin down on a board and sprinkle the flesh with the lemon juice and thyme and season it well with salt and pepper. Heap the stuffing along the centre and sew it up (see Galantine, p. 86).

Steam the chicken for 1 hour or until the juices run clear when the thigh is pierced with a skewer. If you are going to eat it hot the light avgolemono sauce (p. 114) can be made while it is steaming.

Chicken Breasts
with Tarragon and Tomato

I give several recipes for chicken breasts, but not without reason, as they are easily obtainable, steam beautifully and mix and match well with so many different flavours, herbs and sauces. This is one of the easiest and quickest dishes in the book but it has great subtlety and is well worth trying.

I have frequently advocated that vegetables should be steamed in a top basket, or that they should be steamed and three-quarters cooked and then transferred to the top to finish off while the meat or fish are steamed in the bottom basket. With chicken breasts, I have found that if smallish new potatoes are steamed in a bottom basket, the chicken and green vegetable (I use calabrese piled up so that it takes a little longer to cook) will take exactly the same time in a top basket.

Serve the potatoes with butter, sprinkled with chopped parsley and tarragon, and the calabrese with butter and a squeeze of lemon juice. There is no need for a further sauce as the chicken will be very moist and permeated with the flavour of the tarragon.

4 chicken breasts
1 tomato
salt and pepper
8 sprigs of fresh tarragon

Under a piece of cling film, beat the breasts with a rolling pin to flatten them slightly. Quarter the tomato, discard the pips and then cut each quarter into 3 or 4 'new moons'.

Sprinkle the inside of each breast with salt and pepper and lay 2 sprigs of tarragon and 3 or 4 pieces of tomato on one half of each one. Fold the other half over and put the breasts in the steaming basket with the fold upwards to stop the tomato falling out. You may find that it is easiest to balance one against another.

If you are steaming the breasts on the bottom, immediately over the water, they will take 12–15 minutes. If you are steaming them with calabrese, over potatoes, everything will take from 30–35 minutes and you will need to remember to salt the vegetables after 5 minutes.

Chicken Breasts Stuffed
with Curd Cheese
and Pine Nuts

This is slightly fiddly to make as you have to be very careful not to pierce the flesh and make a hole when cutting the pocket in the chicken breasts. The filling, however, is easily made and you can stuff the breasts ahead and refrigerate them until needed.

The sauce is on the rich side and, if you wish, you could serve rather less of it and therefore reduce the cream and butter content.

4 chicken breasts, skinned and boneless
3 oz/75 g curd cheese or half cottage cheese and half thick natural yoghurt
white part of 4 small or 2 large spring onions, chopped
2 tablespoons pine nuts, lightly toasted
salt and pepper
sauce
2 tablespoons dry vermouth
¼ pt/150 ml double cream
2 oz/50 g cold butter, diced
fresh chives, chopped

Drain any liquid from the curd cheese and beat it until smooth. If you are using cottage cheese and yoghurt make sure that they are well amalgamated. Stir the spring onions in to the cheese, together with the pine nuts and salt and pepper to taste. This stuffing can also be made quickly and easily in a food processor.

Take a very sharp pointed knife and carefully, starting at the thick end, cut into each breast to make a pocket. Spoon the stuffing into the pockets and secure with a cocktail stick.

Steam the breasts over a small amount of water for 15 minutes, or until the juices run clear when pierced with a skewer. Remove the breasts to a dish, cover and keep warm.

To make the sauce, place ¼ pt/150 ml of the steaming liquid in a small saucepan with the vermouth. Bring to the boil and, over a high heat, reduce the liquid by two thirds. Stir in the cream, bring it to the boil and let it bubble for 3 minutes. Stir in the butter piece by piece and continue cooking, stirring all the time, until the sauce has thickened. Serve the chicken breasts, on individual plates, sprinkled with a few chopped chives and with the sauce poured round them.

Chicken Breasts
with Mango and Coriander

Mango goes beautifully with chicken breasts and I like it spiced with a little fresh coriander. This is a very healthy dish as it doesn't need a sauce and therefore has remarkably little fat. Try to find a mango that is just ripe, but still firm and possible to cut into neat cubes.

Many supermarkets sell ready skinned chicken breasts, usually with the fillet attached. For this dish, as the chicken breasts need to be beaten very thin, I find it easiest to buy big ones and to use just the main breast cutting off the fillet and keeping it for some other dish.

Serve with rice, which could have been steamed in advance and then kept warm in a top basket.

4 chicken breasts, skinned
small handful of coriander leaves, finely chopped
juice of 1 lime
1 tablespoon sunflower or vegetable oil
salt and pepper
1 mango

Flatten the chicken breasts by placing them between a double thickness of cling film and beating with a rolling pin until they are thin and at least half as big again, then put them in a dish (it won't matter if they overlap).

Mix the coriander with the lime juice, oil and salt and pepper and pour it over the chicken. Leave the breasts to marinate for at least 2 hours, turning them over at 30 minute intervals.

I find that the easiest way to prepare mango is to hold it upright on a board and to take a slice off each flat side, cutting down as near to the stone as you can, and then to cut the 2 smaller wedges off the ends. It is then possible, using a very sharp knife, to take each piece and skin it, but do it over the dish of chicken so that any juices are caught in the marinade. On a chopping board cut the flesh into cubes and reserve in a bowl until needed.

Put the chicken breasts in your steamer basket and put a quarter of the cubed mango on top of each one. If your basket is small, let them overlap and just distribute the mango over the top. Bring the water to simmering point, put the basket over it and immediately spoon half the marinade over the chicken.

Check the chicken after steaming for 5–6 minutes – the beaten breasts will cook quickly and they need to be taken from the heat before the mango has gone tasteless and mushy. Serve with the remaining marinade spooned over the chicken.

Feuilleté of Chicken Veronique

A good dinner party dish and one that can be speedily made, the only fiddly part being peeling the grapes; but if you use large juicy ones it shouldn't take too long.

This dish is one that would, I think, be marred rather than complemented by the addition of a vegetable; so I would serve vegetables as a separate course or make a large salad to go with the cheese.

To make puff pastry you need lots of time and care. Time is, for most of us, the most difficult of these requirements so I have resorted to bought frozen puff pastry. You can now buy frozen sheets of puff pastry which are made from vegetable oils, and the rather nasty aftertaste which was caused by the use of animal fat in larger blocks of frozen puff pastry seems to have been eliminated. The sheets are also amazingly easy; all one has to do is defrost them, cut them to size and bake them.

For an attractive presentation you could cut rounds of puff pastry with a large cutter; you will need more pastry than for rectangles, although there will be trimmings which can be used in another dish.

4 chicken breasts, skinned and boned
8 oz/250 g (or 2 thin sheets) puff pastry, defrosted if frozen
8 oz/250 g white grapes
1 oz/25 g butter
1 oz/25 g flour
¼ pt/150 ml light chicken stock
¼ pt/150 ml white wine
salt and pepper
3 tablespoons cream or thick yoghurt

Bring your steamer to simmering point and blanch the grapes by steaming them for 3 minutes. Leave them to cool slightly, then skin them and remove the pips. Keep them on one side until needed.

In a small saucepan, melt the butter and stir in the flour. Gradually add the stock and then the wine, stirring constantly. Season to taste then pour in the cream or yoghurt and leave the sauce until needed.

Preheat the oven to gas 6/200° C/400° F.

If necessary roll out the pastry to a thickness of ½ in/1 cm and then cut out 4 rectangles or circles. Place the pieces on a wet baking sheet and put into the hot oven. They will take about 12 minutes to cook.

With a sharp knife cut each chicken breast lengthwise into 4 slices, but do not detach them at the end. Sprinkle each breast with a little salt and pepper. Lay the breasts in your steamer basket and fan them out slightly. Steam for 8–10 minutes or until cooked.

Add the grapes to the sauce, check the seasoning and warm it over a low heat.

Assemble the dish by cutting the cooked puff pastry in half horizontally and putting the bottom part on each of 4 hot plates. Spoon a little of the sauce onto each one and cover with the top half. Fan out the chicken pieces, arrange them on the plates and spoon the remaining sauce around them.

Chicken Quarters on a Potato Bed

A good dish for cheering up bought chicken quarters. The potato and onion bed will have received all the delicious drips from the chicken above, and all you need to add is a vegetable such as cauliflower or steamed whole tomatoes. Wash it all down with a rough red wine and you will have a delicious dinner for a winter's evening.

This is another dish that needs a big steamer. Alternatively it can be cooked in two layers, but if you do that, it will take around 40 minutes and you will need to remember to swop the baskets round half way through.

4 chicken quarters
1 lb/500 g Spanish onions
1½ lb/750 g new potatoes
4 tablespoons olive oil
salt and pepper

It is probably nicer if the chicken quarters are skinned, but you can just slash through the skin in several places so that the oil can penetrate underneath it.

Peel the onions and potatoes, cut them into slices of about ¼ in/5 mm thick and lay them in the bottom of your steamer basket. Place the chicken quarters on top and drizzle the oil over them. Steam them for 25 minutes or until the juices run clear when the thigh is pierced with a skewer and the onions and potatoes are soft. If you have a nice-looking basket you can serve everything from it, otherwise transfer it to a dish.

Twice Cooked Chicken

A northern Chinese dish, and a useful one, as except for the last minute frying it can be cooked ahead. Serve with rice.

4 chicken joints
vegetable oil for frying
marinade
2 tablespoons finely chopped spring onions
2 teaspoons finely chopped ginger
1 teaspoon sugar
1 tablespoon thick soy sauce
1 tablespoon rice wine or dry sherry
1 teaspoon sesame oil
salt and black pepper
sauce
2 tablespoons cider vinegar
1 tablespoon thick soy sauce
1 teaspoon sugar

Mix all the marinade ingredients together with ½ teaspoon salt and a good grinding of black pepper, and spread it over the chicken joints. Leave them for at least 1 hour, spooning the marinade back over the top at intervals. Bring your steamer to simmering point and steam the chicken for 35–40 minutes, spooning any leftover marinade on top of the joints half way through cooking.

Put the steamed joints on a rack and leave for at least 2 hours, to allow the skin to dry.

Make the sauce by mixing the ingredients together with ¼ teaspoon salt.

Heat about 2 in/5 cm vegetable oil in the bottom of a wok or deep frying pan and when it is hot (a piece of bread will sizzle and cook immediately) put the chicken pieces in. Fry them skin side up for 3 minutes, then turn them over and fry for a further 3 minutes or until the chicken is hot and the skin is brown and crisp.

Drain the chicken pieces briefly on kitchen paper, then sprinkle them with the sauce.

Ricotta and Spinach
Chicken Thighs

Chicken thighs are, I think, often underestimated, for they are cheap, tender and have a good flavour. Many supermarkets now sell them already skinned and boned, but if you can't find them it is easy and quick to do it yourself.

Ricotta cheese can be bought in many supermarkets and delicatessens and is worth looking for. However, you can, if necessary, replace it with sieved cottage cheese.

Serve with potatoes and, if liked, the mushroom sauce given below.

12 chicken thighs, skinned and boned
8 oz/250 g fresh spinach or 4 oz/125 g cooked frozen spinach
1 oz/25 g butter
2 shallots, finely chopped
1 clove garlic, crushed
4 oz/125 g ricotta cheese
1 oz/25 g freshly grated Parmesan cheese
nutmeg
salt and pepper
to serve (optional) mushroom sauce (see below)

Follow the instructions for Spinach Pudding (p. 45) to steam the spinach and squeeze it dry. Melt the butter in a small frying pan and gently cook the shallots and garlic until they are soft and transparent.

Put the spinach in a food processor or blender and process until it is coarsely chopped. Add the cheeses, process to mix them in, and finally pulse in the shallots and garlic and their juices, a little grated nutmeg and salt and pepper.

Lay the chicken thighs out flat and place a tablespoon of stuffing on the inside then turn the ends over to meet on the top. Place the thighs, seam side uppermost, in your basket and steam them for 12–15 minutes.

Mushroom Sauce

2 oz/50 g button mushrooms
1 oz/25 g butter
1 oz/25 g flour
½ pt/300 ml light chicken stock
2 tablespoons cream
salt and pepper

Wipe over the mushrooms and slice them thinly. In a small saucepan melt the butter, add the mushrooms and sweat them for 1–2 minutes. Take the pan from the heat and stir in the flour. Return it to the heat and gradually add the stock, stirring all the time. Bring it to the boil and simmer for 3–4 minutes. Add the cream, season with salt and pepper and serve.

Stuffed Chicken Drumsticks

These are quite fiddly to prepare, but if you use a really sharp pointed knife they shouldn't take too long.

The first version should be eaten when the flesh is fully cooked but the stuffing still slightly crisp; the mushrooms used to stuff the second version are pre-cooked so the drumsticks will need a minute or two less in the steamer. The lightly spiced tomato sauce given below goes well with them, perhaps with noodles and a green salad on the side.

8 chicken drumsticks
½ small red pepper, deseeded and cut into strips
8 button mushrooms
4 small spring onions
salt and pepper

Bone the drumsticks by working from the thick end. Cut away the flesh from the bone and as you advance peel back the already released flesh. Be very careful not to pierce the flesh and skin. After removing the bone and any obvious sinews, turn the drumsticks back the right way and pull the skin back into position.

Bring your steamer to simmering point and, if you want, make some light stock by adding the bones to the water. Steam the red pepper for 15 minutes. Cool the pepper for 5 minutes, then peel off the skin, discard it and chop the flesh finely.

Make the stuffing by chopping the spring onions (use the white part with a little of the green) and the mushrooms finely and mixing them with the chopped pepper. Season with a little salt and pepper and, using a teaspoon, stuff each boned drumstick. Try to keep each one in its original shape and lay it carefully in the steamer basket.

Steam for 15 minutes, or if you are steaming them in 2 layers, for 20 minutes, swopping the baskets round half way through.

Variation

8 chicken drumsticks (or 4 large ones)
1 oz/25 g butter
3 oz/75 g mushrooms, roughly chopped
salt and pepper
8 rashers streaky bacon

Follow the directions above to bone the drumsticks.

Melt the butter in a small frying pan, add the mushrooms and when they begin to sweat turn up the heat. Cook until they are soft and the juices have been boiled away. Season to taste.

Leave the mushrooms until cool then, using a teaspoon, stuff the boned drumsticks with the mixture. Cut any rind from the bacon and wrap a rasher (or 2, if the drumsticks are large) round each stuffed drumstick.

Steam them for 12–15 minutes.

Lightly Spiced Tomato Sauce

Tomato sauce is always a good standby and goes with endless dishes. This one with a little bit of curry and slightly sweetened with dried apricot is good and just a little bit different. I always try to use fresh tomatoes but in the middle of the winter canned are an adequate substitute.

1 tablespoon olive oil
2 shallots or 1 small onion, chopped
1 small carrot, chopped
2 dried apricots, chopped
1 clove garlic, crushed
¼–½ teaspoon garam masala or curry paste
1 lb/500 g tomatoes, roughly chopped

Heat the olive oil in a saucepan, add the shallots or onion, the carrot, apricots and garlic and leave to sweat for 5–10 minutes. When they have softened add the garam masala or curry paste and stir it in. Mix in the roughly chopped tomatoes, bring to simmering point and cook for 20 minutes or until the sauce has thickened. Pass it through a sieve and if it is still a little too liquid, cook it to reduce it further. It is better, even if accompanying a cold dish, if it is served slightly warm.

Hot Chicken Breasts Vinaigrette

Warm salads have become very fashionable in recent years, but are usually quite small and served as a first course or instead of a cheese course. This one is definitely a main course and with the juxtaposition of colours and shapes is, I find, a very satisfying dish to make.

4 chicken breasts, skinned and boned
oil for brushing over the chicken breasts
4 potatoes
8 baby carrots
8 florets of calabrese
vinaigrette 2 tablespoons white wine vinegar
6 tablespoons light oil (e.g. sunflower or peanut) or 4 tablespoons light oil and 2 tablespoons walnut oil
salt and pepper
Garnish bunch of chives, snipped

Prepare the chicken breasts, by cutting off any pieces of membrane or fat, slitting each one in half and brushing it with oil. Peel the potatoes, slice them and leave in cold water. Leave a little bit of green end on each carrot, peel them and, using a sharp knife, slit each into 3 or 4 slices, stopping about ½ in/1 cm from the top. Cut any tough stalk from the calabrese.

Use the vinegar, oil and salt and pepper to make a vinaigrette dressing.

Fill the steamer base with water and put it on to boil. If you have a small steamer, steam the vegetables first and keep them warm while the chicken is cooking, otherwise cook everything to finish at the same time. The potato slices, depending on thickness, will take around 15 minutes, the carrots and the calabrese about 10 minutes. The chicken breasts, if sliced in half, will take 6–8 minutes.

Arrange the cooked chicken and vegetables on individual plates, fanning out the carrots. Drizzle the vinaigrette over everything and sprinkle the chicken thickly and the potatoes thinly with snipped chives.

Duck with Liver and Orange Sauce

Steaming a whole duck works well as the fat doesn't seem to penetrate the meat during steaming, thereby giving an ordinary Aylesbury duckling a stronger taste, which is much more akin to a wild duck. If you only have a small steamer or Chinese baskets you could joint the raw duck and steam it in 2 layers.

2 oranges
4½ lb/2.25 kg Aylesbury duckling
1 carrot, roughly chopped
1 onion, roughly chopped
6 peppercorns
1 oz/25 g butter
the duck's liver, coarsely chopped
1 oz/25 g flour
2 tablespoons Grand Marnier, orange curaçao or brandy
salt and pepper

Pare off the zest of 1 orange, leaving the pith behind, and cut half of it into strips. Using a sharp knife make incisions in the duck's skin and insert a piece of orange zest in each.

Pour at least 1 pt/600 ml water into your steamer base and add the zest from the other half of the orange, the carrot, onion and peppercorns. Bring the water to the boil and steam the duck for 1 hour and 20 minutes. Strain the stock and leave it to cool.

Carve the flesh from the duck and cut it into bite sized pieces. Grate the zest from the second orange and reserve it. Remove and keep the segments from both oranges, taking care to discard all skin and pith. Remove the fat from the stock either by carefully pouring it off or by sucking up the stock from under it with a bulb baster. Let it settle again and remove any fat that is left by pulling a piece of kitchen paper over the surface of the stock. If you have time you could refrigerate the stock and then just remove the hardened fat with a spoon. You will need ½–¾ pt/300–450 ml stock to make the sauce.

In a large saucepan melt the butter, add the duck's liver, cook it for 1 minute, then sprinkle on the flour. Slowly pour in half the stock and, stirring all the time, bring to the boil and cook it for 2 minutes. Pour the sauce into a food processor or blender and process it to purée the liver, then return it to the saucepan, add the remaining stock, the Grand Marnier, orange curaçao or brandy, the grated orange zest and salt and pepper and simmer for a few minutes. Add the duck and the orange segments and heat through before serving.

This dish can be made ahead and then quickly heated through, covered, in the oven, but try not to cook it any more, otherwise the duck will toughen and the orange will be overcooked.

Warm Salad of Duck Breasts in Radicchio

The lovely rounded bowl-like shape of the separated leaves of radicchio make ideal containers for stuffing. Unfortunately, radicchio loses a lot of its colour when cooked but this does not matter with this dish as the parcels are served on a bed of mixed green leaves interspersed with the remaining little red leaves from the heart of the radicchio. Try to use raspberry vinegar and walnut oil for the dressing, for they really add something to this dish and lift it out of the ordinary.

Duck breasts are available from supermarkets and the removal of the skin makes them virtually fat free.

4 small duck breasts (6 large ones would be enough for 8 people)
1 good head radicchio
salt and pepper
1 clove garlic, crushed (optional)
2 tablespoons raspberry or wine vinegar
3 tablespoons walnut oil and 2 tablespoons sunflower or grapeseed oil or 5 tablespoons olive oil
1 oz/25 g walnuts, chopped
mixed green salad leaves, e.g. lettuce, batavia, rocket, lambs lettuce
8 or 12 small new potatoes
1 teaspoon chopped parsley
small bunch chives, snipped

Using a sharp knife ease the skin away from the duck breasts, discard it and cut each breast into 3. Cut out the base of the radicchio and gently unwrap it leaf by leaf: after every 2 or 3 leaves you will have to cut another slice from the stem. Take the 12 best leaves, or if they are small 24 leaves. Keep the remaining leaves for the salad. Lightly season the pieces of duck with salt and pepper and, if liked, a tiny piece of crushed garlic. Wrap them up, in either 1 or 2 leaves, tie into a neat parcel with a double thread of cotton, then keep them covered in the refrigerator until you are ready to cook them.

Make the dressing using the vinegar, oils, seasoning and perhaps a touch of garlic, stir the chopped walnuts into it and keep until needed. Arrange the salad leaves decoratively on 4 individual plates, leaving spaces for the duck parcels and the potatoes.

About 20–25 minutes before you want to eat heat up your steamer and put the potatoes on to cook, then 10–15 minutes later put in the duck parcels—you may have to put the potatoes to finish cooking on a top layer. (If you only have a small, one layer steamer finish cooking the potatoes before starting the duck parcels and keep them warm in the oven.) The parcels, depending on how pink or well done you like your duck, will take 8–10 minutes to cook.

Cut the cotton from the cooked duck parcels then place them and the potatoes on the salad leaves. Slit the top of each parcel and open it up. Pour the dressing over the top, sprinkle on the parsley and some snipped chives and serve immediately.

Chicken Liver Pâté

An exceedingly quick and easy pâté; the ingredients are chopped, put into a bowl, steamed until cooked and then puréed. The finished pâté is slightly loose in texture, but a slicing pâté can easily be achieved by resteaming it, after puréeing, for a further 15 minutes. Marsala is sometimes difficult to obtain, but it can easily be replaced with port or a sweet sherry, in which case I would substitute pistachios for the almonds.

8 oz/250 g chicken livers
4 oz/125 g mild smoked streaky bacon
2 shallots or 1 small onion, chopped
1 clove garlic, crushed
2–3 tablespoons Marsala
1 teaspoon chopped fresh tarragon or ½ teaspoon dried tarragon
1 oz/25 g butter
2 oz/50 g blanched split almonds
salt and pepper
a little aspic jelly or melted butter (optional)

Trim any discoloured or fatty pieces from the chicken livers. If the bacon has rinds cut them off and roughly chop the rashers. In a small basin mix the chicken livers, bacon, shallots, garlic, Marsala and herbs together. Put the butter on the top, cover with a double piece of cling film and steam for 30 minutes. While it is steaming, toast the almonds under a hot grill, turning them once or twice to brown them evenly.

Use a food processor or blender to purée the contents of the basin, season to taste, spoon in about three-quarters of the almonds and pulse them in. Pour the pâté into a serving dish, cover and refrigerate.

When the pâté is firm, sprinkle on the remaining almonds and, if you wish, finish it off by pouring a thin layer of aspic jelly over the top. Alternatively, seal the top with some melted butter.

Warm Chicken Liver Mousses

These little mousses are very light and delicate tasting. They can either be eaten with a teaspoon direct from the ramekins or, for something more special, they can be served as a warm salad, turned out into the centre of a lightly dressed mixed green salad. A salad made with a mixture of leaves such as oak leaf, rocket and the radicchio would look attractive, and if served this way the amounts given here are enough for 8 people. If you are going to turn the mousses out you might find it easier if you line the ramekins with cling film.

2 oz/50 g sultanas
zest of 1 orange

3 tablespoons brandy
2 tablespoons orange juice
8 oz/250 g chicken livers
2 eggs
½ pt/300 ml double cream
salt and pepper

Put the sultanas and orange zest to soak for at least an hour in the brandy and orange juice. Cut any fat or greenish bits off the chicken livers and drain them to get rid of any excess juices.

The chicken livers, eggs and cream should be used straight from the refrigerator. Purée the livers and eggs in a food processor, adding the cream through the feed tube while the machine is running. Season with salt and pepper, add the soaked sultanas and their juices and pulse the machine briefly to mix them in.

Divide the mixture between 4 or 8 greased ramekin dishes making sure that the sultanas are evenly distributed. Cover them with foil or cling film and steam them for 20 minutes. Unless you have one of the bigger steamers you may have to cook them in 2 batches. They are best if they are left to cool for 15–20 minutes and eaten warm rather than hot.

MEAT

You can steam any joint of meat and although you won't have an outside that is browned or crisp, neither will you have one that is tough or burnt. Steamed meat is also very low in fat as any in the meat is melted by the steam and then drips down into the water.

Steaming cooks meat quickly so it should not be used for a stewing cut that needs long slow cooking. With a joint it is quite a good idea to leave it, when cooked, in the turned off steamer for 10 minutes or so for the juices to run back and give you meat that is both tender and easy to carve.

In the recipes I have given suggested timings which should be used as a guide. The cooking time will be governed by whether you like your meat well done or rare, as well as its thickness and shape and its temperature; a piece of meat from the refrigerator will take longer to cook than a piece that is at room temperature.

Meat steaming times

Beef

joints	10–12 minutes per lb/500 g plus up to 15 minutes depending on size of joint
steaks	thin cut sirloin – medium rare – 3 minutes thick cut sirloin – medium rare – 4 minutes
	fillet – 4½–5 minutes

Lamb

joints	15 minutes per lb/500 g plus up to 15 minutes depending on size of joint
cutlets	6–8 minutes
chops	10–15 minutes

Pork

chops	15–18 minutes

Veal

chops	18–20 minutes

Calf's Liver in Red Peppers

Liver and red peppers are a good combination. This makes an easy supper dish that is probably best served with plain rice. Liver can be steamed by itself, but it is inclined to dry out and I would only recommend it to those on a strict fat free diet.

Raspberry vinegar, if you can find it, or make it, is a delicious and unusual addition, but otherwise red wine vinegar or lemon juice are perfectly acceptable.

10–12 oz/300–375 g calf's liver
¼ pt/150 ml milk
2 large red peppers
2 oz/50 g mushrooms
2 oz/50 g butter
1 shallot, finely chopped
1 clove garlic, crushed (optional)
2 tablespoons raspberry or red wine vinegar or lemon juice
4 tablespoons chopped parsley
salt and pepper

Cut the liver into thin slices, then into strips and put it to soak in the milk for 1 hour. This will remove some of the juices from the liver and tenderize it.

Cut the peppers in half lengthwise and remove the stalk and any seeds, leaving a shell in which the liver will be steamed. Peel the mushrooms and cut them into 4 or 6 depending on their size.

Drain the milk from the liver (either throw it away or give it to the cat) and pat the liver with kitchen paper to remove the remaining moisture. Melt the butter and add the shallot and garlic, if using. Cook until the shallot is soft, then add the vinegar or lemon juice. Mix it in, then add the liver, mushrooms and parsley together with a generous sprinkling of salt and pepper. Toss the mixture to mix, then spoon it into the pepper shells.

Balance the filled peppers in your basket and cover with a tea towel to stop any condensation dripping back onto the peppers. Steam for 20–25 minutes or until the peppers are soft and cooked.

Lamb Cutlets in Mint Jelly

Glazed lamb cutlets are a pretty dish for a summer dinner party, when they can be arranged on a plate with some salad or cold french beans with a little vinaigrette drizzled over them. Steaming is an ideal way to cook them, as you do not get any hard brown edges but it is a good idea to cut off most of the fat before you start. They should be eaten quickly as the mint jelly is inclined to slide off, but if you want to keep them for longer, make the mint jelly stiffer by adding a little melted gelatine to it.

8 small lamb cutlets
salt and pepper
2 oz/50 g mint jelly
½ teaspoon gelatine

Bring the water to the boil and steam the cutlets for 3 minutes. Sprinkle a little salt and pepper over each one then turn them over, season the second side, and steam for a further 3–5 minutes, depending on the thickness of the meat. Test with a skewer — they should be slightly pink in the centre — then leave them until completely cold.

Melt the gelatine in 2 teaspoons water. Put the jelly in a small saucepan and, over moderate heat, stir it until it has melted, add the gelatine then refrigerate it until it is thickening and on the point of setting. Spoon the jelly carefully over the cutlets and put them in the refrigerator or even better the deep freeze, for 10 minutes or so to set. Serve them immediately.

Lamb Noisettes with Fresh Herbs

Little lamb noisettes, which are just the cutlets with the bone removed, are somehow just that much more elegant than a straight cutlet. They steam well but they need quite a lot of seasoning and the herbs, which can be varied, should be fresh if possible. Serve with a selection of vegetables (p. 118).

8 lamb noisettes, 2½–3 oz/65–75 g each
a good handful of parsley, finely chopped
1–2 sprigs of tarragon, finely chopped
1–2 cloves garlic, crushed
zest and juice of ½ lemon
salt and pepper
16 fresh mint leaves

Mix together the parsley, tarragon, crushed garlic, lemon zest and juice, salt (sea salt if possible) and freshly ground black pepper. Press the noisettes into the herbs so that each side is well covered. Arrange a bed of mint leaves in your steamer basket, put the noisettes on top and steam for about 6 minutes. You may have to cook them in 2 layers, in which case you will need a few more mint leaves. You will also have to swop them around half way through steaming or cook the top layer rather longer. Discard the mint leaves before serving.

Stuffed Crown of Lamb

A stuffed crown of lamb with white cutlet frills on the ends looks most impressive. It steams well, but you will not get the brown crisp outside that is achieved when you roast it. Cut off as much excess fat as you can—there is usually quite a lot in the centre—and steaming the joint will dissipate most of the rest; you will then have a joint that is pleasant to eat.

You could use my stuffing; this is one of our family favourites which seems to suit steamed meat well and has its flavour sharpened up with lemon juice and mint.

You may find that a crown is rather too tall for your steamer, but you could take some off the length of the bones. Otherwise, if you don't have a domed lid, you could make extra height by turning a saucepan upside down over the top of your steamer basket.

1 crown of lamb, about 2 lb/1 kg
½ oz/15 g butter
1 tablespoon vegetable oil
1 small onion, finely chopped
1 small stick celery, chopped
2 oz/50 g button mushrooms, peeled and chopped
a few mint leaves, finely chopped
3 oz/75 g fresh white breadcrumbs
juice of ½ lemon
1 egg
salt and pepper

Melt the butter and oil in a small pan and gently fry the onion for 2 minutes. Add the celery and fry for a further 3 minutes before stirring in the mushrooms and frying for a final 2 minutes. Remove the pan from the heat.

Stir the mint into the breadcrumbs, then add the fried vegetables, the lemon juice and the egg. Mix them well together and season to taste with salt and pepper.

Cut any flaps of fat from the inside of the crown and spoon the stuffing into the centre. Steam it, depending on its size and the thickness of the bottom meat, for 35–45 mintues. Remove it from the steamer and serve with the cutlet frills slipped onto the ends of the bones.

Leg of Lamb with Caper Sauce

When I was first married one of my favourite dinner party dishes was a boiled leg of lamb with caper sauce. When I started work on ideas for this book the thought of steaming lamb brought it back to me; nowadays it is rather unusual. It is a good entertaining dish as the leg can be cooked and then kept warm for quite some time; small potatoes and cabbage or another green vegetable can be steamed while you are making the sauce.

I give instructions for a large leg of lamb which will feed 10 people. The leg will need a large steaming basket, especially as it seems to swell during cooking. Use a large Chinese basket or an electric steamer or a fish kettle, but watch the water level and replenish it if necessary.

For fewer people you could use half a leg and steam it in a smaller basket.

serves 10

5 lb/2.5 kg leg of lamb
1 clove garlic (optional)
salt
1 onion, chopped
1 carrot, chopped
a few peppercorns
sauce 1½ oz/40 g butter
1 oz/25 g flour
3 tablespoons capers
juice of 1 lemon
pepper

If you are using garlic, cut the clove into slivers. With the point of a sharp knife, make incisions in the leg of lamb and insert a sliver of garlic in each. Sprinkle salt all over the leg. Add the onion, carrot and peppercorns to the steaming water, bring it to the boil and steam the lamb for 15 minutes per lb/500 g plus 5–15 minutes depending on how pink or well done you like it. Keep it warm, well covered with foil, in the oven, or in the steamer, with the water hot but well below boiling point, while you make the sauce.

Melt the butter, stir in the flour, then slowly add ¾ pt/450 ml of the hot, strained stock. If you don't have enough stock to make the sauce, make it up, if you have it, with chicken stock or with water and a scrap of stock cube. Bring to the boil, stirring, and when it has thickened add the capers and lemon juice and season with salt and pepper.

Serve the lamb, carved into thick slices, with the sauce on the side.

Steak with a Red Wine, Mushroom & Caper Sauce

Steak remains tender and cooks well in a steamer. This particular dish is good accompanied by oven baked potatoes and a green vegetable.

4 pieces sirloin steak
2 shallots, very finely chopped
¼ pt/150 ml red wine
2 fl oz/50 ml wine vinegar
¼ pt/150 ml single cream or crème fraîche (p. 126)
3 teaspoons capers
1 teaspoon Dijon mustard
salt and pepper
2 oz/50 g butter
4 oz/125 g button mushrooms, thinly sliced
2 teaspoons flour

to garnish (optional)
chopped parsley

Put the shallots in a saucepan together with the red wine and the vinegar. Bring to the boil and keep boiling until the liquid has reduced by about two thirds. Strain out the shallots, return the reduced liquid to the pan, reheat it, stir in the cream or crème fraîche, then bring it back to the boil and simmer, stirring frequently, for 3 minutes. Take the pan off the heat, stir in the capers and mustard and season well. Leave the pan on one side while you prepare the mushrooms.

In another pan melt the butter, then add the mushrooms and sauté them over a fairly high heat, stirring constantly, until their juices have started to run. Stir in the flour and when it has amalgamated, pour in the wine mixture, stirring until it is smooth and thick.

Put the steaks on to steam, following the timings on p. 104, and having regard as to the thickness of the meat and whether you like it rare or well done. If necessary, gently reheat the sauce while they are cooking. Spoon a pool of sauce onto each plate and place a steak in the centre, sprinkled, if you wish, with a little chopped parsley.

Paupiettes of Veal with Prosciutto

These little paupiettes are one of the simplest ways of cooking veal escalopes. This is a dish that one often meets in one form or another in Italy where they are sometimes known as messicani. After steaming, the paupiettes are inclined to be a dull colour and to look slightly insignificant, and therefore need to be served carefully. Place them on a dish, with a tiny sprig of fresh thyme on top of each one, and surround them with some potatoes with snipped chives and 2 or 3 colourful and interestingly shaped vegetables such as french beans, broad beans, peas, spring carrots, baby corn.

If you have a good sized steamer with 2 baskets this is an ideal dish, as the vegetables can all be steamed, in 1 or 2 baskets, then put together on the top layer to keep warm while the paupiettes are cooked. There is no need to use any extra saucepans or hot plates.

4 veal escalopes, 3–4 oz/75–125 g each
2 shallots, very finely chopped
1 oz/25 g butter
4 thin slices prosciutto
salt and pepper
sprigs of fresh thyme

Sauté the shallots in the butter until they are soft, then leave the pan on one side to cool. Put the escalopes between 2 pieces of cling film and beat with a rolling pin until they are very thin, then cut each escalope and each slice of prosciutto into 4. Lay a piece of prosciutto in the centre of each escalope, spoon a little of the cooked shallot and butter onto it, season with a grinding of pepper and very little salt and finish by adding a tiny sprig of thyme. Roll the escalopes into neat parcels, use a cocktail stick to hold them together, then cover and keep them refrigerated.

When you are ready, steam them for 5 minutes.

Medallions of Pork Tenderloin in Cabbage Leaves

Pork tenderloin is probably the leanest cut of pork there is and can now be bought already cut into medallions; however, it is just as easy to buy the whole tenderloin and slice it yourself. The pork, together with a simple stuffing, is wrapped in cabbage leaves before being steamed. The pork and stuffing go so well with the cabbage that it is worthwhile serving the inside leaves as a vegetable: shred them and steam them, either round the edge of the basket or for 15–20 minutes on a top layer. Add the cabbage to a basket of half cooked potatoes and everything will be ready at the same time.

1 medium green cabbage – Primo is good
12 oz–1 lb/375–500 g pork tenderloin
stuffing
4 oz/125 g streaky bacon, chopped
1 medium onion, chopped
6 tablespoons fresh breadcrumbs
good bunch herbs (parsley, thyme and a little sage), chopped
salt and pepper

Remove and discard any outside damaged leaves of the cabbage, then cut off 8 good sized ones. Steam the 8 cabbage leaves for 4 minutes, remove and keep on one side.

To prepare the stuffing, cook the bacon in a small frying pan and when the fat is running add the onion. Continue cooking until the onion is soft and transparent, adding a little oil if necessary. Stir in the breadcrumbs, cook them for a few minutes, then remove the pan from the heat and stir in the herbs and season to taste.

Cut the pork into 16 even slices (if you have bought ready cut medallions they will probably be thick and need cutting in half). Taking each cabbage leaf in turn, cut out any tough stalk, place a piece of pork in the centre, spoon on some stuffing, cover it with another piece of pork and finally a little more stuffing. Turn in the bottom, the sides and then the top of the cabbage leaf and carefully transfer each parcel to the steaming basket. Steam for 10 minutes, or if your steamer is small, steam it on 2 layers for 15–18 minutes, swopping the baskets round half way through.

Chops

Chops—lamb, pork or, more extravagantly, veal—are the easy supper dish; a few minutes under the grill and there you are. Carefully cooked and simply served they represent the best of plain English cooking.

One of the problems of grilling chops is that they can all too easily end up with a hard, overbrowned outside and a tough inside and I find that steaming them is a very good solution; you may not get the crispness, but the fat seems to melt away and the meat retains both its flavour and succulence. The chops can just be laid in the basket and steamed; however if you do this you will lose any of the juices that may flow from the meat and I prefer to place them on a bed of vegetables. The vegetables cook with the meat, retain the juices and save you having to cook them separately or on another layer.

If you only have a small steamer don't worry; either use two layers, swopping the baskets round about half way through, or put the chops one on top of each other on a thick layer of vegetables and use tongs to swop them round half way through. If you use either of these methods the steaming time will be considerably longer, depending on how close together the chops are, but reckon on just under double the time given in the recipe.

Lamb Chops on a Potato Bed

This recipe uses dried herbs so it can be made at any time of year. I suggest 1 lb/500 g potatoes, but this is just a guide and can be altered to fit in with your family's appetite or diet.

4 good sized lamb chops or 8 cutlets
1 lb/500 g potatoes
1 teaspoon dried oregano or Italian mixed herbs
salt and pepper

Peel the potatoes and cut them into slices of up to ¼ in/5 mm thick. Lay the slices in your basket—it will not matter if they overlap or if there are gaps—and sprinkle them with half the herbs and the salt and pepper. If you are using thick chops, put them on top of the potatoes, sprinkle them with pepper and herbs and steam for 20–25 minutes, or until the potatoes and the chops are cooked, sprinkling the chops with salt 5 minutes before the end. If the chops seem cooked before the potatoes are ready you can always take them out and leave the potatoes to finish cooking. However, I find that they do cook in more or less the same time.

If you are using cutlets they will cook more quickly than the potatoes, so steam the potatoes for 10 minutes, lay the cutlets on top of them, sprinkle with pepper and herbs, and continue steaming for a further 10–15 minutes, by which time they should both be cooked. Again the cutlets will be better if salted a few minutes before they finish cooking.

Pork Chops with Sage and Onion

Pork chops on a bed of onions and herbs. You could put some sliced potatoes underneath the onions, but if you do so, remember to increase the steaming time.

4 pork chops
3 medium onions, thickly sliced
4–6 sage leaves, finely chopped
salt and pepper

Lay the onions in the bottom of your steamer basket and sprinkle with the sage, salt and pepper. Place the chops on top and steam for 20–25 minutes, or until the onion is soft and the chops cooked, seasoning the chops after about 15 minutes.

Pork Chops with Orange

I like to make this early in the year when the Seville oranges are available; their taste is quite different from other oranges and the juice makes an excellent sauce. When the orange skins are boiled in the water the resulting steam is so strongly flavoured that it will penetrate the meat and give it a pleasant orange scent.

The sauce has a strong flavour, so you only need a tablespoon of it with each chop. Good accompaniments with such a sweet sauce are plain buttered noodles, carrots and calabrese.

4 pork chops, well trimmed
2 Seville oranges
1 oz/25 g sugar
1 teaspoon cornflour, dissolved in 1 tablespoon water

Squeeze the oranges and reserve the juice. Cut the remains of the oranges into strips and place them in the bottom of your steamer with no more than 1 pt/600 ml water. Bring to the boil, then leave them to simmer for about 20 minutes before placing the basket with the chops over the top. The chops, depending on their size, will take about 10 minutes to cook.

Meanwhile, make the sauce by heating the orange juice and sugar. When the sugar has dissolved, stir in the dissolved cornflour. Stirring all the time, bring to the boil and let it bubble gently for a minute or two for the sauce to thicken.

Veal Chops with Fennel

4 veal chops
2 bulbs fennel
a few sprigs of lemon thyme, thyme or rosemary, finely chopped
salt and pepper

Cut the bottoms off the fennel bulbs and remove any brown outside leaves. Slice the fennel, lay the slices in the steamer basket and sprinkle them with half the herbs and the salt and pepper. Place the veal chops on top of the fennel and sprinkle them with the remaining herbs. Steam them for 20–25 minutes, or until the juices run clear when the chop is pierced with a skewer, seasoning them with salt and pepper after about 10 minutes.

Dolmathes with a Meat and Rice Stuffing

Dolmathes are essentially Greek but are also part of the Middle Eastern tradition of stuffed vegetables. They are, when stuffed, either steamed or casseroled, but I find that steaming is preferable as you then have no difficulties with them falling apart when they are removed from the pot.

Any Greek or Cypriot greengrocer worth his salt will have packets of pre-served vine leaves and, if you buy one, he will almost certainly take 10 minutes telling you exactly how you should use them, stuff them and cook them.

In the early summer it is sometimes possible to buy fresh vine leaves from Greek delicatessens, and they will have a wonderful sweet flavour. (Blanch them in boiling salt water for a couple of minutes before laying them out to dry on a tea towel).

Dolmathes take a bit of time to make, but are not difficult once you have got the hang of rolling them. Depending on the size of the vine leaves you will need 3–5 each for a first course and 5–8 for a main course. The avgolemono sauce given below has a lovely fresh taste and is frequently served in Greece with meat stuffed dolmathes, but not with vegetable ones. The dolmathes are often eaten warm, rather than hot or cold and if you do not want to make the sauce just spoon a little extra olive oil over them.

8 oz/250 g can or packet vine leaves
4 oz/125 g long grained rice
1 large onion, chopped
3 tablespoons olive oil
12 oz/375 g lamb, minced or ground
3 tablespoons chopped parsley
2 tablespoons chopped dill or fennel or 1 teaspoon dried dill weed
zest of ½ lemon and juice of 1 lemon
salt and pepper

to serve
avgolemono sauce (see below)

To prepare the vine leaves, rinse them in cold water, put them in a large bowl, pour over a kettle of boiling water, and leave for 10 minutes. Drain off the hot water and refill the bowl with cold water. The leaves by now should have separated and you will be able to take them out one by one when you are rolling the dolmathes.

Wash the rice well and soak it for a few minutes in cold water. Sauté the onion in the olive oil. When the onion is transparent, raise the heat, add the meat and stir it round with a wooden spoon until it has separated and coloured. Lower the heat, stir in the rice and pour in 3 fl oz/75 ml water. Simmer gently for 10 minutes, then turn the heat up, and stir constantly until most of the liquid has evaporated. Add the herbs, lemon zest and juice, salt and pepper and leave on one side to cool a little.

Take the leaves one by one and lay them, right side down, on a flat surface, nip off any stalk with your finger nail and put a dessertspoon of the stuffing in a small heap near the stalk end. Turn up the bottom of the leaf, then turn in the sides and roll the leaf into a small sausage. You may find that the leaves vary enormously in size, and therefore the amount of stuffing each one needs will also vary, but do not overstuff them as the rice will swell during cooking.

Lay the stuffed leaves seam side down in your basket and when you have completed a layer, sprinkle a little salt and pepper over the top. Continue until you have used all the stuffing and probably all the leaves (each packet contains 30–40 leaves). The stuffed dolmathes will fit flat in only the biggest sized basket, but they will cook perfectly well if they are layered and in a small steamer you will need to arrange them in 3 or 4 layers.

Steam for 45 minutes or until the rice is soft and cooked. As in the recipe for dolmathes with spinach and rice (p. 162), you can make these without pre-cooking the stuffing, but they will need to be steamed for up to 1 hour longer.

Serve in a little pool of avgolemono sauce: the contrast between the dark green vine leaves and the yellow sauce is very pretty.

Avgolemono Sauce

1 tablespoon cornflour
½ pt/300 ml light stock
3 egg yolks
juice of 1–2 lemons
salt and pepper

Mix the cornflour to a paste with 2 tablespoons of the stock. Heat the remaining stock and gradually stir in the cornflour paste. When you are sure that there are no lumps, bring it to simmering point and cook, stirring constantly, until it has thickened, then remove the pan from the heat.

Beat the egg yolks and add the lemon juice to them. Add 2 tablespoons of the stock, beating hard, then gradually, still stirring, pour it into the main mixture, which has been returned to a low heat, but don't let it boil or it will curdle.

Keema Stuffed Cabbage Rolls

Keema is the Indian word for any dish that is made with minced meat. It is dry-cooked and then served with dal and one of those lovely Indian breads, or used as a filling for samosas or vegetables. These keema stuffed cabbage rolls can be made ahead and steamed just before you need them. I would serve them as part of an Indian meal accompanied with a lightly spiced aromatic rice (p. 172), dal (p. 174), and some raita (see below). For a reasonably hot curry use 2 chillis, a little extra turmeric and garam masala to taste, but if you like something milder cut back to one chilli and less spice. If you are into Indian cooking, you will, no doubt, make your own garam masala, but the bought ready mixed jars (buy them in a shop that has a quick turnover) are perfectly good as long as you don't let them languish at the back of the cupboard; ready ground spices should be used fresh.

2 tablespoons vegetable oil
3 cloves garlic, crushed
1–2 green chillis, seeded and finely chopped
1 in/2.5 cm fresh ginger root, finely chopped
1 lb/500 g lamb, minced
1 teaspoon salt
½ teaspoon turmeric
1–2 teaspoons garam masala
12 outside cabbage leaves

to serve
tadka (p. 174, but make at least double the quantities)

Heat the oil in a frying pan add the garlic, chillis and ginger and let them sizzle for a minute or two. Stir in the minced lamb and continue stirring until it has browned all over. Sprinkle on the salt and turmeric and pour over 8 fl oz/250 ml water. Bring the mixture to the boil and simmer, stirring frequently to stop it burning, for 25–30 minutes or until all the moisture has evaporated. Stir in the garam masala and leave to cool.

Steam the cabbage leaves for 5–8 minutes or until they are floppy; unless you have a large 2 layered steamer you will probably have to do this a few leaves at a time. Put 1–2 dessertspoons of the keema into each leaf and fold over the top, the sides and then the bottom to make a neat parcel. Arrange them in your steamer, in 1 or 2 layers, on top of each other or however you can fit them. Steam them for 30–40 minutes and serve them on a dish with the tadka strewn over the top.

Raita

1 cucumber
2 ripe tomatoes, peeled and deseeded
salt
½ pt/300 ml thick natural yoghurt (Greek yoghurt is good)
2 sprigs of fresh mint, chopped

Peel the cucumber, grate it and put it in a sieve, leaving it to drain for 30 minutes or so. Cut the tomato flesh into narrow strips.

Sprinkle some salt over the yoghurt, beat it until smooth, and a few minutes before serving stir in the cucumber, tomato and mint.

Meatballs

Spiced and flavoured meatballs steam well and are tender and not overcrisp on the outside or overfatty in the middle. I give two versions: a simple European one, which can be altered and spiced or flavoured as you wish, and a Chinese one, which has the addition of cornflour and egg white which act to lighten the mixture and hold it together.

Serve the first version with buttered noodles and the tomato sauce on p. 96, and the Chinese version with plain steamed rice.

12 oz/375 g beef, minced
1 small onion
1 tablespoon tomato purée
1 teaspoon Dijon mustard
small bunch of parsley, chopped
1 egg
salt and pepper

Combine all the ingredients except the beef. Put the beef into a bowl, break it up with a fork and, if necessary, knead it with your hands until it is soft, then add the remaining ingredients and mix them in. You can do all this in a food processor, in which case you may find it more satisfactory to start with some lean stewing beef which can then be processed to the fineness that you like.

Form the prepared mixture into balls, each no bigger than a small onion, and steam them for 20 minutes.

Chinese Meatballs

12 oz/375 g pork, minced
1 egg white
2 teaspoons cornflour mixed with 2 teaspoons cold water
1 tablespoon soy sauce
3 spring onions, finely chopped
a few sprigs of coriander, finely chopped
salt and pepper

In a bowl, use a fork to break up the minced pork, then beat in the egg white followed by the cornflour and all the other ingredients. Using your hands—you will find it easier if they are wet—shape about 16 meatballs, each one the size of a ping-pong ball. Put the meatballs into a shallow dish or onto a plate and steam them for 20 minutes. Pour off the juices before serving.

VEGETABLES

Vegetables come in all shapes, sizes and colours, but there are few that don't steam well; generally it is the very best way of cooking them.

Steamed vegetables retain their taste, and they also retain many of the vitamins and minerals that are frequently lost when they are boiled. However, steamed green vegetables, contrary to popular opinion, do not keep their colour very well and are best if they are cut into small pieces and steamed for a very short time. If you are going to use any steamed green vegetable in a salad it is best if you set the colour by plunging them directly from the steamer basket into a bowl of cold water.

This chapter, which is far and away the longest in the book, lists, alphabetically, all the usual as well as some of the less usual vegetables together with ideas for using them.

Each vegetable has a description with suggestions for preparation and steaming times. This is followed by a list of any recipes in other sections of the book that use that vegetable. Finally, in the majority of cases, there is a recipe, or recipes, using the vegetable as the principle ingredient. Some of the recipes are not much more than a serving suggestion and some of them use the vegetable with other ingredients to make a complete dish or main course for a vegetarian meal. I have tried to make it as easy as possible to look up a particular vegetable and then to find all the uses suggested for it throughout the book.

I have kicked off with a dish of mixed vegetables, a three vegetable terrine and a selection of vegetables in a puff pastry case. Such dishes have been popularised by nouvelle cuisine, which has encouraged us to use many different vegetables at a time. Steaming seems to me to be the perfect and easy way of cooking them.

A Dish of Mixed Vegetables

One of the real joys of steaming vegetables is the ease with which you can produce a dish like this. There is nothing nicer than being served with a beautifully presented piece of meat or fish and then, on the side, several vegetables of varying shapes and colours. Sometimes the vegetables can be intermingled, looking as if they were put together by an impressionist painter; alternatively, they can be carefully arranged in separate and colourful piles to look more like a disciplined, modern still life.

In the days of boiling vegetables this would have been a labour of love, with probably 6 individual saucepans on the go. However, if you have a steaming basket of a reasonable size, or if you have 2 baskets to layer on top of each other, it really is easy to do.

I give instructions below for 6 different vegetables and at the end 2 other suggested mixtures. These lists, of course, do not have to be rigidly followed; just use a selection of vegetables that are fresh and different in colour and shape. It will look better if the vegetables are small, or cut into small pieces, for instance calabrese or cauliflower need to have all the stalk cut off and then to be divided into tiny florets.

Before you start cooking, list the vegetables you are using and mark the steaming time against each one, remembering that anything that has been cut into tiny pieces will cook very quickly. You can then work out when to put each vegetable into the basket so that they are all ready at the same time.

Another advantage of these vegetable mixtures is that they can be eaten hot, warm or cold. If you are eating them hot, a little melted butter can be poured over; if warm, try dressing them with some lemon juice spiked with garlic, and if cold, use a vinaigrette.

4 baby carrots
6 pods broad beans
12 pods peas
1 head calabrese
12 mange-touts
1 medium courgette
salt

Prepare the vegetables as follows and keep them separate.

Wash the carrots, scrape them if necessary, cut off the bottom of the root and most of the green, leaving about ¼ in/5 mm of it. Pod the broad beans and peas. Cut the stalk off the calabrese and divide the head into florets. Top, tail and string the mange-touts. Cut the courgette into matchstick-sized pieces, sprinkle them with salt and leave them to drain.

The steaming times for this selection will probably be: 8 minutes for the carrots, broad beans, peas and mange-touts; 6 minutes for the calabrese; and 3 minutes for the courgettes. (If they are piled up or the basket is very full everything may need a minute or two longer.)

Fill the steamer with water and bring to the boil. When it is simmering put the first 4 vegetables on. Add the calabrese after 2 minutes, and the courgettes 3 minutes after that. When the time is up test to make sure they are cooked and then divide the vegetables, making sure that all the colours and shapes show up, between 4 dishes or plates. (You may find that it is worthwhile spending a few seconds to pop the broad beans out of their skins).

Variation for late summer
baby sweet corn or asparagus tips, french beans, little onions, cherry tomatoes, cauliflower, broad beans

Variation for winter
tiny leeks, carrot sticks, brussels sprouts, potato slices, pieces of parsnip

Three Vegetable Terrine
(with Tomato Coulis)

This not only looks like the Striped Fish Mousseline (p. 56), it also shares with it the problem of having been overdone and over-exploited by both restaurants and cookery books. It is an attractive dish and can be made with practically any vegetable—just remember to choose 3 different colours so that you have contrasting stripes. I have used potatoes, which, surprisingly, work rather well; calabrese; and turnips to which I have added, both for taste and colour, a little tomato purée. More conventional, and also good, would be to use spinach, cauliflower and carrots. The fresh tomato coulis given below goes well with the terrine.

8 oz/250 g potatoes
8 oz/250 g turnips
8 oz/250 g calabrese
9 tablespoons double cream
3 eggs, separated
salt and pepper
1 tablespoon tomato purée

to serve
fresh tomato coulis (see below)

Peel the potatoes and turnips and cut them into chunks. Cut any stalks off the calabrese. Steam all 3 vegetables: the calabrese will take about 10 minutes and the potatoes and turnips from 12–15 minutes. Keep the vegetables separate and remove each one from the steamer as it is cooked. Meanwhile, prepare 1½ lb/750 g loaf tin by lining it with cling film.

In a bowl (don't use a food processor or blender or it will become gluey) mash the potatoes, then when they are lumpfree beat in 3 tablespoons cream and 1 egg yolk. Season well with salt and pepper and leave on one side.

In a food processor or blender purée the turnips together with 3 tablespoons cream, 1 egg yolk and the tomato purée. Season, scrape the mixture into a bowl and leave on one side.

There is no need to wash the food processor bowl or blender, just wipe it round with a piece of kitchen paper. Purée the calabrese together with remaining egg yolk and cream and season.

Whisk the egg whites until stiff then, using a metal spoon, fold approximately one third into each of the vegetable mixtures. Spoon the potato mixture into the prepared tin. Smooth it over, then add the turnip mixture followed by the calabrese one. Cover loosely with foil or a double layer of cling film and steam for 40 minutes.

Turn it out and serve, while still warm, in slices. Spoon a little tomato coulis onto the side of the plates.

Fresh Tomato Coulis

1 lb/500 g tomatoes
juice of ½ lemon
1 teaspoon sugar
salt and pepper
1–2 tablespoons cream (optional)

Blanch the tomatoes in boiling water and skin them. Halve them, cut out any hard stalks and discard them together with the pips. In a food processor or blender purée the tomato flesh and season to taste with lemon juice, sugar, salt and pepper. If you like you can also add a tablespoon or two of cream.

Feuilleté aux Légumes

A triangle of light puff pastry with colourful 'chips' of 3 different vegetables cascading from it. An onion and wine sauce is served on the side. This all sounds like a description from the menu of a rather pretentious restaurant, but it does work, is not difficult and makes an arresting first course or, with the amounts given below, main course for 2 people. For something less rich you could replace the onion sauce with the fresh tomato coulis given opposite, warmed through just before serving.

As mentioned on p. 91, you can now buy frozen sheets of puff pastry made from vegetable oils, which do not need rolling out—simply defrost and cut them out as required.

1 Spanish onion
1 oz/25 g butter
8 oz/250 g carrots
8 oz/250 g celeriac
2 tablespoons wine vinegar
8 oz/250 g courgettes
salt and pepper
¼ pt/150 ml white wine
8 oz/250 g (or 2 thin sheets) puff pastry, defrosted if frozen
¼ pt/150 ml double cream
nutmeg

Peel the onion, cut it in half, then lay each half flat on the chopping board and cut it into very thin slices. In a small saucepan melt the butter, stir in the onion slices, turn the heat to low and cover. The onion needs to cook very slowly for about ¾ hour; it should be a deep yellow and cooked almost to a purée. While it is cooking lift the lid occasionally and give it a stir; if the onion looks like browning or catching add 1 tablespoon of water.

Prepare the remaining vegetables. Peel the carrots and celeriac and cut them into small chips. Leave the carrots in a bowl of cold water and the celeriac in one of acidulated water—use 1 tablespoon vinegar to ½ pt/300 ml water. Top and tail the courgettes, cut them into chips and leave them to drain in a colander, sprinkled with salt.

Set the oven to gas 6/200° C/400° F and put your steamer to heat up.

Remove the onion from the saucepan and keep on one side. Pour the wine into a saucepan, add the remaining vinegar and set it over a high heat. Boil it down until it has reduced by about two thirds. You can then leave it off the heat until you are ready to continue with the sauce.

If necessary, roll out the pastry to ½ in/1 cm thick and cut out 4 triangles. Lay them on a wet baking sheet and put into the hot oven. They will take about 12 minutes to cook.

Drain the celeriac and put it on to steam – it will also take about 12 minutes. After 2 minutes add the drained carrots.

Finish the sauce by returning the reduced wine to the heat, bringing it to the boil, then pouring in the cream. Let it bubble fast for 3–4 minutes; it should become thick enough to coat the back of a wooden spoon. Stir in the reserved onion, season with salt and pepper and a scraping of nutmeg and keep warm until needed.

Wash the salt from the courgettes and add them to the steaming basket—if they are on top of the other vegetables they will need about 3–4 minutes steaming.

Assemble the dish by cutting each puff pastry triangle in half horizontally and putting the bottom half on each of 4 warm plates. Spoon a mixture of the vegetables onto the pastry—they will spill off it but this doesn't matter. Top with the other triangle of pastry and spoon the sauce around the pastry. Serve immediately.

Artichokes – Globe

The artichoke is the most elegant of vegetables, coming from a lovely grey leaved thistle which is frequently grown in the herbaceous border. It is the buds that are picked and eaten and occasionally resisted and left to turn into a spectacular cornflower blue flower. British grown artichokes appear in midsummer, but it is the arrival in March of the imported ones from France that gives me an early bout of spring fever.

To prepare: start by eliminating any dirt or insects by standing the artichokes upside down, for at least 30 minutes, in a bowl of cold salted water. Cut off the stem and the bottom few leaves and immediately, to stop it browning, rub ½ a lemon over the botton. You can leave the artichoke as it is or you can even it up by cutting off the top of the leaves. I think a whole artichoke looks much nicer, but if you are going to remove the choke from the artichoke to serve it stuffed, it is easier to get to the centre if the sharp ends of the leaves have been cut off.

Steaming time: 40–50 minutes
Sprinkle with salt after 5 minutes

Artichokes filled with a Chicken Liver Mousse

A filling first course, so it is probably better to choose fairly small artichokes, but try and find ones that are fresh and have no brown edges to the leaves. The artichokes should be eaten with the the chicken liver filling just set, so that the individual leaves can easily be dipped into it.

4 artichokes
1 lemon
filling
1 oz/25 g butter

2 shallots, chopped
4 oz/125 g chicken livers, trimmed and coarsely chopped
1 tablespoon brandy
1 egg
¼ pt/150 ml double cream
nutmeg
salt and pepper

Follow the instructions to prepare the artichokes and cut off the top third of all the visible leaves, then when you get to the centre just pull out the remaining leaves; you may have to give quite a hard tug. You will now be able to see the choke, which can be removed by cutting round it, then across it several times with a sharp knife before digging it out with a teaspoon. If you find it difficult to remove the inner leaves and the choke you can always leave it until the artichoke is half cooked: hold it in a tea towel, pull out the centre leaves and use a teaspoon or fork to remove the choke. Whenever you do it you must make absolutely sure that all the choke has been removed.

As you finish preparing each artichoke, put it into a bowl of water with the juice of ½ lemon squeezed into it; this is to stop any discoloration.

To make the filling, melt the butter in a frying pan, add the shallots and cook until they are transparent, then add the chicken livers and cook them, stirring, for about 3 minutes or until the outsides are browned. Raise the heat, add the brandy and stir for another minute. Transfer the contents of the pan to a food processor or blender, break in the egg, add the cream, and season with a scraping of nutmeg, salt and pepper. Blend until smooth and then refrigerate until needed. Steam the artichokes, depending on size, for 15–20 minutes, sprinkling them with salt after 5 minutes. Spoon in the filling and steam them for a further 20 minutes: they are cooked when one of the bottom leaves pulls out easily.

Two Artichoke Salad

An interesting marriage of flavours; a cold globe artichoke stuffed with diced Jerusalem artichokes in a mayonnaise dressing. Try and use smetana, which is now available from many supermarkets, in the dressing, for its very slight sweetness goes especially well with the Jerusalem artichokes. You can make more dressing and serve it separately to be spooned on top of the artichokes as you eat them.

4 globe artichokes
12 oz/375 g Jersusalem artichokes
3 fl oz/75 ml light mayonnaise
3 fl oz/75 ml smetana or yoghurt
salt and pepper

Follow the instructions to prepare and steam the globe artichokes. Leave them to cool for a few minutes, then remove the central leaves and chokes and leave until cold.

Peel the Jerusalem artichokes, cut them into bite size cubes and steam them, sprinkled with a little salt, for 15–20 minutes or until tender.

Mix the mayonnaise and smetana or yoghurt together and season to taste. Toss the cooled Jerusalem artichokes in the dressing.

To serve, place a globe artichoke on each plate and spoon the Jerusalem artichokes into the centre.

Artichokes – Jerusalem

Jerusalem artichokes are best known as a soup vegetable but they are good eaten in other ways, for example in a white parsley sauce or, more extravagantly, with a hollandaise sauce. They are also good topped with garlic breadcrumbs, as suggested for turnips (p. 168).

Even the new smoother varieties of artichokes are knobbly, making peeling boring and difficult. There are 3 alternatives: you can peel them raw and then steam them— when peeled, if you are not going to cook them immediately, put them into acidulated water; you can steam them until they are half cooked, peel them, and then continue the steaming; or you can steam them until they are fully cooked and then peel them, but that is very difficult. As they are a comparatively cheap vegetable, I am inclined to use the first method, chopping off knobs and skin together and finishing with a smooth, rounded tuber. Cube the artichokes or cut them to more or less the same size.

Steaming time: 15–25 minutes
Sprinkle with salt after 5 minutes

Recipes:
Jerusalem Artichoke Soup (p. 29)
Jerusalem Artichoke Soufflé (p. 43)
Two Artichoke Salad (p. 123)

Artichoke and Beetroot Salad

A layered salad, with white artichokes in a jellied mayonnaise topped by the jewel coloured beetroot set in a lemon jelly. Taste wise the two slightly sweet vegetables marry well and the contrasting textures are complementary. The salad is good with cold meats and would brighten the table at Christmas, especially as both vegetables are easily available and cheap at that time.

Make it in a 1½–2 pt/900 ml–1.2 litre round bottomed pudding bowl or jelly mould.

12 oz/375 g raw beetroot
12 oz/375 g Jerusalem artichokes
3 teaspoons gelatine
juice of ½ lemon
1 tablespoon wine vinegar

> salt and pepper
>
> 4 tablespoons mayonnaise

Steam the beetroot (p. 133). Wash and peel the artichokes, cut them into bite sized cubes and leave them in acidulated water until needed. When the beetroot has cooked change the steaming water and, if necessary, wash any red colour from the basket. Steam the artichokes until tender and leave on one side.

Top, tail and skin the beetroot and cut it into neat slices. Put ¼ pt/150 ml water into a bowl, sprinkle over 1½ teaspoons gelatine and put it over a pan of hot water to melt. When the gelatine has melted add the lemon juice, vinegar and salt to taste. Pour a little into the bottom of your bowl or mould and put it in the refrigerator, or even better the deep freeze, to set. Keep the remaining gelatine mixture somewhere warm. When the gelatine in the bowl has set, arrange the beetroot slices on it; try and make the first layer with even sized slices so that it will look good when turned out. Pour over the remaining gelatine mixture and refrigerate.

After the beetroot mixture has set continue with the next layer. Pour another ¼ pt/150 ml water into a bowl, sprinkle over the remaining gelatine and put it over a pan of hot water. When the gelatine has melted stir in the mayonnaise and season to taste. Gently stir in the cooked artichoke pieces and spoon the mixture over the beetroot jelly. Smooth the top and leave to set.

To serve, dip the bowl or mould into a bowl of hot water, then turn it out onto a plate.

Asparagus

It is now easy to buy tall asparagus steamers, which enable you to cook perfect asparagus, with the stalks cooked in a very little water while the tips are slowly steamed. Otherwise you will need an electric steamer or a good sized round one. The asparagus spears can be cooked flat or, perhaps even better, propped at a slight angle across the basket so that the tips are further away from the simmering water than the stalks. Prop them up on a few new potatoes, which, as well as helping to slow up the speed that the tips cook at, will absorb some of the asparagus flavour and make delicious eating.

Asparagus is frequently eaten hot or warm with butter, salt and pepper and perhaps a squeeze of lemon juice, but it is equally good eaten cold with a vinaigrette. If it is going to be eaten cold it is best to arrest the cooking and help preserve the colour by plunging it straight from the steamer into a bowl of cold water.

To prepare, cut off the woody stems and use a damp cloth to wipe off any mud.

Steaming time: 7–20 minutes.

Asparagus varies in thickness from the sprue or grass to the very thick white French variety and the cooking time varies just as much. Test it by piercing the stalk with a sharp knife; the thickest part should be tender.

Sprinkle with a little salt after about 2 minutes or when the spears are wet.

Recipe

Asparagus Soup (p. 25)

Asparagus and Crème Fraîche Tartlets

One of the prettiest of first courses and although rather time consuming and fiddly it can be made in advance and just heated briefly in the oven at the last minute. Crème fraîche, which is the very light French version of our sour cream, has become quite easy to find, but it is simple to make and I give a recipe for it, which should be made a day ahead. For a slightly sharper taste you could use half yoghurt and half crème fraîche or you could mix a thick yoghurt with a little double cream or a low fat soft cheese.

I like the slightly nutty taste wholewheat flour gives the pastry, but if you prefer it, you could use an ordinary shortcrust. Kitchen shops sell little individual tartlet tins with a diameter of 3–4 in/7–10 cm and the bigger ones are best for this dish.

pastry

3 oz/75 g plain flour
2 oz/50 g wholewheat flour
3 oz/75 g cold butter plus extra for greasing tins
2 oz/50 g Cheddar cheese, grated
salt and pepper
1 small egg yolk

filling

½ pt/300 ml crème fraîche – or make your own with ½ pt/300ml single cream and 2 tablespoons sour cream
12, 16 or 20 asparagus spears (depending on their thickness and the size of the tartlets)
¼ red pepper

To make your own crème fraîche, all you need to do is to mix the two creams together, then cover the bowl and leave it overnight in a warm place, such as an airing cubboard, by which time it should have set and be the consistency of a thick yoghurt.

The pastry is most easily made in a food processor: put the flours in the bowl together with the butter, cut into cubes, cheese and seasonings and process for about 5 seconds or until you reach the breadcrumb stage. Add the egg yolk and a few drops of water and process for a further 10 seconds, and if the pastry has not turned into a ball add a little more water and process for a few more seconds or until it does. Turn it out, divide it into 4 balls, flatten each one slightly, wrap in cling film and refrigerate for up to 30 minutes.

Roll each pastry ball out into a thin circle, fit into the greased tins and, using the rolling pin, trim off the edges neatly. Prick the bases all over with a fork, line each one with a piece of foil and refrigerate again for about 20 minutes. Bake in a preheated oven, gas 6/200° C/400° F for 10–15 minutes or until crisp and light golden. Leave to cool. These pastry cases can be made ahead and then stored for a day or two in an airtight tin.

Prepare the asparagus by cutting off the woody stems and then laying the spears side by side in the steamer. Add the piece of red pepper and steam for 8–10 minutes, depending on the thickness of the asparagus spears; remember to sprinkle them with a little salt after 2 minutes steaming. Leave them to cool, but if you are not going to use them straight away, cover them to stop them drying out. (The steaming liquid and the leftover parts of the spears can be used to make the soup on p. 25.)

To assemble: stir some salt and pepper into the crème fraîche, or whatever mixture you are using, and then spoon it into the pastry tartlets. Cut the bottom part off the asparagus spears to use for soup, and arrange 3, 4 or 5 tips in each case – bunch the stalks together and spray them out as if they were a bunch of flowers. Cut a thin strip from the pepper and lay it over the stalks, using a teaspoon to push it under at the ends, so that it resembles a ribbon. Lay the tartlets on baking sheets, cover with foil, and just before serving heat for 5 minutes in a preheated oven at gas 2/150° C/300° F.

Aubergines

Missing out the almost obligatory preliminary frying of aubergines and steaming them instead is most satisfactory. You don't have the colour of the fried slices but neither do you have globules of oil seeping out all over the plate. Aubergines are real sponges when fried and I find it a great relief to be able to add oil at the final stage of the dish without having to think about the enormous amount that has already been soaked up by the vegetable.

I have tried steaming a whole aubergine and, although it worked, I think they are better if they are halved, salted and drained of the bitter juices before cooking (see below, Aubergine Purée).

Steaming time: 25–30 minutes (halved, salted and drained)

Recipe Poisson Provençale (p. 69)

Aubergine Purée

An aubergine purée is found throughout the Middle East, and is often referred to as Poor Man's Caviar. It has many variations: you could add a tablespoon of tahini or some yoghurt and chopped mint leaves. Serve with fingers of pitta bread to dip into it.

1 large aubergine
salt and pepper
juice of ½ a lemon
1 tablespoon olive oil
1 shallot, finely chopped

Prepare the aubergine by cutting it in half lengthwise. With a sharp knife, being very careful not to pierce the skin, cut round the flesh of each half and then make several cuts crosswise in both directions to give you a diamond pattern. Sprinkle each half liberally with salt and leave for half an hour. Under a running tap, wash out the juices and salt and then pat the tops dry with a piece of kitchen paper. Put the halves to steam for 25 minutes or until the flesh is soft, then leave them upside down for a few minutes for any water to drain out.

Spoon the flesh from the skins and mash it with a fork or in a food processor or blender, together with the lemon juice, olive oil and shallot. Season to taste and transfer the purée to a serving dish.

Stuffed Aubergines

These are very good either hot or cold and they are also used as the base for Poisson Provençale on p. 69. If you are eating them alone you can always jazz them up a bit by adding some crushed coriander seeds to the shallots and garlic when you are frying them, or you could stir in extra olive oil together with some pitted and chopped black olives. For something slightly more substantial, lay a lattice of 4 or 5 anchovy fillets over the top of each aubergine half, then drizzle on a little more olive oil and sprinkle with chopped parsley.

2 medium sized, long shaped aubergines
salt and pepper
1 tablespoon olive oil
3 shallots or 1 small onion, peeled and chopped
2 cloves garlic, crushed
8 oz/250 g tomatoes, peeled, deseeded and roughly chopped
small bunch chopped basil or ½ teaspoon dried oregano
juice of ½ lemon

Prepare and steam the aubergines following the instructions for Aubergine Purée on p. 128.

Melt the oil in a saucepan, add the shallots and garlic and cook until they are transparent. Add the tomatoes and continue frying for no more than 5 minutes, or until they are just cooked. Scrape the flesh from the aubergines, roughly chop it and stir it into the tomato mixture. Add the herbs and lemon juice and season, being careful with the salt.

Spoon the ratatouille mixture into the aubergine shells and either refrigerate them to eat them cold, or put them flat in your steamer basket and steam for about 15 minutes or until they are well heated.

Aubergines filled with Tomato Sauce with Cheese

The Italian name for this dish, which rolls off the tongue beautifully, is Melanzane alla Parmigiana.

The tomato sauce can be made with a can of tomatoes or, even better, a carton or jar of tomato passata. This is becoming more widely available and saves time and trouble as the tomatoes have already been puréed and sieved.

2 medium aubergines
salt and pepper
1 large onion, finely chopped
2 cloves garlic, crushed
2 tablespoons olive oil
14 oz/450 g can tomatoes or 17 fl oz/500 ml packet of passata
a few basil leaves (if available)
a few sprigs of fresh marjoram or 1 teaspoon dried oregano or Italian mixed herbs
4 oz/125 g mozzarella or fontina cheese
1 oz/25 g parmesan cheese, grated

Prepare and steam the aubergines following the instructions for Aubergine Purée (p. 128).

Sauté the onion and garlic for a few minutes in the olive oil before adding the tomatoes, then simmer, stirring frequently, for about half an hour or until the sauce has thickened. Add the herbs, very little salt, some pepper and leave it on one side until needed.

When the water has drained from the aubergines and they are cool, scrape out the flesh, chop it and stir it into the tomato sauce. Cut the mozzarella or fontina into little cubes, mix them in and taste for seasoning.

Put each aubergine skin onto a square of foil, bunch it up round the base and place them flat in the steamer basket. Fill each shell with a quarter of the tomato mixture, sprinkle over the parmesan and steam (if your steamer lid drips the moisture back cover with a tea towel before putting on the lid) for 20 minutes, by which time the filling will be hot and the cheese melted and stringy.

Aubergine Casserole

This is a good family supper dish and you can make it suitable for vegetarians by omitting the ham and using rather more cheese. It is not really a steamed dish but I have included it as the aubergine and pepper have a preliminary cooking, which I always used to do by frying and I now do by steaming which seems to retain their flavour, while reducing the amount of fat in the final dish. I do fry the onions, but I suppose the really fat-conscious could also steam them and then just pour over the tomatoes before the final baking.

2 aubergines
salt and pepper
1 green pepper
2 medium onions, thinly sliced
1–2 cloves garlic, crushed
2 tablespoons olive oil or butter
1 tablespoon plain flour
17 fl oz/500 ml packet passata or 14 oz/450 g can creamed tomatoes
½ teaspoon dried oregano
8 oz/250 g sliced ham, roughly chopped
2 oz/50 g cooking cheese, grated

Cut the aubergines into thick slices, salt them and leave them to drain for half an hour. Cut the pepper in half and remove the stalk, pith and seeds. Pat the aubergine slices dry with a piece of kitchen paper and steam them and the pepper for 15 minutes.

Fry the onions and garlic in the oil or butter until they are soft and yellow, stirring frequently to stop them burning. Sprinkle the flour over the onions, stir it in then pour in the tomatoes. Bring to the boil, season with the oregano, some ground pepper and perhaps a little salt, and simmer gently for about 10 minutes, to thicken it slightly.

Grease an oval ovenproof dish well and cut the green pepper into strips. Place the aubergine slices in one layer (if possible) in the bottom of the dish and spread the green pepper over it. Cover with the ham and then pour the tomato sauce over the top. Sprinkle on the cheese and bake at gas 6/200° C/400° F for 25–30 minutes or until the cheese has melted and is bubbling.

Beans – Broad

One of the best vegetables one could possibly eat are tiny broad beans, served with a little butter, some lemon juice and perhaps a sprinkling of parsley.

Unfortunately very few of us have access to the perfect baby bean and have to make do with large, or frequently, over-large ones.

Large beans can be very good; try them with the avgolemono sauce on p. 114, but the over-large one are really only worth eating in soups or as a purée. Large broad beans are nicer to eat if skinned, which, needless to say, is a boring and time consuming job. It is easiest to do after the beans are cooked and while they are still hot (you may find you need to wear rubber gloves). Take each bean, cut off the scarred end with a sharp knife and squeeze; the bean should just pop out.

3 lb/1.5 kg beans in their pods will give you about 1 lb/500 g of podded beans; after cooking and skinning this will be just enough for 4 people. If you use baby beans you will need at least another 1 lb/500 g.

Steaming times: small beans—6–8 minutes
large beans—8–12 minutes
Sprinkle with salt after 2 minutes

Recipe A Dish of Mixed Vegetables (p. 118)

Purée of Broad Beans in a Bacon Wrapping

Broad beans have a great affinity with pork and this purée of older broad beans with the addition of onion, cream and egg is spooned inside bacon lined ramekins, steamed and then turned out. It can be eaten by itself or you could make it more substantial by serving it with poached eggs. Either way, crusty granary bread is a good accompaniment.

2 lb/1 kg broad beans
8 oz/250 g thin cut streaky bacon
1 small onion, finely chopped
1 oz/25 g butter
1 egg
2 tablespoons cream
salt and pepper

Pod the broad beans and steam them for about 10 minutes or until cooked. Meanwhile line 4 ramekins with the bacon—you will need 2 rashers for each ramekin—lay them across each other and let the ends hang over the sides. The bacon rashers should be very thin and, if necessary, you can stretch them by drawing the back of a knife along them while pulling with the other hand.

Sauté the onion in the butter until it is soft and transparent. Skin the cooked beans and purée them, together with the egg, cream and seasonings, in a food processor or blender. Add the onion mixture and process again to just mix it in.

Spoon the purée into the prepared ramekins, cover each one loosely with foil or a double layer of cling film and steam them for 40 minutes. If you slip a knife round the edge of the ramekins it should be easy to turn them out.

Beans – Green

Green beans now seem to come in many different sizes and with just as many names, french beans, bobby beans and snap beans being just three of them. There is no point in getting muddled over them, for they are all similar and all need the same preparation with the steaming time adjusted to take account of the thickness of the bean.

The little matchstick thin french beans, which are often imported from Kenya, are the best and the most expensive, but provided you choose fresh, crisp and unwilted beans there is no need to buy the most expensive ones. French beans are essential for a salade niçoise and a good addition to many other salads, but if you are going to use them in this way, set the colour by plunging them directly from the steamer into a bowl of cold water. Also, only add the dressing at the last minute, otherwise the beans will soak it up, darken in colour and go limp.

To prepare, top and tail the beans and if there are any strings peel them off.

Steaming times: thin french beans—6–8 minutes
larger beans—8–15 minutes
Sprinkle with salt after 5 minutes

Recipes
Summer Vegetable Soup (p. 26)
Baby Sweetcorn with Green Beans and Red Pepper (p. 164)

Beans with Garlic and Pine Nuts

12 oz/375 g green beans
2 oz/50 g butter
2 oz/50 g pine nuts or split almonds
2 cloves garlic, crushed
salt and pepper

Prepare the beans and put them on to steam. While they are cooking, melt the butter in a small saucepan, add the nuts and, turning constantly, cook them until they start to brown. Stir in the garlic and the salt and pepper and keep warm on one side until needed. Remove the cooked beans to a warm dish, pour over the butter and nuts and serve very hot.

Beans – Runner

Runner beans, with their profusion of red flowers, were originally grown as a decorative plant and indeed they are still a very pretty feature of many an English cottage garden. They are one of the best vegetables of late summer and, I think, often underrated, but they do need harvesting at the right time and not left to grow to be tough and around a foot long.

Prepare them by topping and tailing and, if necessary, de-stringing them. They should then be cut into diagonal strips: this is time consuming with a kitchen knife but it is cheap to buy a bean cutter. They should be served on their own, with just a knob of butter and a grinding of pepper; I do not believe in putting them into soups or casseroles.

Steaming time: 12–15 minutes
Sprinkle with salt after 2 minutes

Beetroot

Like many people I have a horror of sliced or cubed beetroot swimming in an unbelievably strong dose of malt vinegar and, as a result, it has taken me a long time to come round to the virtues of beetroot. It makes, of course, a good soup, but is also worth using as a hot vegetable. The beetroot and orange given below is simple to make and the finished dish has the most stunning colour.

Uncooked beetroot are not always easy to find but bought cooked ones are often inclined to be overboiled and tasteless. In fact, steaming is preferable to boiling when so much of the flavour seems to get washed out in the water.

To prepare: wash the beetroot thoroughly and trim them, being very careful not to let them bleed by puncturing the skins or cutting too closely when you trim off the leaves and roots. Beetroot are cooked when the skin is loose and moves if pressure is put on the outside (wear a pair of rubber gloves when testing them). You can test them with a skewer or sharp knife, but remember that the juice will run out every time you puncture the skin. However, if you are going to use the steaming water to make a sauce this will not matter so much. When they are cooked run them under a cold tap before peeling them.

Steaming times: small beetroot—40–50 minutes
medium beetroot—50–60 minutes
large beetroot—over an hour

Recipes
Chilled Beetroot and Cucumber Soup (p. 24)
Artichoke and Beetroot Salad (p. 124)

Beetroot in an Orange Sauce

1 lb/500 g small uncooked beetroot
2 oranges
2 cloves
1 teaspoon cornflour
salt and pepper

Garnish
1 teaspoon chopped parsley

Follow the instructions to prepare the beetroot and steam them until cooked, having added the orange zest and the cloves to the steaming water. Peel the beetroot and cut into dice.

Strain the orange rind and cloves from the steaming liquid and transfer about 7 fl oz/200 ml to a pan or, over a high heat, reduce the liquid to about this amount. Squeeze the juice from the oranges, mix it with the cornflour and add it to the liquid. Stirring constantly, bring it to the boil to let it thicken. Add the beetroot and its juices, season with salt and pepper and serve, warm, sprinkled with the parsley.

Brussels Sprouts

Brussels sprouts take a little time to prepare as each one needs to have the outside leaves removed; if they are big and old, it is a good idea to cut a cross in the bottom of each one to help the stalk cook as quickly as the leaves.

They are always cooked whole and young ones are good eaten with butter and a squeeze of lemon juice, or a light scraping of nutmeg. At Christmas they are traditionally mixed with whole chestnuts, which can, after peeling, be cooked and softened by steaming them alongside the sprouts. Brussels sprouts, although they are strong tasting, also mix well with other flavours; such as onion and bacon as given below.

If you have large, end of season sprouts they are good made into a purée which can then be scattered with a few grilled split almonds or some little cubes of fried bread.

Steaming times: tiny brussels sprouts—8–10 minutes
                 medium—10–12 minutes
                 large—12–14 minutes
Sprinkle with salt after 2 minutes.

Brussels Sprouts with Onion and Bacon

1 lb/500 g brussels sprouts

4 oz/125 g thinly sliced streaky bacon

1 medium onion, chopped

salt and pepper

Wash and trim the sprouts and steam until just cooked. While they are steaming fry the bacon until it is crisp, then put it to drain on a piece of kitchen paper. Discard all but a tablespoon of the fat and add the onion. Cook over a medium heat and when the onion is soft and yellowing add the sprouts, cut into halves if they are large ones. Season with salt and pepper, turn it all into a serving dish and crumble the bacon over the top.

Cabbage

Due to the bad, overcooked food that used to be the norm for institutional cooking, cabbage suffers from the reputation of being tasteless, smelly and watery. However, the newer varieties and the habit of selling younger and smaller cabbages, means that the cooking time is shorter and that the final result is both full of taste and smell-free. If you are steaming cabbage to eat as a vegetable, the variety doesn't matter, just choose the one that looks freshest in the shop; they are all treated in the same way and steamed for more or less the same time.

Prepare the cabbage by removing any dry outside leaves, quartering it, cutting out the stalk and shredding the remainder. Wash the shreds in a bowl of cold water before putting them into the steaming basket.

Steaming time: 5–10 minutes (depending on type of cabbage and size of shreds)
Sprinkle with salt after 2 minutes

Recipes
Medallions of Pork Tenderloin in Cabbage Leaves (p. 110)
Keema Stuffed Cabbage Rolls (p. 114)

Purée of Cabbage

1 green cabbage
1 oz/25 g butter
1 oz/25 g flour
2 tablespoons white wine vinegar
salt and pepper
a few juniper berries or caraway seeds (optional)

Follow the instructions to prepare and steam the cabbage, then purée it in a food processor or blender. In a saucepan, melt the butter, stir in the flour and cook it for a minute or so. Stir in the vinegar and immediately add the cabbage and stir it altogether. If it seems to be too dry add a little of the steaming water. Season with salt and pepper and, if used, a few crushed juniper berries or caraway seeds, heat through and serve.

Cabbage Pudding

I always think that Savoy is one of the best of the cabbages, its only problem being that water is apt to get caught in its crinkly leaves so that it turns up at the table as a soggy mess. Steaming is therefore ideal, especially if you cover the basket with a clean tea towel to catch the condensation drips before they reach the cabbage. This dish, I call it a pudding for want of a better name, is a very useful one for it can be made ahead and reheated. It goes well with any meat or game, with sausages or grilled bacon rashers.

1 medium Savoy cabbage
2 medium onions
1 carrot, chopped
2 stalks celery, chopped
salt and pepper
1 oz/25 g butter plus extra for greasing basin
1 oz/25 g flour
bouquet garni
¼ pt/150 ml sour cream

Discard the outside leaves and any tough stalk from the cabbage and roughly chop the rest. If it is necessary to wash the cabbage, shake it vigorously in a tea towel to dry it as much as possible. Chop 1 of the onions and put it in the steaming water with the carrot and celery; bring it to simmering point. Steam the cabbage for 5 minutes, sprinkle it with ½ teaspoon salt, stir it in and steam for a further 5 minutes or until it is just cooked but still crisp to the bite. Leave it, covered, until needed.

Finely chop the second onion and sauté it with the butter, until it is soft and transparent. Sprinkle on the flour and cook briefly before slowly adding ½ pt/300 ml of the strained steaming liquid and stirring until it thickens. Add the bouquet garni, a good grinding of pepper and a little salt and cook for 5 minutes. Leave the sauce to cool slightly before stirring in the sour cream and finally the cabbage. Turn it all into a greased basin, making sure the bouquet garni is on the top, cover with cling film and steam again for about 20 minutes or until the cabbage is hot. Remove the bouquet garni and turn the pudding out onto a serving dish.

Whole Stuffed Savoy Cabbage

Chou farci is the French farmer's wife's version of the English shepherd's pie, in that it is frequently cooked on Monday with Sunday's leftovers being chopped up and added to the stuffing. It is also very often made with sausage meat and Jane Grigson says how good it is made with the best quality Cumberland sausage. More sophisticated, and a classic dish, is a cabbage stuffed with a partridge, for the flavours merge together beautifully.

The stuffing I give here is a good, easy to make, midweek one, and if you wish, you can replace some or all of the bacon with sausages.

Use an even shaped Savoy or green cabbage with a good heart; I personally prefer the savoy and it is also easier to peel the leaves back to stuff it. A 3–3½ lb/1.5–1.8 kg cabbage should hold this amount of stuffing and happily feed 4 hungry people. Steaming keeps the cabbage very moist which means that a sauce is a pleasant, but not absolutely necessary, addition. The tomato and carrot sauce (p. 138) is good, or you could reduce the steaming liquid, thicken it with beurre manié and flavour it with more herbs and parsley.

1 large cabbage
3 oz/75 g long grained rice
bouquet garni or ½ teaspoon mixed herbs
8 oz/250 g carrots, shredded
8 oz/250 g green streaky bacon rashers, rinds removed
1 onion, chopped
salt and pepper
1 egg, beaten

Make sure that the cabbage is clean and mud free, remove any broken outside leaves and steam the whole cabbage for 20 minutes; you will need a deep steamer to do this, or you might be able to reverse the second basket so that it is upside down over the bottom one. If you do this place the lid over the top. After 20 minutes, remove the cabbage and leave to cool.

Put the rice and the bouquet garni or mixed herbs with 3 fl oz/75 ml water in a shallow dish. Steam it for 20 minutes or until the water has been absorbed and the rice is cooked. Keep it on one side.

When the cabbage is cool enough to handle, gently bend back about 3 layers of the outside leaves, and, using a small sharp knife, carefully cut out the heart, leaving a flat platform of stalk to hold the stuffing. Cut away and discard any stalk or tough pieces attached to the heart, chop the remainder and keep on one side.

Steam the carrots for 5 minutes and keep on one side.

Cut the bacon into pieces and slowly fry it until it is just cooked, but not crisp. Using a slotted spoon remove the bacon from the pan and, in the remaining fat, fry the onion until it is soft.

In a large bowl—I find it is easiest if I use my hands—mix the rice, carrots, bacon, onion and any remaining fat, and chopped cabbage leaves. Season with salt and pepper and mix in the beaten egg.

Take 2 new 'J' cloths, lay them on a flat surface at right angles across each other and place the cabbage in the centre. Shape the stuffing into a ball, put it into the middle of the cabbage and fold the outside leaves up and over it. Fold over the 'J' cloths to make a neat parcel. Steam for 2 hours, unfold the cloths, reverse the cabbage into a bowl or back into the steaming basket, and then reverse it again to get it the right way up into a serving dish.

Tomato and Carrot Sauce

1 tablespoon vegetable oil
1 small onion, finely chopped
1 clove garlic, crushed with a little salt (optional)
14 oz/450 g can creamed tomatoes or 17 fl oz/500 ml packet of passata
1 large or 2 medium carrots, grated
½ teaspoon sugar
1 bay leaf
1 teaspoon chopped fresh thyme or ½ teaspoon dried thyme
pepper

Heat the oil, stir in the onion and garlic and let them sizzle gently until the onion is soft and transparent. Add all the remaining ingredients, bring the sauce to the boil and simmer, stirring frequently, for 20 minutes. If the sauce is too thin boil it rapidly to reduce it further. Remove the bay leaf and taste for seasoning.

Calabrese or Broccoli

Large headed green calabrese has in recent years been imported in quantity from countries like Spain and is often sold, a few stems at a time, wrapped up in a piece of cling film. Its British grown close relation, purple sprouting broccoli, can, if eaten young and fresh, be delicious, but it is inclined to be stringy. Sometimes one comes across Cape broccoli, which is a large headed purple broccoli; it is very tender and delicate tasting and cooks slightly more quickly than the other varieties.

You can either cut off the florets and steam them with a tiny piece of stem attached to each one, or retain the big heads, just peeling the stems. Peeled broccoli dries up and toughens very quickly, so only prepare it just before cooking.

Steaming times: little florets—5–6 minutes
heads—8–14 minutes
Sprinkle with salt after 2 minutes

Recipes
Hot Chicken Breasts vinaigrette (p. 96)
A Dish of Mixed Vegetables (p. 118)
Three Vegetable Terrine (p. 119)
A Mould of Cauliflower and Calabrese (p. 141)

Calabrese with Cherry Tomatoes

4 oz/125 g cherry tomatoes
1 lb/500 g calabrese

salt and pepper

1 oz/25 g butter or margarine

Peel the little tomatoes by steaming each one for a few seconds, then briefly plunging into cold water. Keep them on one side.

Discard any tough stalk from the calabrese then steam for 8–12 minutes, or until it just starts to become tender. Add the tomatoes, sprinkle with salt and steam for a further 1–2 minutes or until the calabrese is cooked and the tomatoes are heated, but not cooked and mushy.

Transfer to a serving dish. Put the butter to melt over the top and give it all a good grinding of pepper.

Carrots

One of the most cheering and prettiest of spring sights is to go to the greengrocer and see bunches of young carrots with their wispy leaves hanging out of the box or over the counter. We are not the first generation to appreciate the leaves; Carolean ladies wore them pinned to their dresses or as decoration, perhaps cheaper and more easily obtainable than peacock's feathers, for their hats. Really fresh little carrots are also a joy to eat, washed but unpeeled, steamed, and served with butter and a good sprinkling of parsley. In fact they are such an essential and good looking part of nouvelle cuisine that, in the winter, many chefs cut larger and older carrots down into baby look alikes.

As well as being a vegetable or salad ingredient, carrots are an essential addition to numerous other dishes for, rather like onions, they add a good background flavour. Carrots steam well, whole or cut into any shape or size that might take your fancy. I give steaming times for whole baby carrots and for sliced older carrots; and if you are going to cook grated ones or curls you will have to reduce the time accordingly.

Steaming times: whole baby carrots—7–10 minutes

medium sliced carrots—5–7 minutes if spread out, longer if the basket is full

Sprinkle with salt after 2 minutes

Recipes
Summer Vegetable Soup (p. 26)
Mount Koya Mushi (p. 37)
Fish and Vegetable Terrine (p. 52)
Boned Trout with a Julienne of Vegetables (p. 69)
Hot Chicken Breasts Vinaigrette (p. 96)
Lightly Spiced Tomato Sauce (p. 96)
A Dish of Mixed Vegetables (p. 118)
Feuilleté aux Légumes (p. 121)
Tomato and Carrot Sauce (p. 138)
Courgette Boats with a Carrot Stuffing (p. 146)
Leek and Carrot Terrine (p. 150)
Timbale of Parsnip and Carrot (p. 156)

Carrot and Stilton Tart

Carrot and Stilton are a good combination and this tart which is finished with slices of carrot arranged in circles on the top, also looks very attractive. Serve it with a green salad and it makes a good main course vegetarian dish.

I find that a food processor makes excellent pastry, but if you don't own one use the amounts given and make the pastry by your normal method. I give instructions for making one tart in a 9 in/23 cm flan or quiche tin, but you could make individual tartlets in which case you would need to reduce the cooking time slightly.

pastry
6 oz/175 g plain flour
3 oz/75 g cold butter, cubed
salt
1–2 tablespoons cold water
filling
1¼ lb/600 g carrots
4 oz/125 g Stilton cheese
3 egg yolks
cayenne pepper
a little melted butter

Make the pastry by putting the flour, butter and a pinch of salt into a food processor and processing until you reach the breadcrumb stage. Stop the machine, sprinkle on the ice cold water and process again until the pastry draws into a ball. Turn it out, knead it into a smooth ball, wrap it in cling film and refrigerate for 20 minutes.

Roll the cooled pastry out and use to line a 9 in/23 cm flan tin. Prick the bottom with a fork, cover the pastry with a piece of foil and weigh it down with dried beans. Bake it in a preheated oven, gas 6/200° C/400° F, for 15 to 20 minutes or until it is just becoming crisp.

Meanwhile top, tail and peel the carrots. Cut 8 oz/250 g into cubes, and leave the remainder, which will be used for the topping, whole. Steam them for 12–15 minutes or until the cubes are very soft and the whole carrots just cooked.

Purée the cubed carrots in a food processor or blender. Add the cheese, egg yolks, salt and a pinch of cayenne pepper and whiz them all together until the mixture is smooth. Pour it into the pastry case.

Cut the whole carrots into even slices and arrange them, with the slices slightly overlapping, in circles on top of the cheese mixture. Brush the melted butter over the top and bake in a medium oven, gas 4/180° C/350° F, for 20 minutes or until the cheese mixture only just wobbles if you agitate the tin. If the carrot slices look like burning cover the tart with a piece of foil for the last few minutes.

Like most quiche mixtures this is best if it is served warm.

Cauliflower

Cauliflower can be cooked whole, cut into quarters or, quickest of all, in florets. Boxes of ready cut florets are now available from supermarkets, but if you should buy one do cook them immediately for a cut up cauliflower will very quickly dry up.

Cauliflower goes well with many sauces and is often served covered with a béchamel or a cheese sauce. It is also good sprinkled with fried breadcrumbs, either on their own or mixed with chopped hard-boiled egg. Cauliflower makes a very good salad ingredient and is often used raw; however, in some salads, such as the one with anchovies given below, it is better if it is slightly cooked.

If you are going to cook the cauliflower whole, trim off the outside leaves and dig into the base to remove some of the tough core.

Steaming times: whole cauliflower—14–18 minutes
florets—8–12 minutes
Sprinkle with salt after 3 minutes

Cauliflower and Anchovy Salad

1 medium cauliflower, divided into florets
1 tablespoon wine vinegar
3 tablespoons olive oil
1 clove garlic, crushed
salt and pepper
4–6 anchovy fillets, chopped
6 black olives, stoned and quartered
1 tablespoon capers
1 tablespoon chopped parsley

Steam the cauliflower florets, to slightly soften them, for 4–5 minutes. Make a dressing with the vinegar and the oil, stir in the garlic and season it with salt and pepper. Toss the cauliflower, anchovy fillets, olives and capers together, pour over the dressing and sprinkle the top with parsley. Leave for at least half an hour, not refrigerated, for the flavours to blend, before eating.

A Mould of Cauliflower and Calabrese

In this dish the slightly cooked florets of cauliflower and calabrese are arranged in a pudding basin, flower side out. The centre is filled with a little parsley sauce and the whole is covered with a piece of foil and steamed.

The hot mould is then turned out onto a dish, giving a rounded pudding made up of the white and green florets. It looks unusual and has the advantage that it can all be made ahead and steamed just before serving.

You will need a pudding basin with a capacity of 1½ pt/900 ml.

1 medium cauliflower
8 oz/250 g calabrese
1 oz/25 g butter + extra for greasing the pudding basin
1 oz/25 g plain flour
¼ pt/150 ml milk
salt and pepper
bunch of parsley, chopped

Cut any stalks from the cauliflower and calabrese and steam the florets for 4–5 minutes (sprinkle them with salt after 2 minutes), then leave them on one side to cool.

Use the butter, flour and milk to make a thick white sauce. Season it well and stir in a good handful of chopped parsley.

Grease your pudding basin, then arrange the florets, flower side out, inside it and up the sides, using cauliflower and calabrese alternately. Spoon the sauce into the centre and fill the basin with any leftover florets. Cover the basin with foil or a double layer of cling film and steam it for 20–25 minutes.

Turn the hot mould onto a dish and serve immediately.

Celeriac

To keep its colour celeriac usually has lemon juice added to the cooking water, but I find that it stays white after peeling and cutting into chunks, if I soak it for 10 minutes or so in acidulated water and then put it directly into the steamer basket. When cooked it makes a good purée, just add some butter and perhaps a tablespoon of cream. Try serving it side by side with a parsnip purée as the flavours blend well.

Steaming time: 15–20 minutes cut into chunks of about 1 in/2.5 cm
Sprinkle with salt as you put it in the steaming basket

Recipes
Celeriac and Red Pepper Soup (p. 27)
Feuilleté aux Légumes (p. 121)

Timbales of Celeriac

This makes a pleasant tasting first course which is best eaten warm. I give instructions for a light avgolemono type sauce, which tastes good but gives no colour contrast, so serve them on bright plates with perhaps a black olive on top of the timbales and a small sprig of coriander on the side. You could serve them with a fresh tomato coulis, but you would need very little or it would overpower the timbales. Otherwise you could try a light sunflower oil mayonnaise, coloured with some chopped tarragon or lovage and sharpened up with a couple of tablespoons of yoghurt or smetana.

These timbales can also be served as a vegetable with your main course and they go particularly well with a casserole of pheasant or any rich gamey dish.

serves 6–8

1 celeriac, about 1 lb/500 g
2 tablespoons lemon juice or wine vinegar
2 shallots, finely chopped
butter plus extra for greasing ramekins
2 eggs
1 egg yolk
4 tablespoons double cream
½ teaspoon Dijon mustard
salt and pepper
light avgolemono sauce juice of ½ lemon
2 eggs

Peel the celeriac, cut it into chunks measuring about 1 in/2.5 cm and immediately put them into acidulated water—2 tablespoons lemon juice or wine vinegar to 1 pt/600 ml water—and leave for 10 minutes or so.

Bring your steamer to simmering point, drain the celeriac and put it into the basket. While it is cooking sauté the shallots in the butter until they are transparent.

Steam the celeriac until it is very soft, about 20 minutes, then remove it to a food processor or blender. Purée the celeriac and the shallots, then add the eggs, the extra yolk, the cream, mustard and seasonings. Divide the mixture between 6 or 8 well greased ramekins or moulds and steam, either with the moulds loosely covered with cling film or foil, or with a tea towel between the moulds and the lid of the steamer, for 15 minutes. Turn them out and surround with a sauce or serve as an accompaniment to a main course.

To make the sauce, take 7 fl oz/200 ml of the steaming liquid, add the lemon juice to it and beat in the eggs. Heat it very slowly, stirring all the time, until it thickens. Season with salt and pepper and serve while still warm.

Celery

Braised or cooked celery is a dish that one comes across much more frequently in France than in England and although canned celery hearts, again much used in France, can be good, fresh celery is much better. Braised celery is usually cooked in a stock or a sauce, but halved or quartered hearts steam well and can then be eaten either hot, with a squeeze of lemon juice, a knob of butter and a sprinkling of parsley, or cold—they make a good light first course with the walnut dressing given below.

To steam celery, cut off the top and trim off and discard any tough looking root, outside sticks and leaves. Cut it lengthwise into halves or quarters, destring the outside sticks and wash it well. If your steamer basket is large you will be able to cook it laid flat on the bottom or perhaps propped across it, otherwise you could cut each piece into half, or you could cook it with the sticks cut into pieces. Place the celery in the basket and sprinkle it with salt.

Steaming times: halved or quartered celery—20–30 minutes
chopped celery—15–20 minutes

Recipe
Boned Trout with a Julienne of Vegetables (p. 69)

Celery and Walnut Vinaigrette

2 heads celery, halved or quartered
2 oz/50 g walnuts
1 tablespoon wine vinegar
3 tablespoons walnut oil
2 tablespoons vegetable oil
salt and pepper

Garnish
small bunch parsley, chopped

Follow the instructions to prepare the celery and steam until tender. Leave to drain and cool down, then place a half or two quarters on each plate and sprinkle the walnuts over the top. Make a dressing from the vinegar, oils and seasonings, spoon it over the celery and sprinkle with parsley.

Chicory

When shopping choose chicory that is white and crisp, for if it has been stored in the light and the outside leaves are yellow or turning green it will have become too bitter to make pleasant eating.

Chicory needs little preparation, just cut off the bottom, remove any damaged outside leaves and wipe it over with a damp cloth. Don't soak it in water, as this will increase the bitter taste. Put the prepared chicory in your steaming basket, either whole and preferably propped at an angle so that the bottom part is nearer to the steam and will cook more quickly, or otherwise, in a large basket, split in half lengthwise. Before cooking, sprinkle the heads with a spoonful of mixed oil and lemon juice, a little salt and a grinding of pepper.

Steaming times: whole chicory—15–20 minutes
halved chicory—8–12 minutes

Buttered Chicory

4 small or 2 large heads chicory
2 teaspoons oil
2 teaspoons lemon juice
salt and pepper
2 oz/50 g butter
1 tablespoon chopped parsley

Prepare the chicory and if you are using large heads cut them in half lengthwise. When in the basket sprinkle with the oil, lemon juice and seasonings and steam until it is just tender. Melt the butter in a frying pan, add the parsley and the cooked chicory and fry, turning frequently, until it is a light brown. Remove the chicory to a serving dish and pour the juices from the pan over it.

Chinese Leaf or Chinese Cabbage

Chinese leaf is a brassica that comes from South East Asia and is very suited to stir-frying and Chinese cooking. In the last few years, since Israel started to grow Chinese leaf as an important crop for export, it has become familiar in Britain, where it is used in a variety of ways. It makes a good salad green and in the winter, especially, is a nice change from the ubiquitous coleslaw. It can also be cooked and used like any other cabbage and has a particular affinity with nutmeg or juniper berries; try using it for the Purée of Cabbage on p. 135.

Chinese leaf, with its delicate flavour, is a vegetable that steams well, but needs careful watching as it is much better if it is eaten while still slightly crisp. Prepare it by removing any outside or yellowing leaves and shredding it. Wash the shreds in cold water before steaming. Serve it as it is or with a knob of butter and a scraping of nutmeg or, perhaps, with a little grated ginger and soy sauce.

Steaming time: 6–8 minutes
Sprinkle with salt first

Recipe
Marinated Cod wrapped in Chinese Leaves (p. 73)

Courgettes

Little courgettes are sometimes cooked and served whole, but I prefer to eliminate the bitter taste that they can have by cutting them and draining them sprinkled with salt for about half an hour. Just before cooking the courgettes rinse off the salt and juices under a cold tap.

They can be split lengthwise into halves or quarters, sliced, cut into dice or strips, or grated.

Steaming time: 2–5 minutes
No extra salt is needed
Test with a sharp knife, they should be slightly crisp and not mushy. If you are going to eat them cold arrest cooking by plunging them from the steamer into a bowl of cold water.

Recipes
Summer Vegetable Soup (p. 26)
Petits Pots aux Courgettes (p. 34)
Shrimp and Courgette Salad (p. 52)
A Dish of Mixed Vegetables (p. 118)
Feuilleté aux Légumes (p. 121)

Courgette Boats with a Carrot Stuffing

2 large or 4 medium courgettes (the courgettes should lie flat across the steaming basket)
salt and pepper
2 oz/50 g raisins
zest and juice of 1 orange
4 oz/125 g carrots, coarsely grated
2 tablespoons yoghurt
1 oz/25 g hazelnuts or almonds, toasted and chopped (optional)

Cut the courgettes in half lengthwise and scoop out the seeds and flesh. Discard the seeds and any tough bits but keep the pieces of flesh. Sprinkle the inside of the prepared courgette boats with salt and leave them upside down, for at least half an hour, to drain.

Put the raisins to soak in the orange juice for half an hour.

Mix the carrots with the reserved courgette flesh, the raisins and juice, the orange zest and salt and pepper. Wash the courgette boats, pat dry with kitchen paper and spoon in the stuffing. Put them flat in your steaming basket—you may need to use 2 levels—and steam them for 15–20 minutes or until the carrot shreds are just cooked.

Leave them until cold and serve them with a little yoghurt drizzled along the top of each one, scattered, if liked, with the nuts.

Courgettes with Tomato Stuffing

7 medium courgettes
salt and pepper
4 tomatoes, peeled and deseeded
½ Spanish onion, chopped
1 clove garlic, crushed
2 tablespoons olive oil
8 black olives, stoned and chopped
½ pt/150 ml stabilised yoghurt (p. 27–8) or crème fraîche (p. 126)
2 tablespoons chopped parsley

Take four of the courgettes, cut them lengthwise in half and use a spoon to hollow them out into boats. Discard any seeds, but keep the good flesh. Salt the courgette boats and leave them to drain, upside down, for about half an hour. Meanwhile cut the remaining courgettes into cubes and put them in a sieve with the other courgette flesh, salt them and also leave them to drain.

Cut the tomato flesh into cubes. Fry the onion and garlic slowly in the oil until they are soft. Take the pan off the heat and stir in the cubed tomato, olives, yoghurt or crème fraîche, parsley, courgette pieces—with most of the salt rinsed off them—and then season; you will need very little extra salt.

Rinse out the courgette shells, dry them with kitchen paper and spoon in the stuffing. Put them flat in your steamer basket and steam them for 10–12 minutes. You may need to use 2 layers, when they will need to be steamed for 15–20 minutes with the baskets being switched round half way through. Serve hot as a first course or cold as a salad.

Cucumber

For a long time cucumbers have been avoided by many people as they were inclined to be both bitter tasting and indigestible. However, this problem has largely been overcome by the breeding of new varieties which eliminate much of the bitter-gene as it is called.

Cucumbers and their uses have been imported from a variety of countries and we are now all familiar with tzatziki, the Greek cucumber and yoghurt salad, and with raita, the Indian equivalent, which does, so well, the job of cooling the mouth from the heat of the chilli. Cucumber can also be eaten as a hot vegetable, either steamed and then simply tossed in a little butter, or more substantially, as given below, in a béchamel sauce with dill or chives—the perfect accompaniment to hot salmon.

Peel the cucumber, cut into 4 lengthwise and then into pieces of about 2 in/5 cm. Sprinkle with salt as you put it into the steaming basket.

Steaming time: 8–10 minutes (adjust the time for pieces of a different size.)

Recipes
Cucumber Soup with Dill (p. 23)
Chilled Beetroot and Cucumber Soup (p. 24)
Trout Stuffed with Cucumber and Dill (p. 63)
Raita (p. 115)

Cucumber with a Béchamel Sauce

This also makes a good vegetarian dish if it is served with a covering of grated cheese.

1 large cucumber
1 oz/25 g butter
1 oz/25 g flour
¼ pt/150 ml milk
¼ pt/150 ml cream
2 teaspoons chopped fresh dill or chives or ½ teaspoon dried dill weed
salt and pepper

Prepare and steam the cucumber following the instructions above. While the cucumber is steaming make the sauce. Melt the butter, stir in the flour and slowly add the milk and cream. Add the herbs and seasoning and then carefully, so as not to break the pieces, stir in the cooked cucumber.

Fennel

We use the name fennel to describe both the herb and the bulbous vegetable. Although the plants are closely related they are not the same, and the vegetable should really be called Florence fennel. The herb and the vegetable share the same anise flavour and both accompany fish beautifully.

Fennel is very often served raw as part of a salad, but it cooks well and can then be finished off with butter and lemon juice as suggested for chicory on p. 145. It is also frequently used as a substitute for celery and is good served with walnuts and a vinaigrette sauce as given on p. 144.

Prepare the bulb by cutting off the brown base and removing any old looking outside leaves. Cut off and keep the feathery leaves, for they make a pretty decoration for the finished dish. Cut the bulb, from top to bottom, into half or if the bulb is big 3 or 4 slices. You can, if you prefer, keep it whole and cut it up after cooking.

Steaming times: slices—8–12 minutes
                       whole bulb—30–40 minutes
Sprinkle the slices with salt as you put them on to steam or the whole bulb after 5 minutes.

Recipes
Salmon Filled Watercress Cake (p. 58)
Red Mullet with Fennel and Anchovies (p. 68)
Veal Chops with Fennel (p. 112)

Kohlrabi

The French bracket kohlrabi and celeriac together, one being called chou-rave and the other celéri-rave. Kohlrabi is a German word which literally means cabbage-turnip, a translation that is sometimes used in English. My French dictionary gives rave as radish or turnip, although a turnip itself is a navet and there is no mention of rave under the entry for turnip. I can only presume that rave is only used, hyphened with another name, to indicate a turnip flavour.

The kohlrabi plant is a member of the cabbage family, the vegetable itself being an above ground swelling of the stem. It should be eaten small, no bigger than a tennis ball, otherwise it will be tough, fibrous and have an overwhelming smell and taste of turnip.

To prepare, cut off the root and any stalks that may be projecting from the vegetable. Leave the skin on and peel after cooking. Serve with butter and lemon juice or a light béchamel sauce.

Steaming time: 30–40 minutes

Leeks

Leeks in village flower shows are always of an almost inconceivable size. They look quite wonderful, but I rather dread to think how they taste. Leeks, like the majority of vegetables, are at their best harvested small and young, but they are very versatile and the bigger ones make a marvellous soup or a good addition to a casserole with other vegetables or meat.

Whole small leeks look attractive, but if they are gritty and muddy it is probably best to slice them or cut them in half lengthwise before washing them. Otherwise, wash them under a running tap and then stand them upside down in a jug of water, and if you are lucky the grit will fall out of them.

I like to eat leeks with just a little butter, either by themselves or with a few baby carrots. They can be served with many sauces, including a plain or cheese flavoured béchamel and they are good, as below, eaten warm with a vinaigrette. Otherwise, you could pour cold vinaigrette over the hot leeks and leave them until cold, then sprinkle some chopped hard-boiled egg over the top just before serving.

Steaming time: 12–20 minutes
Sprinkle with salt after 5 minutes

Recipe Fish and Vegetable Terrine (p. 52)

Leeks with a Warm Vinaigrette Sauce

8 leeks, or 12 if they are very small
1 tablespoon white wine vinegar
3 tablespoons olive oil
salt and pepper

Garnish
1 tablespoon chopped parsley

Prepare the leeks and put them on to steam. Mix the wine, vinegar, oil, salt and pepper in a small saucepan and put it to warm over a gentle heat. When the leeks are cooked, take the basket from the steamer and leave it on one side for a minute for the leeks to dry out. Remove the leeks to a serving dish, pour over the hot vinaigrette and sprinkle the top with parsley.

Leek and Carrot Terrine

A leek terrine which cuts into colourful slices has become rather a cult dish in recent years. It is also a problem dish, for however much it is weighed down while the liquid is drained off it still remains a devil to cut and seems to fall to pieces more often than not. I have tried to get round this by holding it together with a gelatine mixture. It helps, but you still need to use a razor sharp knife when cutting it.

6 fat or 12 thin leeks
12 oz/375 g carrots, shredded
salt and pepper
2 teaspoons gelatine
3 tablespoons white wine vinegar
3 tablespoons white wine

Garnish (optional)
olive oil

snipped chives

Remove and discard the outside leaves from the leeks and wash the leeks thoroughly. Steam the carrot shreds for 5 minutes, remove them, sprinkle with a little salt and leave them on one side. Steam the leeks, sprinkled with a little salt, until they are cooked; about 10 minutes for thin ones and 15 for thick ones. If you steam the vegetables at the same time, with the carrots in a top basket, you will probably find that they take about the same time to cook.

Line with cling film, or well grease, a 2 lb/1 kg terrine or loaf tin and cut the leeks to the length of the tin. Spread about a third of the carrot over the bottom and cover with a layer of leeks, 3 large or 4 small, arranged nose to tail followed by a grinding of black pepper. Continue with the layers: if using big leeks you will only have 1 more layer of leeks; if using small ones, 2 more. Finish with a layer of carrots. Cover the terrine with a double layer of cling film and push it down hard, leaving it weighted for half an hour or so for the terrine to consolidate before pouring over the gelatine mixture.

Dissolve the gelatine in 2 tablespoons water in a bowl in the steamer. Mix in the vinegar and the wine, and add enough vegetable steaming water to make it up to ½ pt/300 ml, season with salt. Drain any water from the terrine then pour the gelatine mixture over the carrots, gently pushing with a fork to let the gelatine soak down between them; if it won't take all the mixture don't worry. Cool and then refrigerate for at least 2 hours to set the gelatine. Turn it out onto a dish and serve on individual plates, cut into slices and sprinkled, if you like, with a little olive oil and a few snipped chives.

Mange-Tout Peas

These are sometimes sold as sugar peas and in the States they are called snow peas. They are now well known in this country, for intensive growing and importation has made them easily available for most of the year. Nouvelle cuisine and food photographers have also done a lot for them, as their bright green colour and pretty shape look good as part of a plate of carefully arranged food.

The preparation is easy, for they just need topping, tailing and de-stringing. They are usually served simply with a small knob of butter, a grinding of black pepper and perhaps a squeeze of lemon juice. They also make a very good salad ingredient but, if you are going to use them in this way, preserve the colour by plunging them from the steamer into a bowl of cold water.

Mange-touts should have a crisp bite to them and in order to achieve this many people cook them for only 2 or 3 minutes. I much prefer to cook them for considerably longer, and I am glad to see that Jane Grigson feels the same, for I find that the pod still retains its bite and that the whole becomes very tender. The cooking time is also, of course, governed by the age and size of the peas.

Steaming time: 8–12 minutes
Sprinkle with salt after 2 minutes

Recipes
Mount Koya Mushi (p. 37)
Fish and Vegetable Terrine (p. 52)
A Dish of Mixed Vegetables (p. 118)

Mange-Touts with Garlic and Olives

8 oz/250 g mange-touts
salt and pepper
2 oz/50 g butter
2 cloves garlic, crushed with a little salt
4–6 green olives, chopped
2 teaspoons chopped marjoram plus 2 teaspoons chopped parsley or 1 tablespoon chopped parsley

Prepare the mange-touts and put them to steam. While they are cooking heat the butter and gently cook the garlic and olives. Transfer the mange-touts to a heated serving dish, pour the butter over them and sprinkle the top with the herbs and a good grinding of pepper.

Mushrooms

Mushrooms take up the flavour of butter, cream or oil so well that they are nearly always cooked in one of them. When steamed they retain their own distinctive flavour but are inclined to go slightly rubbery so are better used as part of another dish rather than eaten alone. Spinach and mushrooms go well together and the little timbales given below make a good appetiser.

Steaming times: button mushrooms—3–5 minutes
flat mushrooms—4–6 minutes
Sprinkle with salt after 1 minute

Recipes
Chawan Mushi (p. 35)
Marinated Cod Wrapped in Chinese Leaves (p. 73)
Mushroom Sauce (p. 94)
Stuffed Chicken Drumsticks (p. 95)
Stuffed Crown of Lamb (p. 106)
Steak with Red Wine, Mushroom and Caper Sauce (p. 108)

Mushroom and Spinach Timbales

8 oz/250 g spinach or 4 oz/125 g packet of frozen spinach
4 oz/125 g button mushrooms
2 eggs
4 tablespoons cream
nutmeg
salt and pepper
butter for greasing the ramekins

Wash the spinach well, cut the bottom of the stalks off the mushrooms and wipe them clean. Steam the spinach for 10 minutes or, if using frozen spinach, steam it until it has defrosted and is cooked. Steam the mushrooms for 6 minutes or until soft.

Purée the cooked spinach in a food processor or blender. Add the eggs, the cream, a scraping of nutmeg and salt and pepper and process until you have a smooth mixture. Add the mushrooms and process again to chop them roughly.

Grease the ramekins with butter and spoon the mixture into them. Cover with foil or a loose piece of cling film and steam them for 10 minutes.

Okra

Okra, or more prettily, ladies' fingers, are the mucilaginous seed pods of the tropical *Hibiscus esculentus*. A member of the mallow family, which comes from Africa. But okra is probably best known as an essential ingredient (the juices act as a natural thickener) of gumbo, the famous stew of the southern American states. It is also frequently used in spicy stews in both the Middle East and India.

Choose pods that are fresh looking, crisp and bright green, rejecting any with a brownish tinge. Whether you cook okra whole or cut is a matter of choice, but I think that the finished vegetable is slightly less sticky if it is treated like an aubergine. Split the okra in half, sprinkle the cut side with salt and leave for at least half an hour. Under a running tap, wash off the salt and as much of the stickiness as you can, then thoroughly dry the pod between a double layer of kitchen paper.

If you steam the okra whole the only preparation needed is the removal of the conical cap; don't cut any further down the pod or you will release the juices and increase the stickiness of the cooked vegetable. The other method is to soak the split okra in acidulated water, but I find that this makes them yellow and limp.

Serve the cooked okra with butter and lemon juice or leave them until cold and serve with tomatoes and a vinaigrette dressing.

Steaming time: 6–9 minutes

Onions

Onions, as the universal flavouring medium with a myriad of uses, are the one vegetable that any cook always has in stock. Even so, other than baked or roast, they are comparatively seldom eaten as a vegetable on their own. Onions steam well and, as they are not agitated by boiling water, they stay whole and keep their shape. Whole steamed onions are good served sprinkled with cheese and grilled until brown and bubbling.

Don't be frightened of using what may seem to be an enormous amount of mustard in the glazed onion recipe below; it blends in well and makes a vegetable that is particularly good served with roast beef or steak.

Steaming times: little pickling onions—15–20 minutes
medium onions—25–30 minutes
large Spanish onions—35–45 minutes
Sprinkle with salt after 2 minutes

Mustard Glazed Onions

1 lb/500 g pickling onions
2 oz/50 g butter
salt and pepper
2 tablespoons English or strong mustard

Peel the onions and steam them until soft. Melt the butter in a small saucepan, add the onions, together with salt and pepper, and toss them in the butter. Finally spoon in the mustard and stir to coat the onions with it. Serve at once.

Spanish Onions with a Parsnip Purée

Lightly curried parsnip soup has long been a family favourite and this dish of Spanish onions stuffed with a curried parsnip purée is a derivation of it. It makes a filling first course or you could cut the onions in half and serve them as an accompaniment to pork chops or a rice stuffed shoulder of lamb.

I don't bother to mix my own spices for a simple dish like this, for very good quality curry paste is available at most Indian grocers.

4 Spanish onions
12 oz/375 g parsnips
2 oz/50 g butter
1 tablespoon sunflower oil
1–2 teaspoons curry paste
2 oz/50 g raisins
2 tablespoons pine nuts (optional)
salt and pepper

Cut the tops off the onions, peel them and, using a sharp knife, dig out the centre leaving a shell of about ½ in/1 cm thick. Coarsely chop the centre of the onion and keep it on one side. Peel the parsnips and cut them in half lengthwise. Steam the onion shells and the parsnips for 15–20 minutes or until they are soft; the onion shells will probably take slightly longer than the parnsips.

Meanwhile, in a frying pan, melt half the butter and the oil and fry the chopped onion for a couple of minutes. Stir in the curry paste, the raisins and, if you are using them, the pine nuts and fry for a further 2 minutes. Purée the cooked parsnip in a food processor or blender, add the fried onions and all the juices and pulse the machine once or twice to mix them in.

Place each onion shell on a square of foil and crumple it up round the base so that it will hold the onion and catch any overflow of the stuffing during the final steaming. Spoon in the parsnip purée and put the onions flat in the steamer basket. If you are using a steamer with a metal or plastic lid you will need to stop the water dripping back onto the onions by covering the basket with a tea towel before putting on the lid. This is not necessary with a Chinese basket as the woven lid allows any excess steam to escape.

Put a nut of butter on top of each onion and steam for 20 minutes or until the onions are heated through.

Parsnip

Parsnips are one of my favourite vegetables; I love their slightly sweet taste and their surprising versatility which I find fun to experiment with. They are one of the vegetables that has benefited enormously from the advent of the food processor, for puréed parsnips, served on their own or mixed with potatoes, carrots, or both, make a really attractive vegetable. The parsnip salads and variations given below are easy and cheap in the winter and the ginger one, especially, is good around Christmas time as an accompaniment to cold ham and other meats.

Parsnips are also good cut lengthwise into quarters, steamed until tender, and served with a good grinding of black pepper, some butter and a squeeze of lemon juice.

Steaming time: 12–20 minutes. Steam parsnips, depending on their size, cut lengthwise into halves or quarters, or cut across into reasonably even sized chunks. Sprinkle with salt after 2 minutes.

Recipe
Spanish Onions with a parsnip Purée (p. 154)

Parsnip Salad

12 oz/375 g parsnips
1 teaspoon Dijon mustard
4 tablespoons mayonnaise
salt and pepper

Garnish
1 teaspoon chopped parsley

Peel the parsnips, cut them into halves or quarters and steam until tender. Mix the mustard into the mayonnaise and season it to taste. Cut the cooked parsnips into cubes, fold them into the mayonnaise, cover and refrigerate. Just before serving sprinkle the parsley over the top.

Parsnip Salad with Nuts and Yoghurt

1 tablespoon hazelnuts or walnuts
12 oz/375 g parsnips
2 tablespoons walnut or sunflower oil
2 teaspoons wine vinegar
2 tablespoons natural yoghurt
2 spring onions, finely chopped
salt and pepper

Grill the nuts for a few minutes, but watch them carefully and don't let them burn. If you are using hazelnuts, put them onto a clean tea towel and rub off the skins. Coarsely chop the nuts and keep until needed.

Steam the parsnips and cut them into cubes. Mix oil and vinegar together, then stir in the yoghurt, spring onions and nuts and season to taste. Fold in the parsnips, cover and keep in the refrigerator until needed.

Parsnip Salad with Ginger

12 oz/375 g parsnips
2–3 knobs stem ginger, finely chopped
2 teaspoons of the ginger syrup
1 tablespoon natural yoghurt
3 tablespoons mayonnaise
salt and pepper

Steam the parsnips and cut them into cubes. Mix the stem ginger, syrup and yoghurt into the mayonnaise. Stir in the parsnips and, before serving, check for seasoning.

Timbale of Parsnip and Carrot

This timbale is unusual in that the sweetness of the parsnips and carrots has been heightened by the addition of grated orange zest and marmalade. It tastes good, but I am not quite sure when it should be eaten; for it is hardly substantial enough for a first course or sweet enough for a pudding, so I am led to think that it is probably at its best with a meat that marries well with orange, such as duck or pork.

12 oz/375 g parsnips, halved or quartered
4 oz/125 g carrots, coarsely grated
oil for greasing basin
2 tablespoons marmalade

2 eggs, beaten
zest of 1 orange
salt and pepper

Steam the parsnips and carrots until tender; the parsnips will probably take about 15 minutes and, if you have the carrots above them, on a top layer, they will take 8–10 minutes.

Take a pudding basin that will fit into your steamer and prepare it by greasing it and lining it with cling film. Spoon the marmalade into the bottom and then spread it around and up the sides as much as you can.

Put the parsnips into a food processor or blender and process them until smooth, while slowly pouring the eggs in through the feed tube. Add the carrot, orange zest, salt and pepper and briefly pulse the machine to mix them in.

Transfer the mixture to the prepared basin, cover with cling film and steam it for 30 minutes. Turn it out onto a plate and serve hot.

Peas

Really fresh young peas, unless you are lucky enough to have a vegetable garden, are difficult to come by. Slightly lower your standards and you will find that there are times when the greengrocer will have acceptable peas; if you see them, buy them, cook them that day, and eat them with butter and chopped chervil or a little chopped mint mixed with ½ teaspoon sugar. If your peas are bigger and older they need to be cooked for longer and below I give a recipe for Steamed Peas à la Français.

Unless they are amazingly small, peas have to be podded, which is a slow job, but if one sits, preferably outside in the sunshine with a cup of tea on the side, a happy one. You will probably lose about half the weight of the peas when podding them.

Steaming time: 6–15 minutes. Size and age make a lot of difference to the steaming time.

Sprinkle with salt and, if you like, sugar and herbs after 2 minutes.

Recipe
A Dish of Mixed Vegetables (p. 118)

Steamed Peas à la Français

1 lettuce heart or 6 large lettuce leaves
10–12 oz/300–375 g podded peas
4 spring onions, chopped
small handful of parsley, chopped
1 teaspoon sugar
1 oz/25 g butter
salt and pepper

Use the lettuce leaves to make a bed in the bottom of your steamer basket and on it put the peas, spring onions, parsley, sugar, salt and pepper. Steam over just simmering water for 20–30 minutes. Remove the peas and spring onion bits to a dish, chop the lettuce and add it and the butter to the peas. Check the seasonings and serve.

Peppers

One of the joys of peppers are their lovely colours, which prompt evocative thoughts of sun soaked Mediterranean food; dishes such as ratatouille or a salad niçoise made with thick olive oil, juicy black olives and strips of shining red, green and yellow peppers interspersed with bright green and pungent basil leaves.

Peppers, except for stuffed ones, are not ideal for the steamer. However, if you are using them in salads and if, like me, you prefer to peel them, you can cut them in quarters, remove seeds and pith and steam them to cook them slightly, making them more digestible and also loosening the skin. The skin is also often removed by charring the peppers under a grill; this gives them a slightly different taste, perfect for some dishes, but not so good for others—the method you use is up to you.

Steaming times (for skinning peppers): red peppers—10–12 minutes
green and yellow peppers—12–15 minutes
Do not steam for longer than is necessary to remove the skin, as the colour, especially with green peppers, starts to fade with excess cooking.

Recipes

Celeriac and Red Pepper Soup (p. 27)
Soufflé with Shrimps in Rouille (p. 44)
Stuffed Chicken Drumsticks (p. 95)
Calf's Liver in Red Peppers (p. 104)
Baby Sweetcorn with Green Beans and Red Pepper (p. 164)

Multi-Coloured Pepper Salad

1 red, 1 green and 1 yellow pepper
1 tablespoon lemon juice
2 tablespoons olive oil
1 clove garlic, crushed with a little salt
pepper
1 tablespoon chopped parsley

Quarter the peppers and remove the stalks, seeds and any pith. Steam them and while they are still warm peel off the skin and cut the flesh into long, narrow strips. Make a dressing with the lemon juice and oil and stir in the garlic, some freshly ground pepper and the parsley. Pour the dressing over the pepper strips, cover the dish with cling film and refrigerate until needed.

Stuffed Peppers

Peppers can be steamed with an uncooked stuffing and I find that the rice cooks perfectly while the pepper shells become soft and sweet tasting. You can, if you prefer, partially pre-cook the stuffing by gently sautéeing the onion, adding the meat, browning it, then stirring in the well washed rice and some water before bringing it briefly to the boil and stirring in the flavourings. But do not overcook, or the rice will turn to a mush when you steam the peppers.

The addition of cinnamon and mint is very Middle Eastern and gives an interesting flavour. As with most rice stuffed vegetables the peppers can be served either hot or cold. If you are going to eat them hot you might like to serve them with the lightly spiced Tomato Sauce given on p. 96. If served cold they are good topped with a tablespoon or two of thick yoghurt and a sprinkling of mint or parsley.

4 medium red or green peppers, 6–7 oz/175–200 g
4 teaspoons olive oil
stuffing
6 oz/175 g lean lamb or beef, finely chopped
3 oz/75 g long grained rice
1 medium onion, finely chopped
1 tablespoon chopped parsley
1 teaspoon chopped fresh or dried mint
¼ teaspoon ground cinnamon
1 tablespoon raisins (optional)
salt and pepper

Cut the tops off the peppers and remove and discard the stalks, seeds and any pith. If they are uneven shave a piece of the bottom of each one to make it stand up straight, but be careful not to puncture the skin.

Mix all the stuffing ingredients together (including, if used, the raisins) and spoon into the peppers. Do not fill the shells more than two thirds full as the rice will expand during cooking. Spoon a teaspoon of olive oil into each and add water to come to the top of the rice. Stand them upright in your steamer basket, do not cover with the lids but place them on their sides by the peppers. Steam for 25–30 minutes, by which time the rice should have fluffed up and absorbed all the liquid..

Potatoes

There is a definite division between new and old potatoes and I have tackled them separately.

Old potatoes

I find that the best way to steam winter potatoes (I usually use King Edwards as they seem to cook evenly and keep their shape) is to peel them and then cut them into slices of about ¼ in/5 mm thick. The slices when steamed are beautifully moist and can be eaten as they are, or, if steamed for slightly longer, used for mashed potatoes. Very floury potatoes do not steam quite so well and are inclined to go gluey if you try to mash them.

Steaming times: sliced—12–18 minutes
halved—25–30 minutes
Sprinkle with salt after 5 minutes.

Recipes
Hot Chicken Breasts Vinaigrette (p. 96)
Warm Salad of Duck Breasts in Radicchio (p. 98)
Lamb Chops on a Potato Bed (p. 111)
Three Vegetable Terrine (p. 119)

New potatoes
New potatoes are now imported from a wide variety of countries and are available all the year round. However, the baby Jersey and English potatoes with that wonderful, elusive flavour that is inclined to fade so quickly after digging, lend themselves particularly well to steaming and being served simply.

Varieties of waxy salad potatoes are now sometimes available in the shops and, if you see them, are well worth buying, for they are much the best potatoes for eating in a cold dressing and they steam beautifully. Occasionally in the late summer you see the old English variety, pink fir apple, for sale (the name is descriptive, for they are pink, shaped rather like a fir cone and have a texture that does not fall apart). These also are a good buy as they have a delicious flavour and need no more than washing, steaming, a knob of butter and possibly a sprinkling of parsley.

It is difficult to give anything more than a guide as to timings, as new potatoes vary enormously in size and the cooking time is very likely to be lengthened by the steaming basket being full. Whether you just wash them or scrape them is a matter of choice, but I always think that the whiteness of scraped ones looks better in a salad.

Steaming times: small—12–18 minutes
medium—18–22 minutes
large—23–30 minutes
Sprinkle with salt and, if you like, a little chopped mint after 5 minutes.

Recipes
Cold New Potato soup with Raw Tomato and Basil (p. 23)
Chicken Quarters on a Potato Bed (p. 92)
Hot Chicken Breasts Vinaigrette (p. 96)
Warm Salad of Duck Breasts in Radicchio (p. 98)

Salsify and Scorzonera

These two vegetables are very close cousins and are treated in the same way. They also taste very similar, although it is salsify that has the nickname vegetable oyster which comes from its reputation of tasting of seafood. Although the vegetable has a delicate and interesting taste I would not equate it with an oyster or indeed with anything else.

Both vegetables are liked and eaten a lot in mainland Europe, and they are becoming better known now in England. Early spring is the time that you are most likely to find them.

Both salsify and scorzonera turn black when cut or peeled so it is best to just wash them, steam them and peel them while hot. The peel should be easy to push off and if you have difficulty with it sticking, it means that the vegetable is overcooked. Serve, like asparagus, with melted butter poured over the top or cook the butter until dark brown, but not burnt, before pouring it over them.

Steaming time: 20–30 minutes
Sprinkle with salt after 5 minutes

Salsify Fritters

The French frequently serve salsify this way. The cooked salsify is dipped in a batter and deep fried and it makes a crispy coated vegetable with an unexpected flavour.

3 oz/75 g plain flour
salt
1 tablespoon olive or sunflower oil
1 egg white
1 lb/500 g salsify
deep fat for frying

Make a batter by sifting together the flour and a pinch of salt, then making a well in the centre and pouring in the oil and 3 fl oz/75 ml warm water. Stir the flour gradually into the liquid and then beat until smooth. Leave in a cool place for 30 minutes, then, just before using, whisk the egg white until stiff and fold it in.

Steam the salsify, push off the skin and cut the stalks into bite sized pieces. Dip each piece into the batter, then carefully drop it into the hot fat. Fry until it is golden, 3–4 minutes, then remove with a slotted spoon and drain on kitchen paper.

Spaghetti Marrow

This is a fun vegetable that is amusing to serve when you have children or teenagers around. It is also easy to cook and tastes good; to my mind much better than a vegetable marrow.

A whole spaghetti marrow is quite large and although it can be cut in half is still only suitable for the bigger steamers: electric ones, the biggest Chinese basket or a fish kettle. It can otherwise be boiled, but again you will need a big saucepan.

If you cut it in half before steaming (it can then be cooked in 2 layers), remove the seeds and seal the top of each half with a piece of cling film. Steam until tender then use a fork to comb the flesh and it will separate into spaghetti-like strands. Season with salt and pepper, pour over some hot melted butter and, if liked, add a good handful of grated cheese. Serve immediately.

Steaming time: 40–50 minutes according to size

Spinach

It is always recommended that spinach is cooked without extra water and that it is just steamed in a saucepan with any water thay may be clinging to it after washing. Steaming it in a basket is slightly simpler and works very well. If you are cooking a large quantity don't try to squash it all in together but begin by puting about half to three-quarters of the leaves on to steam and them, after 3 or 4 minutes, turn the half steamed spinach over and add the remainder.

Steaming time: 10–12 minutes
Sprinkle with salt as you put it into the basket

Recipes
Lightly Spiced Spinach and Lentil Soup (p. 28)
Oeufs Fiesole (p. 33)
Spinach Pudding (p. 45)
Fish and Vegetable Terrine (p. 52)
Striped Fish Mousseline (p. 56)
Lemon Sole and Salmon with Spinach (p. 65)
Ricotta and Spinach Chicken Thighs (p. 94)
Mushroom and Spinach Timbales (p. 152)

Dolmathes with Spinach and Rice

This is a lovely dish for a hot day and really makes one think of the sea, beaches and holidays. These dolmathes are best served cool either with some olive oil drizzled over them or with a tablespoon of thick Greek yoghurt with some fresh mint chopped into it.

8 oz/250 g can or packet vine leaves
8 oz/250 g fresh spinach
4 oz/125 g long grained rice
1 large onion, finely chopped
2 tablespoons chopped parsley
1 tablespoon chopped mint
juice of 1 lemon
4 tablespoons olive oil
salt and pepper

Steam the spinach for 10–12 minutes, squeeze it dry and chop it. Soak the rice in a bowl of cold water for 10 minutes.

In a mixing bowl combine the spinach, drained rice, onion, herbs, lemon juice and oil and season with salt and pepper.

Prepare the vine leaves, filling them and rolling them following the instructions for Dolmathes with a Meat and Rice Stuffing (p. 113). Place the rolled dolmathes in layers in your basket and steam them for 2 hours or until the rice is cooked. If you want to cut the steaming time you can partially pre-cook the rice before mixing it with the other ingredients.

Swedes

Not, I must admit, my favourite vegetable, but one that in the winter can have its uses. It is one of those vegetables that is inclined to become watery when boiled and, therefore, steams well. I think the best way of eating it is mashed with an equal quantity of potato.

To prepare, peel the swedes and cut them into ½ in/1 cm cubes.

Steaming time: 15–20 minutes
Sprinkle with salt after 5 minutes

Sweetcorn

Freshly cooked corn on the cob seasoned with salt and black pepper and served with lots of melted butter is a delicious starter to any meal. It is messy to eat, and can, as people suck at the butter, be noisy, so it is perhaps best kept for family and close friends: I once made the disastrous mistake of giving it to somebody with a beard! You also need to provide large napkins that can be tucked in or tied round the neck and a finger bowl.

It is always said that sweetcorn should go straight from the plant to the cooking pot, as the sugar in the sweet tasting kernel starts to convert to starch the moment it is picked. Modern varieties are much better at retaining their sweetness and providing you buy cobs with plump, light yellow kernels and cook them on the same day, you should have a very good dish.

If you want to make a dish using only the kernels you can scrape them from the cob with a knife, either before or after it has been cooked, but, unless you happen to have a glut of corn in the garden it is hardly worthwhile, for frozen or even tinned sweetcorn kernels are both very good.

Sweetcorn steams well and the time needed is dictated not only by size of the cob but by variety and by freshness. It does need fairly careful watching and frequent prodding as overcooking makes the corn tough.

Prepare by cutting off the bottom of the stalk and removing the leaves and the silky inside covering.

Steaming time: 12–20 minutes
Test for tenderness by piercing a kernel with a skewer.
Sprinkle with salt after 5 minutes

Recipe
Sweetcorn Pudding (p. 46)

Baby Sweetcorn

The little baby sweetcorn that is flown in from South East Asia is one of the 'new' vegetables that has been an instant success and they can now be found in many supermarkets.

It is one of the easiest of vegetables, needing no preparation, and as it is so small and tender the whole cob is eaten. Just steam it, season it and serve with butter and possibly a squeeze of lemon juice. It also makes a wonderful salad ingredient; visually the yellow colour is marvellous at breaking up the more usual greens and reds. The little bundles given below, with green beans and held together with a ring of pepper, can be eaten hot but, I think, are best as a salad.

Steaming time: 10 minutes
Sprinkle with salt after 5 minutes

Baby Sweetcorn with Green Beans and Red Pepper

24 thin green beans
½ red pepper
8 baby sweetcorn
salt and pepper
melted butter or vinaigrette dressing

Top and tail the beans and check on the cooking time; if they are not the very finest they will need to be steamed for as long as the sweetcorn. Cut the pepper into 4 rounds. Steam the sweet corn for 4 minutes, sprinkle it with salt and pepper and add the beans and pepper to the steaming basket. Steam for a further 6 minutes, seasoning the beans and pepper after 2. Take 2 pieces of sweetcorn and 6 beans and thread them into a pepper ring. If the ring is too big cut out a section and join it at the back when you lay the bundle onto the plate. Repeat with the rest of the corn and beans and either serve the bundles hot with a little melted butter or cold sprinkled with a vinaigrette dressing.

Sweet Potatoes

Sweet potatoes originated in South America. They grow easily in a hot moist climate and are a very important crop, being the staple source of both starch and carbohydrate for the poor in many tropical countries. Sweet potatoes are the roots of the trailing vines of a plant belonging to the convolvulus family.

The American treatment of the sweet potato is very similar to the British treatment of the parsnip and the Thanksgiving roast turkey is frequently presented surrounded by roast sweet potatoes.

Sweet potatoes are good steamed, especially as their flavour is inclined to be washed out by boiling. They can be served like a baked potato, slit along the top and with a knob of butter and possibly some grated cheese, or candied, to accompany ham or pork.

Steaming time: whole, unpeeled sweet potatoes 35–50 minutes (depending on size and shape)

Candied Sweet Potatoes

1½ lb/750 g sweet potatoes
2 oz/50 g soft brown sugar

| 2 oz/50 g butter plus extra for greasing dish |
| ¼ teaspoon powdered cinnamon |
| salt |

Steam the sweet potatoes until nearly cooked then peel them, cut into thick slices and lay them in a greased baking dish. Combine the sugar, butter, cinnamon and salt and 2 tablespoons water in a small saucepan; bring the mixture to the boil and, stirring frequently, simmer for 3–4 minutes. Pour the syrup over the prepared sweet potatoes and bake, uncovered, in a hot oven, gas 5/190° C/375° F, basting once or twice, for 20 minutes.

Tomatoes

Tomatoes are one of the most frequently used vegetables, or more correctly fruits, in the British kitchen. Even in the winter, when fresh tomatoes are both hideously expensive and tasteless, a can of plum peeled tomatoes or a jar or packet of the newer passata, or creamed tomatoes, makes an excellent tomato sauce or a very acceptable soup. I have used tomatoes in many of the recipes in this book, usually peeled tomatoes, and a steamer is an ideal way of peeling them.

Steaming time (for peeling tomatoes): 30 seconds–3 minutes depending on type and ripeness of tomatoes
Immediately after steaming, plunge them into a bowl of cold water and slip off the skin

Recipes
Cold New Potato Soup with Raw Tomato and Basil (p. 23)
Summer Vegetable Soup (p. 26)
Shrimp and Courgette Salad (p. 52)
Turbot with Saffron, Tomato and Basil (p. 62)
Poisson Provençale (p. 69)
Chicken Breasts with Tarragon and Tomato (p. 89)
Lightly Spiced Tomato Sauce (p. 96)
Raita (p. 115)
Fresh Tomato Coulis (p. 120)
Stuffed Aubergines (p. 129)
Tomato and Carrot Sauce (p. 138)
Calabrese with Cherry Tomatoes (p. 138)
Courgettes with Tomato Stuffing (p. 147)

Tomato Custard

This tomato custard is a simple dish, but if you have some really sweet tomatoes and some fresh herbs, a very good one.

12 oz/375 g ripe tomatoes
2–3 tablespoons chopped fresh herbs (parsley, basil, chervil, chives, marjoram) or 2 teaspoons dried Italian mixed herbs
salt and pepper
2 eggs
8 fl oz/250 ml single cream
butter for greasing the dish or ramekins

Use the steamer to peel the tomatoes, then cut them in half and remove and discard the pips. Finely chop the flesh and put it in the bottom of a well greased 1 pint/600 ml dish or 4 ramekins and sprinkle it with half the herbs and a little salt and pepper. Whisk the eggs and the cream together, add the remaining herbs, season it and pour it over the tomatoes. Cover with cling film or foil and steam for approximately 30 minutes for 1 dish or 12–15 minutes for individual ramekins, or until the custard has just set.

Garlic and Herb Stuffed Tomatoes

I have dreadful childhood memories of tomatoes stuffed with soggy heavy breadcrumbs overflavoured with musty dried thyme and, as a result, it has taken me a long time to come round to the fact that stuffed tomatoes can be very good.

It is a temptation, to be avoided, to use marmande tomatoes for this dish, as the flesh is inclined to be pulpy and it is very difficult to remove the seeds. Use instead the sweetest, good sized ripe tomatoes you can find. Frying the breadcrumbs makes them crisp, keeps them light and means that they soak up the flavours of the garlic and olive oil.

8 tomatoes
salt and pepper
1 small onion, chopped
2–3 cloves garlic, crushed
3 tablespoons olive oil
5 oz/150 g fresh breadcrumbs
2 tablespoons pine nuts
6 anchovy fillets, drained and chopped
small bunch parsley, finely chopped
1 teaspoon chopped or fresh oregano or ½ teaspoon dried oregano

Wipe the tomatoes clean and cut a lid off each one. Spoon out all the flesh with a teaspoon, sprinkle a little salt inside each tomato shell and put them upside down to drain for about half an hour. Remove and discard the seeds and roughly chop the remaining flesh.

Fry the onion and garlic in the olive oil. When they are soft and transparent add the breadcrumbs and pine nuts and, stirring frequently, continue frying until the breadcrumbs are golden and crisp. Stir the anchovy fillets into the breadcrumbs with the tomato flesh and herbs and give a good grinding of pepper.

Spoon the mixture into the shells and place the lid back on each one. Pack them upright into your steaming basket and steam for 12–15 minutes.

Pasta Stuffed Tomatoes

I find that pasta makes a good fresh tasting stuffing for vegetables and that it blends well with the cream cheese and nuts that are used in this dish. Use one of the small pastas, the little pasta wheels are ideal, otherwise the very smallest macaroni.

2 oz/50 g small pasta pieces
2 tablespoons pine nuts or chopped walnuts
4 large tomatoes
salt and pepper
small bunch parsley
4–5 basil leaves
2 oz/50 g cream cheese
1 clove garlic, crushed
2 tablespoons olive oil

Follow the instructions on the pack and cook the pasta until it is al dente. You can also cook it in a bowl of water in the steamer, but it will take about double the recommended time; however, it is simple for a small amount of pasta and does save on utensils and washing up. Rinse the cooked pasta under cold water, drain and leave until needed. Lightly toast the nuts by placing them under the grill or on a tray in a preheated oven for a few minutes. But watch them carefully for they will burn very easily.

Cut the tops off the tomatoes and use a teaspoon to remove all the pips and flesh; discard the pips and any hard core and roughly chop the remaining flesh. Sprinkle a little salt inside each tomato shell and leave them upside down to drain.

Put the parsley and basil into a food processor and process until they are finely chopped. Add the cream cheese, garlic and seasoning and then, with the machine running, pour the oil in through the feed tube. Remove to a bowl and stir in the pasta, nuts, chopped tomato flesh and check for seasoning. Spoon the mixture into the tomato shells and put the tops back on. Arrange them upright in your steamer basket and steam them for 10–12 minutes. Once cooked this dish will not keep very well, but you can make the stuffing ahead then fill the tomatoes and steam them when needed.

Turnips

Turnips are frequently used in small amounts to add flavour to a stew or vegetable soup (see Couscous, p. 175) but are seldom served as a vegetable in their own right. People automatically turn up their noses at turnips; I think because they only know the big ones which have lost all delicate flavour and are both strong and overpowering, and are even past bashing up to serve with a haggis!

Turnips, when very small and very fresh make good eating. The long shaped ones are best. Steam them until they are tender and serve them with a little white sauce, flavoured with a bay leaf and with some chopped parsley stirred into it.

Steaming times: small, whole—15–20 minutes
cubed—12–15 minutes
Sprinkle with salt after 5 minutes

Recipes
Boned Trout with a Julienne of Vegetables (p. 69)
Three Vegetable Terrine with Tomato Coulis (p. 119)
Couscous (p. 175)

Turnips topped with Garlic Breadcrumbs

1 lb/500 g small turnips
1 oz/25 g butter
1 tablespoon vegetable oil
1 clove garlic, chopped
2 oz/50 g fresh breadcrumbs
2 tablespoons double cream
handful of fresh herbs (parsley, rosemary, chives, tarragon)
salt and pepper

Top, tail and peel the turnips and, unless they are minute, cut them into ½ in/1 cm cubes. Put them to steam, and meanwhile heat the butter and oil in a small frying pan, add the garlic and, when it has sizzled for a few seconds, the breadcrumbs. Continue frying, turning the breadcrumbs constantly, until they are golden and crisp. In another small pan, heat the cream, stir in the herbs and season it well with salt and pepper.

Transfer the cooked turnips to a serving dish, pour over the cream and top them with the crisp breadcrumbs.

Watercress

Watercress is really a salad ingredient but steamed and served in much the same way as spinach, it makes an interesting and unusual vegetable. When cooked it still retains a peppery flavour so it is probably best in small quantities as part of a selection of vegetables.

A milder version of the moulds below could be made substituting spinach for the watercress.

Wash the watercress and sprinkle with salt before steaming.

Steaming time: 4–6 minutes

Recipes
Watercress and Yoghurt Soup (p. 27)
Salmon Filled Watercress Cake (p. 58)

Hot Watercress Moulds

Cooked watercress does lose some of its bitterness but it still retains a certain bite and subtlety. For these little moulds the watercress is picked over and trimmed, but not puréed, which, in the days of the food processor, makes a nice change. Try to buy really fresh, bright green watercress and avoid the bunches that have roots growing out all over the place. Although it is much more expensive, the ready trimmed watercress sold in supermarkets is often a good buy.

1 lb/500 g fresh watercress
salt and pepper
½ oz/15 g butter plus extra for greasing the dishes
½ oz/15 g flour
¼ pt/150 ml milk
1 egg
2 tablespoons double cream
1 oz/25 g strong cheese, grated
nutmeg

Well grease 4 ramekin dishes and if you want to turn the moulds out to serve them, you may find it a good idea to line each ramekin with a piece of cling film.

Wash the watercress, pick it over and remove any yellow bits or tough stalks and chop it coarsely. Steam it, sprinkled lightly with salt, for 4 minutes.

While it is steaming use the butter, flour and milk to make a béchamel sauce. Cook the sauce for a minute or two then remove it from the heat and let it cool slightly before beating in the egg, cream and cheese and seasoning it with salt and pepper and a scraping of nutmeg. Stir the watercress into the béchamel mixture, turn it into the prepared ramekins, cover each one tightly with foil and steam them for 20–25 minutes.

DIMSUM, RICE AND PULSES

Rice

Rice steams well and in this chapter I give instructions for a plain steamed rice using a normal long grained rice and for a spicy one using Basmati rice. Basmati rice needs treating with care as it can easily become sticky, but I find that the method I give below works very well. Naturally you can cook it without the spices or with more, and perhaps different spices. A sprinkling of turmeric or the addition of a little grated ginger are both good, or you could serve it with the tadka given with dal on p. 174.

Although I give a creamed rice in the pudding section I would not, for savoury dishes, recommend steaming a short grained or

Italian risotto rice as they are much better if they are fried briefly before the water is added and they are brought to the boil.

Plain Steamed Rice

8 oz/250 g long grained rice

salt

Wash the rice thoroughly with cold water then measure the volume. Put the rice in a bowl that will fit into your steaming basket and pour over slightly more than the same volume of water. Sprinkle some salt over the top and steam for 20–25 minutes, by which time the water in the bowl will have evaporated. You can serve it immediately just fluffed up with a fork but I find that it is better if it is then transferred to a strainer and held under the hot tap for a minute or so to wash any surplus starch from the rice grains. Then, if necessary, you can warm it up again by putting it back in the steamer, with the lid propped half open, for 5 minutes, and then, if you wish to keep it you can turn off the steamer, replace the lid, and leave it. You can also leave it and eat it cold with a salad or reheat it when you need it.

You can also steam brown rice but it will take about 15 minutes longer to cook.

Spiced Rice

8 oz/250 g Basmati rice

10 cardamom pods

½ teaspoon cumin seeds

1 teaspoon mustard seeds

1 stick cinnamon

salt

Wash the rice very thoroughly. Turn the rice into a shallow dish which will fit into your steaming basket and pour over twice its volume of cold water. A good rule of thumb is 1 oz/25 g rice has the volume of 1 fl oz/25 ml, so 8 oz/250 g rice would need just over ¾ pt/450 ml water. Leave it to soak for 30 minutes, then add the spices and the salt and put it on to steam.

Steam it, without stirring, for 15–20 minutes, or until it has absorbed the water and a grain, if bitten, is very nearly cooked. Prop the lid up at an angle and leave it, with the steaming water still simmering, 5–10 minutes. This final stage seems to get rid of any excess water and to help the grains to separate. Fluff the rice up with a fork before serving. I remove the cinnamon but leave the remaining spices for people to pick out themselves, but, you may prefer to remove them with a teaspoon.

You can keep the rice hot and ready to serve for 20–25 minutes and to do this cook it to the final stage and fluff it up. Then take the steamer from the heat, fit the lid back on the top and leave it until needed.

Pulses

Many pulses can be cooked in a steamer, but they take a long time and it means that the water has to be watched and replenished. I am also slightly wary about which pulses I steam, for you do not get the hard boiling that is necessary with some of them to remove the toxins and if you are going to start by boiling them it is hardly worthwhile changing from a saucepan to a steamer.

However there is the plus point that pulses need little watching while steaming as they won't dry up and burn. If they are soaked the cooking time is considerably reduced and the steaming water is then also unlikely to need any replenishing. I give below a short list of pulses which are worth steaming, with instructions and cooking times.

Chick peas – Soak overnight—place directly in the steaming basket and steam for at least an hour. Salt after cooking.

Lentils – Unsoaked—in a bowl in the steamer with their own volume of water (see plain steamed rice above), 40–45 minutes.
Soaked—place directly in the steaming basket and steam for 25–30 minutes. Salt after cooking.

Split peas – Soak overnight—in a bowl in the steamer with half their volume of water (see plain steamed rice above) 30–35 minutes.
Soak 1–2 hours—in a bowl in the steamer with their own volume of water, 40–45 minutes. Salt when cooked.

Dal

Dal cooks surprisingly quickly (the masoor dal or red lentil given below is the quickest) and is a very good candidate for the steamer, for it slowly absorbs the water put with it and then just needs fluffing up with a fork before serving. I give a simple, only slightly spiced recipe, but you can, of course, add more spices, or omit them altogether. The tadka needs to be fried at the last minute, but it is good and worth doing.

Dal can be eaten as a dip, either with raw vegetables or with strips of pitta bread, or more traditionally as an accompaniment to an Indian meal. Try it with the Keema Stuffed Cabbage Rolls on p. 114.

8 oz/250 g red lentils (masoor dal)
a slice of fresh ginger, peeled
½ teaspoon turmeric
salt
tadka
2 tablespoons vegetable oil
1 teaspoon cumin seeds
1 medium onion, cut into long strips
¼ teaspoon chilli powder (optional)

In a sieve under a cold running tap thoroughly wash the lentils, at the same time picking out any little pieces of foreign matter. Leave them to soak for at least an hour.

Choose a dish that will fit into your steamer basket. Measure the soaked lentils and put them into the dish together with just under half their volume of water and the ginger. Steam the lentils for half an hour, remove the ginger, sprinkle on the turmeric and 1 teaspoon salt and stir the dal into a paste with a fork; if the lentils still haven't disintegrated steam them for a few minutes longer.

While they are cooking make the tadka. Put the oil to heat in a small frying pan and when it is hot sprinkle in the cumin seeds, fry them until they brown, which will only take a few seconds, then add the onion and continue frying, stirring frequently to prevent burning, for 15–20 minutes or until it is dark brown. If you are using it, stir in the chilli powder and then pour the whole lot over the cooked dal and serve it immediately.

Pease Pudding

A real old fashioned dish, but not one to be dismissed lightly; it is very good on a cold winter's day served with hot ham, sausages or roast pork. In spite of the nursery rhyme I think it would be horrible cold and and I would not dream of eating it 9 days old!

8 oz/250 g yellow split peas
1 small onion, finely chopped

bouquet garni
¾ pt/450 ml chicken stock or water
salt and pepper
1 oz/25 g butter plus extra for greasing the pudding basin
1 egg

Soak the peas for an hour or two and then drain them. Put them, with the onion and bouquet garni, into a dish that fits your steamer basket and pour over the stock or water and season well with salt and pepper. Steam for an hour or until the peas are really soft and cooked.

Remove the bouquet garni and drain off most of the liquid, then in a food processor or blender, purée the peas together with the butter. Check the seasoning and if the purée is too thick add a little more of the steaming water. You can, if you wish, serve it now as a purée.

To make the pudding, add the egg to the peas and process it in. Spoon the mixture into a well greased pudding basin, cover with a loose piece of greased foil and steam for an hour. Serve it turned out on a dish.

Couscous

Any book on Middle Eastern cookery carries a recipe for couscous, but this is geographically incorrect, for couscous comes, not from the Middle East but from the western North African countries bordering the Mediterranean. These are generically known as the Mahgreb and are made up of Morocco, Algeria, Tunisia and Libya. However, one should not be too pedantic, for they are all Arab countries and the food, to us at any rate, has about it the feel of the Middle East.

Couscous is made from an amalgamation of 2 ground semolinas, which in turn are made from hard durum wheat, the same wheat that is used in Italy for making the flour for pasta. The couscous that can be bought in this country is all prepared and part-cooked, needing no more than 10 minutes soaking and 30–40 minutes further steaming.

Ready prepared couscous can be bought in the markets of North African countries, but naturally enough the preparation is still frequently carried out in the home, the newly harvested and ground down semolina being dried outside on a sheet and then stored until needed. A mixture of coarse and fine ground dried grain is steamed, and then, while still hot, sprinkled with salted water and rolled, with the palm of the hand, in butter. This process is repeated twice more by which time the couscous will have softened, soaked up a considerable amount of butter and be ready for its final cooking in the top of the couscousière, over an aromatic vegetable, meat or fish stew. Sometimes a little mutton fat is substituted for the butter and sometimes the process omits the fat and just uses water, but oil is never used.

The couscousière is a large double layered pot or saucepan. The stew is cooked in the bottom half and the couscous is steamed above it. I have seen lovely traditional earthenware couscousières, but even in North Africa they are becoming a thing of the past, and are being replaced by aluminum ones, which are cheap, easy to clean and dent rather than break. There is no need to have a special couscousière: a big saucepan with a colander set into the top of it will do, but keep in the steam by packing a damp tea towel round the perimeter to seal any gaps. At the same time make sure there is good clearance below the colander or steaming basket, for the couscous must cook in steam alone and it will be ruined if the gravy bubbles up into it.

Couscous, like all peasant or ethnic foods, relies on ingredients that are easily available, and the basic stew can be made of any meat or fish or just of vegetables. Vegetables are always used: onions are essential and turnips almost essential, but the others will change with the seasons. Chick peas are added to the basic stew and very frequently potatoes as well. All this, combined with a large mound of couscuos, makes a wonderful nourishing dish for the peasant who has been in the fields all day, but one that can be daunting for the sedentary Westerner. I compromise by using chick peas, but not too many of them, and leaving out the potatoes. However, there are no rigid rules and you can do as you wish. When cooking chick peas it is worth remembering that they toughen if the water or stock is salted and that seasonings should be added just before serving.

The spices and flavourings used in couscous alter as you move along the African coast, with each country or area producing its own individual version. Harissa, a very hot chilli paste, which can be found here in specialist shops, is used everywhere, in varying amounts; the hottest couscous being found in Morocco and the mildest in Algeria. The Tunisians often use tabel, which is milder and more aromatic than harissa, being made from fresh coriander, garlic, caraway and red peppers. Harissa is also sometimes replaced with saffron or turmeric, and in Morocco, sultanas and pine nuts are then frequently added to the couscous.

Libya, being the most eastern of these countries, will produce a stew much akin to one you would get in Egypt, flavoured with cumin and coriander and, in both Libya and Tunisia, steamed cracked wheat or bulgar wheat will sometimes replace the couscous.

The Algerians, more often than not, will add the outside leaves and stems of artichokes to the stew. They will also frequently make a very rich gravy by leaving the lamb on the bone and then cleaving it into chunks before serving it. In Algeria one also comes across a sweet couscous; the grain is mixed with raisins and dates, steamed and then sweetened by having a sugar syrup poured over it.

I give 3 recipes for couscous: a very mild one made with fish and flavoured with saffron, a peasant type one with lamb and harissa, and a more sophisticated one which omits the chick peas and uses either fresh dates or dried apricots as a flavouring.

Fish Couscous

This would normally be made with any available Mediterranean fish, but other mixtures can be used; cod, haddock and whiting is an easy one but red and grey mullet is the one that I prefer. The amount of couscous you cook will depend on how hungry everybody is likely to be.

serves 6–8 people
4 oz/125 g chick peas

1½–2 lb/750 g–1 kg fish, skinned, boned and cut
into large pieces

2 tablespoons cooking oil
2 onions, finely chopped
8 oz/250 g tomatoes, peeled and chopped
1 teaspoon tomato purée
3 cloves garlic, crushed
½ teaspoon saffron powder
½ teaspoon paprika
salt and pepper
1–2 turnips, peeled and quartered
4 young carrots, peeled and cut in four lengthwise
4 medium courgettes, quartered
¾–1 lb/375–500 g couscous
2 tablespoons butter

Cover the chick peas with water and leave them to soak for several hours or overnight. If you have the heads and tails of the fish, boil them up with an extra onion to make a stock.

Warm the oil in the bottom part of your couscousière and cook the onions until they are soft and golden. Add the drained chick peas, the tomatoes, and tomato purée, and cook, stirring, for a minute before pouring in 1¾ pt/1 litre strained fish stock or water. Bring to the boil and boil hard, uncovered for 10 minutes. Lower the heat and simmer for 40 minutes.

While it is simmering mix the garlic, saffron powder and paprika together with 1 teaspoon of salt and a good grinding of black pepper. Rub it into the fish and leave it to marinate.

After 40 minutes add the turnips, carrots and courgettes to the pan and leave to simmer.

Place the couscous in a bowl and pour over just enough salted hot water to cover it; leave it to swell for 10 minutes. Drain the couscous, stir it to get rid of any lumps that may have formed, and put it over the simmering vegetables to steam. Leave the couscous uncovered—it is cooked when you see the steam coming through it. Depending on the diameter of your couscousière, the couscous will take about 30 minutes to cook. About 15 minutes (or less if the pieces of fish are small) before you think the couscous will be done, add the fish and all its juices to the bottom pot.

When the couscous is cooked, fluff it up with a fork, add the butter in small lumps and let it melt in. Season the stew, then transfer it to a deep dish and serve separately from the grain.

Couscous with Lamb and Harissa

A basic family couscous, which can be made as hot or as mild as you like. A boned shoulder of lamb with any excess fat cut off is a good joint of meat to use.

serve 6–8

4 oz/125 g chick peas
1–2 teaspoons harissa, or 1–2 teaspoons chilli powder and 1 clove garlic crushed
2 tablespoons tomato purée
salt and pepper
2 lb/1 kg lamb, off the bone with the fat removed and cut into cubes
1½ lb/750 g onions, finely chopped
¼ pt/150 ml olive or cooking oil
8 oz/250 g young carrots, peeled and quartered
8 oz/250 g turnips, peeled and cubed
¾–1 lb/375–500 g couscous
4 oz/125 g podded peas or broad beans
8 oz/250 g courgettes, cut into chunks
8 oz/250 g tomatoes, peeled and quartered
2 oz/50 g butter

Put the chick peas into a bowl, cover them with water and leave to soak for several hours or overnight. Mix ½ teaspoon harissa, or the chilli powder and garlic mixture, and some salt and pepper with the tomato purée and rub it into the meat. Put the meat, the drained chick peas and the onions into the bottom of the couscousière, pour over the oil and an equal amount of water, bring it to the boil and simmer for 15 minutes. Add the carrots and turnips, pour over enough boiling water to just cover them and leave to simmer for a further 15 minutes.

Pour hot salted water over the couscous and leave it to stand for 10 minutes. Drain the couscous and stir it to remove any lumps. Add the peas, courgettes and tomatoes to the lamb in the bottom of the couscousière and put the couscous to steam on the top. Do not cover, but stir the couscous occasionally and, after about 30 minutes, or when the steam starts to come through, it should be cooked.

Turn the couscous into a dish, fluff it up with a fork and stir in the butter, a little salt and a grinding of pepper and heap it up into a pyramid shape. Remove or drain the meat and vegetables from the stew and, if the dish is big enough, put them round the couscous, or use a separate dish.

The sauce, which is served separately, can then be divided in half. One bowl can be left just as it is and the other one can have more harissa or chilli and garlic added to it. People can then choose between the sauces or blend them to their own particular taste.

Variation

Replace the lamb with a jointed chicken. While the couscous is steaming soak 2 oz/50 g raisins in hot water for 10 minutes. Heat 1 oz/25 g butter in a small frying pan and fry 1 oz/25 g pine nuts and the drained raisins until the pine nuts are golden brown. Add the raisins and pine nuts, with the butter, to the cooked couscous, heap it up into a pyramid and dust it with cinnamon.

Lamb Couscous with Apricots or Dates

Fresh dates are frequently used as a flavouring in Algerian cookery, while dried apricots or prunes are more typical of Morocco. This is one of the few couscous recipes I have come across that uses neither chick peas nor turnips, but it does retain the carrots. As in many of these dishes, lamb and chicken are inter-changeable, or you could use a mixture of both, and it would then be called Couscous Royale.

serve 6–8

8 oz/250 g fresh dates or dried apricots or prunes, halved and stoned
2–2½ lb/1 kg–1.25 kg lamb, off the bone with the fat removed and cut into cubes
2 cloves garlic, crushed
1 teaspoon turmeric
1 teaspoon ground coriander
2 onions, chopped
salt and pepper
2 tomatoes, peeled and chopped
8 oz/250 g carrots, peeled and cut into quarters
8 oz/250 g broad beans, podded
¾–1 lb/375–500 g couscous
2 oz/50 g butter

If you are using dried fruit, put it to soak for several hours or overnight. Put the meat, garlic, turmeric, coriander, onions and seasonings into the bottom of the couscousière. Cover them with water (if using dried fruit use the soaking water), bring it all to the boil and leave simmering. Prepare the couscous by covering it with hot salted water, leaving it for 10 minutes, draining it and stirring it to remove any lumps.

When the meat has been cooking for about 30 minutes add the tomatoes, carrots, beans and dates, apricots or prunes. Put the couscous, uncovered, to steam on the top and leave until the steam starts to penetrate through it, when it should be cooked. Stir the couscous to remove any lumps that may have formed, then remove it to a dish and stir in the butter and some salt and pepper.

The stew should be thick without too much extra gravy but if it is liquid raise the heat and bubble to reduce it a little. Check the seasonings and serve either spooned round the couscous or in a separate dish.

Dimsum

Dimsum are those lovely Chinese snacks that so often live up to their pretty name. The Chinese love the surprise of presenting something unexpected and they have developed different skins—egg, wuntun, beancurd—and doughs to contain the secret at the centre. With their dextrous fingers the Chinese roll, fold, paint and decorate dimsum in many different and delicate ways. We Westerners find it difficult to come up with a result that can compete visually with theirs; however, we can produce something that tastes authentic and will look very pretty served directly from a bamboo steamer.

Here I give recipes for filled egg skins, a type of pancake which you can make yourself, and for wuntun, a pasta type skin that can be obtained from a Chinese grocer. I have not gone into the more complicated forms of dimsum nor have I touched on baozi or stuffed and then steamed buns; the yeast dough is not that easy to make and the fillings are either much the same as the ones I have given or they use ingredients that can only be obtained in Chinatown.

Egg Skins

Egg skins are much used in Chinese cookery; the skins themselves often being described as omelettes, but I always think that they are more like pancakes. The skins are wrapped round a filling and steamed and then usually eaten as a dimsum, but they can also be served as a first course or added to a soup or a vegetable dish. They should be quite small, to enable them to be eaten in one or two mouthfuls, around 3 in/7 cm in diameter; however few of us have a frying pan of that size, so you can either try to make a circle in the middle of a bigger pan or just use the smallest one you own. I use an omelette pan with a diameter of 5½ in/13 cm which produces 8 skins from the 3 egg mixture I give.

The filled skins can be shaped in many different ways: for simplicity you can roll them into sausages or turn them over into half moons or you could shape them in the same way as Italian tortellini by turning them into half moons and then wrapping them round your fingers and sticking the top corners together. If you are really deft with your hands and practised with chopsticks you could try making egg purses. To do this, put a tablespoon of the filling onto the setting skin in the frying pan and draw up the sides with chopsticks, gathering them together so that they stick, in a purse-like shape, before the egg has totally set.

An enormous variety of fillings can be used and I give 3 that are easy to make and good to eat. The Chinese would also use the same fillings for dried beancurd skins; these, if you should happen to find them in a Chinese grocery, should be soaked for a few minutes in hot water, drained on a tea towel and then cut into strips before filling and steaming for about 40 minutes.

1 oz/25 g cornflour
2 teaspoons rice wine or dry sherry
3 eggs
salt
vegetable oil for greasing the pan

Mix the cornflour with 2 tablespoons water and the rice wine or sherry and stir until you have a thin cream. Add the eggs and salt and whisk it all together until smooth.

Heat the pan and pour in enough oil to make a thin film on the bottom. Pour in a little batter, your skins should be no thicker than a pancake, and cook to set the underside. Unless you are making egg purses cook the skins until the top has just set, then remove from the pan and stack them on a plate interleaved with cling film. You need to use a reasonable heat, enough to set the bottom quickly, but not so hot that the batter sizzles up as you pour it into the pan. Leave the skins on one side until you are ready to fill them.

Prawn and Beansprout filled Egg Skins

This should be made with large raw prawns, which can be obtained frozen from Chinese grocers and occasionally from fishmongers. They will need to be defrosted, shelled and de-veined before you chop them. If you can't get raw prawns you will have to use either frozen or fresh cooked prawns.

8 egg skins (p. 180)
filling
1 teaspoon cornflour
2 teaspoons light soy sauce
1 teaspoon finely chopped fresh ginger
1 egg white
salt
4 oz/125 g shelled raw prawns or frozen or fresh cooked prawns
1 rasher streaky bacon
2 oz/50 g beansprouts
oil for basket

Mix the cornflour to a light paste with the soy sauce, then stir in the ginger, egg white and salt. Either mince the prawns and the bacon or chop them very finely by hand or in a food processor. If you are doing it by hand, stir in the beansprouts and then the cornflour mixture. If you are using a food processor, add the cornflour mixture to the chopped prawns and process to mix, then put in the beansprouts and pulse the machine a few times to chop them slightly and to mix them in.

Divide the mixture between the egg skins and roll them tightly. Lightly oil the base of your steamer basket and steam them for 20–25 minutes. Serve them hot with more soy sauce or a dipping sauce (p. 184); if you have used a bamboo basket they can be brought to the table in it.

Vegetable filled Egg Skins

You can fill the skins and roll them as given below or you can make the filling ahead and then spoon it onto them while they are cooking. In this case, immediately fold the skin over into a half moon and remove it from the pan; the filling will then be enclosed as the 2 sides will have stuck together.

8 egg skins (p. 180)
filling
1 small carrot, 1–2 sticks celery and 1 small courgette 5–6 oz/150–175 g total weight
1 tablespoon vegetable oil
1 tablespoon finely chopped spring onion
½ teaspoon finely chopped ginger
½ teaspoon sesame seeds
½ teaspoon sesame oil
1 tablespoon thick soy sauce
1 teaspoon rice wine or dry sherry
½ teaspoon salt
oil for basket

Peel the carrot and chop it into small dice. Chop the celery, having removed any strings, and the topped and tailed courgette into identical sized dice. Keep each vegetable separate.

Heat the vegetable oil in a wok or frying pan, add the spring onion and ginger and stir-fry for 30 seconds. Add the carrot and stir-fry for 15 seconds, then the celery, stir-frying for a further 15 seconds, and finally the courgette and sesame seeds and stir-fry for a final 30 seconds. Remove from the heat and stir in the sesame oil, soy sauce, rice wine or sherry and the salt, and leave until cool.

Divide the vegetable mixture between the egg skins and roll them. Oil the base of your steamer basket and steam them, overlapping if necessary, for 15 minutes. Serve on their own or with a dipping sauce (p. 184).

Pork filled Egg Skins

The Chinese would use a cleaver to chop the meat but for the less practised Westerner it is acceptable to buy minced pork or to chop a piece of boneless belly of pork in a food processor.

8 egg skins (p. 180)
filling
½ teaspoon cornflour
1 teaspoon rice wine or dry sherry

2 teaspoons light soy sauce
2 teaspoons finely chopped spring onions
1 teaspoon grated fresh ginger
¼ teaspoon salt
1 egg white
4 oz/125 g minced pork
oil for basket

Mix the cornflour with the rice wine or sherry and soy sauce, then stir in the spring onions, ginger, salt and egg white. Add the pork and stir it in, breaking it up with a fork until it is all thoroughly mixed. Place a good teaspoon onto each skin, spreading it lengthwise across the skin and then rolling each one up like a pancake. Lightly oil the base of your steamer basket, put in the stuffed skins, overlapping each other slightly if necessary, and steam them for 20–25 minutes.

Serve them very hot, cut into slices if they seem too large, with additional soy sauce or a dipping sauce (p. 184).

Wuntun

Stuffed wuntun are added to and cooked in a soup or are served as a dimsum either steamed or deep fried. I give 2 stuffings; the first is a mixture of prawns and pork, a combination that is much used throughout the whole of South East Asia, and the other a simple vegetarian one that uses easily obtainable ingredients. With a dipping sauce (p. 184) these wuntun make a good first course to a Western meal and you will need to allow 6–8 for each person. The small skins (they are about 3 in/7 cm square) can be bought fresh or frozen, in packets of 30–35, from Chinese grocers. You can make good substitute skins by following a recipe for Italian pasta, rolling it out very thinly, or putting it through a pasta machine, and cutting into little squares. Easiest of all would be to buy some plain lasagne, cook it until pliable, drain it on a tea towel and cut it to size.

Pork and Prawn Wuntun

30–35 wuntun skins

filling
4 oz/125 g pork, minced and 4 oz/125 g shelled raw prawns or frozen or fresh cooked prawns, de-veined if necessary and finely chopped
1 tablespoon rice wine or dry sherry
¼ teaspoon very finely chopped fresh ginger
1 tablespoon egg white
1 teaspoon sesame or vegetable oil
salt and pepper
oil for basket

Mix all the filling ingredients together and stir until they are well amalgamated. Fill the skins by placing 1 teaspoon of the mixture in the centre of each skin and then drawing up the sides so that they look rather like a drawstring bag, but don't close the top.

Oil the base of your steamer basket and stand the filled skins in it. Steam them for 20 minutes until the skins are soft and cooked.

Vegetable Wuntun

30–35 wuntun skins
filling
3 oz/75 g cooked spinach, chopped
2 oz/50 g beansprouts, chopped
2 oz/50 g oyster mushrooms or button mushrooms, chopped
3 tablespoons chopped spring onion
1 tablespoon thick soy sauce
½ teaspoon demerara sugar
1 tablespoon sesame or vegetable oil
salt

Mix all the filling ingredients together and follow the directions in Pork and Prawn Wuntun for stuffing and steaming them.

Chinese Dipping Sauces

Chinese dimsum are frequently served with a dipping sauce, and below I give one or two suggestions for sauces that can be placed in a bowl on the table to accompany stuffed egg skins or wuntun. Once made they will all keep well in a jar in the refrigerator. Alternatively you could just put a bottle of soy sauce on the table and let people shake it on as they want it.

Ginger and Wine Sauce

1 tablespoon finely chopped fresh ginger
3 tablespoons rice wine or dry sherry

Mix the ginger into the rice wine or sherry and leave for at least half an hour for the flavours to blend before using.

Garlic Sauce

1–2 cloves garlic, crushed
1 tablespoon Chinese vinegar or 2 teaspoons cider vinegar

1 tablespoon sesame oil

2 tablespoons light soy sauce

Combine all the ingredients.

Chilli Oil

Chilli oil, which is for those who like their food hot and spicy, can be bought from Chinese grocers, but it is not difficult to make yourself.

6 dried chillis

2 fl oz/50 ml vegetable oil

Put the chillis and oil in a small pan and over a medium heat cook until the chillis are dark and swollen. Leave until cool, then strain off the oil.

Chilli oil can be used as a dipping sauce on its own but it is more usual to combine it with thick soy sauce: 1 tablespoon chilli oil to 2 tablespoons soy sauce or according to taste.

PUDDINGS

Puddings, for many people, are no longer everyday fare and if you have a family that insists on ending a meal with something sweet, it is much easier to give them fruit or yoghurt than to cook a pudding. However, puddings still feature in my family, at least at weekends and when entertaining, and consequently they are anticipated and appreciated as puddings rather than being thought of as something to fill up the odd corners.

Steamed puddings are a traditional part of British cuisine, and very good they are too. Nowadays, with heated houses and more people leading sedentary lives, steamed puddings have become more of a treat than a necessity. However, if they are served, not in mountains but in reasonable quantities, they are very warming and satisfying for Sunday lunch on a cold winter's day. The omission of Christmas pudding is not an oversight, for I don't, like many people, have a special Christmas pudding recipe and the steaming, in a basin, is done in exactly the same way as the suet and sponge puddings that I do give.

Custards and petits pots (I give recipes for several of them) are easily cooked by steaming, rather than in a bain marie in the oven, and provided the water is only just bubbling there should be no trouble with the mixture overheating and separating. Steamed sweet soufflés also work well, but it seemed to be easiest to keep all the soufflés together, so the two that I give will be found in the chapter on soufflés (p. 47 and p. 48).

I also include some summer fruit recipes, a nursery creamed rice pudding and a slight flight of fancy in the shape of the Eight Treasure Rice Pudding. It is a perfectly genuine celebration Chinese pudding, but I have a suspicion that the European version, made with arborio rice and familiar treasures, will go down better with most families. I am in love, name and all, with the fluffy Pudding Celeste, which is beautifully light and makes a perfect finale to rich dinner party food.

Crème Caramel

Crème caramel steams very satisfactorily. It needs to be done slowly and will take up to an hour to cook, but it saves on having to heat up the oven. I give a mixture using 3 eggs, which is the absolute minimum for a custard that is going to set. If you like something richer, which will also cook more quickly, you can use an extra egg or 3 yolks and 2 whole eggs and/or replace some of the milk with cream.

3 oz/75 g granulated sugar
3 eggs
1 oz/25 g caster sugar
1 pt/600 ml milk
few drops vanilla essence

Put the granulated sugar in a small saucepan with 3 tablespoons water. Set it over a low heat and stir until all the sugar has melted, then turn the heat up and boil it fast until it caramelizes to a nice golden brown. Immediately pour it into an ungreased pudding basin, one that will fit into your steamer basket and, holding it with a pair of oven gloves, swirl the caramel around so that it covers the sides.

Beat the eggs and sugar together and add the milk and vanilla essence to taste. Pour the custard into the prepared bowl, cover with foil or a double layer of cling film and put it on to steam. Check to see if the custard has set after 45 minutes and continue steaming for up to a further 15 minutes if necessary.

Leave until cool and then refrigerate until cold. Just before serving the crème caramel turn it out onto a large dish or plate with raised edges.

Crème Brulée

The famous pudding from Trinity College, Cambridge. If you steam it very slowly and carefully there is no need to preheat the cream and then make a custard with the egg yolks. Do, however, have the cooked custard as cold as possible (half an hour in the freezer is a good idea) before grilling it to make the caramel, otherwise it may bubble up and curdle.

The dish or dishes you use will have to be determined by your steamer, but I find that it stays smooth with less likelihood of curdling if it is made in a single dish.

4 egg yolks
¾ pt/450 ml double cream
1 oz/25 g vanilla sugar, or use plain sugar and vanilla essence

for the top
about 3 tablespoons caster sugar

Mix together the egg yolks, cream, sugar and, if using it, vanilla essence and pour into 1 shallow dish or 4 ramekins. Steam, covered with foil, over water that is just bubbling, for 25–30 minutes, or until the custard has set. If your water is boiling properly, leave the lid at an angle so that half the steam can escape. It will not matter if it takes 45 minutes for the custard to set, but if it overheats and takes 15 minutes it will separate and curdle.

Refrigerate the custard until cold. Sprinkle an even layer of caster sugar over the top. Put it under a very hot, preheated grill and, watching and turning if necessary, grill until the sugar has melted and turned to a light caramel. Remove and refrigerate before serving.

Burnt Grand Marnier Creams

These little creams are really crème brulée with the addition of orange and Grand Marnier or orange brandy. They are quite delicious and should be served with langues de chat or similar biscuits.

1 large or 2 small oranges
4 teaspoons Grand Marnier or orange brandy
3 egg yolks
½ pt/300 ml double cream

for the top
about ½ oz/15 g caster sugar

Using a zester or grater take the zest from the orange or oranges and keep it on one side. Remove all the peel and pith and then cut out each segment separately. Reserve any juice. Divide the segments between 4 ramekins, pour over the juice and add 1 teaspoon of Grand Marnier or orange brandy to each ramekin. Mix the egg yolks, cream, sugar and orange zest together and pour it evenly between the ramekins. Cover each ramekin with a piece of foil and steam very gently for 25–30 minutes, as for crème brulée.

Refrigerate until cold, then follow the directions for crème brulée for making the caramel topping.

Pineapple and Passion Fruit Creams

A lovely combination of flavours. It is, without doubt, an extravagant dish and perhaps more worthwhile making for 8 people than 4, as you would still only need to buy 1 small pineapple. The creams can be eaten direct from the ramekins, or, if the ramekins are lined with cling film, they can be refrigerated for a few hours and turned out. They could be accompanied with crisp, vanilla-flavoured biscuits.

4 slices pineapple, skin and core removed
2 egg yolks
¼ pt/150 ml double cream
1 oz/25 g sugar
4 passion fruit

Grease 4 ramekin dishes or line them with cling film. Place 1 slice of pineapple, trimmed if necessary, in the bottom of each ramekin.

Beat the egg yolks, cream and sugar together. Cut each passion fruit in half, dig out the flesh with a teaspoon and add it to the custard mixture. If you really dislike the pips you can push the juice through a sieve, but in doing so you will lose some of the flavour.

Pour the custard on top of the pineapple, cover the ramekins with a double layer of cling film or foil, and steam them slowly and carefully for about half an hour. Cool and refrigerate the custards before serving.

Petits Pots au Chocolat

A steamed chocolate custard which is traditionally cooked and served in the little French petits pots with lids; however, covered ramekins do just as well. The addition of some cocoa may not be conventional, but it adds to the chocolate flavour which otherwise can be rather insipid. Serve with langues de chat or a similar biscuit.

2 oz/50 g plain chocolate
½ pt/300 ml single cream
1 teaspoon cocoa

1 whole egg
2 egg yolks
1 oz/25 g caster sugar

Put the chocolate to melt in a small bowl set over the simmering steaming water. In a small saucepan bring the cream to the boil, letting it bubble for a minute or so. Remove it from the heat and pour about 1 tablespoon onto the cocoa, stirring until smooth. Add the remainder to the melted chocolate, again stirring until smooth. Beat together the egg, egg yolks and sugar, combine the chocolate mixtures and add to the egg mixture. Divide the mixture between four petits pots or ramekins, cover each one with a piece of loose cling film or foil and steam for 12–15 minutes, or until the outside is set and the middle still slightly wobbly.

Cool and refrigerate before serving.

Mexican Mocha Custards

Do not be put off by the fact that the ground coffee is not strained out from the finished custards: it adds a powerful flavour and cuts the richness and smoothness of the cream, but do use very finely ground good quality coffee. Espresso ground, which is almost a powder, is best, but if you can't get that fine filter ground will do. If you really cannot bear the thought of the grounds use a much coarser coffee, infuse it in the cream for at least half an hour, strain it and continue with the recipe.

½ pt/300 ml single cream
2 tablespoons espresso or fine filter ground coffee
2 oz/50 g plain chocolate
2 oz/50 g caster sugar
1 tablespoon Tia Maria, brandy or rum
3 egg yolks

Pour the cream into a small saucepan, mix in the coffee and, stirring all the time, bring it to the boil. The moment it reaches boiling point remove it from the heat and leave it on one side to cool slightly. Break up the chocolate and stir it and the sugar into the cream; you may find that you have to return the saucepan briefly to the heat to melt the chocolate, but do not let it get too hot. Leave it on one side until it is just lukewarm, then stir in the Tia Maria and the egg yolks.

Pour the mixture into 4 petits pots or ramekins, cover each one with a double layer of cling film or foil and steam for 20–25 minutes or until the custard has set. Refrigerate and serve with a swirl of whipped cream topped with a chocolate coffee bean or some grated chocolate.

Pudding Celeste

A delightful fluff of a pudding with an equally delightful name. The recipe, name and all, I found in my mother's kitchen notebook and I suspect that she gleaned it from my grandparents' superb cook when she was first married just before the war. For those who are tired of making meringues, it provides a different and unusual way of using up egg whites.

Serve with a bowl of thick cream.

1 oz/25 g chocolate
2 tablespoons coffee
3 oz/75 g granulated sugar
3 egg whites
butter for greasing the basin

Well butter a 2 pt/1.2 litre pudding basin. Melt the chocolate and the coffee together (this can be done in a small bowl in your steamer or over a small saucepan of boiling water) stir them well and pour into the bottom of the basin.

Put the sugar with 3 tablespoons water in a small saucepan over a low heat, swirl the saucepan round, being careful not to spill the contents, until the sugar has completely melted. Turn up the heat and boil hard for 2 minutes to obtain a syrup. While the syrup is boiling, whisk the egg whites until they are stiff and then, still whisking (you will need an electric whisk or a helper), pour in the syrup. Continue whisking until you have a glossy meringue.

Spoon the amalgamated mixture into the basin, cover it with a loose piece of cling film or a pleated sheet of foil (it will rise considerably) and steam very gently for 10 minutes. Leave to cool, but do not refrigerate, and just before serving, turn it out, letting the chocolate drip down the sides.

Variation

This pudding looks and tastes equally nice if served in a pond of raspberry sauce. Make the sauce by heating some raspberries, fresh or frozen, with sugar and lemon juice to taste. Add 1 teaspoon of cornflour which has been dissolved in a little water. Bring to the boil and stir constantly until the sauce has thickened, then leave to cool a little before sieving out the pips.

Make the pudding as above, leaving out the chocolate, and just before serving it out onto a dish, spooning the sauce around it. Serve a jug of cream separately.

Terrestrial Pudding

Not really a down to earth version of Pudding Celeste, but a variation of it. This uses the egg yolks to give a lemon curd type custard which will flow down the pudding when it is turned out.

3 eggs, separated
3 oz/75 g caster sugar
zest and juice of 1 large or 2 small lemons

1 oz/25 g butter, cubed, plus extra for greasing the pudding basin
3 oz/75 g granulated sugar

Well butter a 2 pt/1.2 litre pudding basin. Mix together the egg yolks, caster sugar and lemon zest and juice, then stir in the butter. Pour the mixture into the bottom of the pudding basin.

Follow the instructions for Pudding Celeste (p. 191) for making the meringue. Spoon this on top of the lemon sauce, smooth it flat, cover with a pleated piece of greased foil—it will rise while cooking—and steam for 15 minutes. Leave to cool before turning it out and serving with cream.

Variation

An île flottante can be steamed in exactly the same way; the only difference is that the lemon sauce is replaced with a vanilla custard. This is made with 3 egg yolks, 3 oz/75 g caster sugar, ¼ pt/150 ml single cream and vanilla essence to taste.

This is a lovely pudding if you slightly reduce the sugar content of the meringue, divide it up and steam it in little individual moulds and finally, just before serving, sprinkle the top of each one with a little praline.

Figs with Red Wine, Orange and Cardamom

I find that steaming the figs works well, for it softens them without making the inside mushy and they stay whole. The syrup has a very good flavour, but it must not be boiled down too much or it will be too sweet.

6–8 cardamom seeds
½ pt/300 ml red wine
½ pt/300 ml water
4 oz/125 g sugar
zest and juice of 1 orange
8 fresh figs

Remove the cardamom seeds from their pods and crush them slightly to release the flavour. Put them, together with the wine, water, sugar and the orange zest and juice in the base of your steamer. Bring it slowly to the boil, stirring to dissolve the sugar. Prepare the figs by wiping them clean and with a pair of scissors snipping off any small piece of tough stalk. Put them upright into the steamer basket and steam them for 10 minutes over the simmering wine mixture.

Remove the figs and leave the syrup to simmer for a further 10 minutes or so; it needs to be reduced to somewhere between a third and half of its original volume. Cool the syrup slightly, then strain it into a serving dish, preferably glass. Arrange the figs in the dish and refrigerate before serving.

Muscat Grape Kissel

A kissel is Russian in origin and traditionally has a wonderful colour, being made with red berries. This grape one, which really needs to be made during the few weeks in the autumn when muscat grapes are available, may miss out on the colour but not, I think, on the taste.

In a really extravagant mood you could make the kissel with Sauternes, but sherry or Marsala are both acceptable and I once used a sweet Malaga wine that I had brought back from Spain.

The thickening and adding of the cornflour needs to be done with care for the finished pudding should just hold together, being neither runny or solid.

1 lb/500 g Muscat grapes, off the branch
4 oz/125 g sugar
zest and juice of 1 lemon
2 tablespoons cornflour dissolved in a little cold water
2–4 tablespoons sherry, Marsala or Sauternes

Steam the grapes, over ¾ pt/450 ml water, for 8 minutes or until the skins start to wrinkle, then leave them on one side to cool slightly. When they are cool enough to handle, skin and de-pip them, returning the skin and pips to the steamer liquid. Add the sugar, lemon zest and juice to the liquid. Stir it over a low heat, until the sugar has dissolved, boil it for 5 minutes then strain off the grape skins, pips and zest. You will now have about ½ pt/300 ml liquid. Add it to the cornflour and, stirring continuously, reheat it and boil for 1 minute. If you think the kissel is still too thin, you can add a little more cornflour and briefly re-boil to thicken it.

Take it off the heat, stir in the grapes and the sherry or wine and pour it into a dish. Refrigerate before serving.

Fluffy Topped Blackcurrant and Nectarine Jelly

This pudding is not steamed, but has been legitimately included as it shows how the steamer can be used to heat up different bowls of ingredients, saving on both saucepans and washing up. The instructions are long, but it isn't complicated to make, it just needs to be done in ordered stages.

The finished pudding is both light and summery but can really only be made in the short season when both blackcurrants and nectarines are available. It looks pretty with some mint leaves around the edge of the serving dish. You will probably find that this makes enough for 6 people.

8 oz/250 g blackcurrants
3 oz/75 g sugar
2 nectarines

1½–2 teaspoons gelatine

topping

¼ pt/150 ml double cream

2 eggs, separated

1 oz/25 g sugar

1½ teaspoons gelatine

butter for the mould

Choose a tin or mould for the pudding with a capacity of 1½–2 pts/around 1 litre. I find that a 1½ lb/750 g bread tin is ideal. Grease it and line it with cling film.

Half fill the base of your steamer with water and bring it to simmering point. Wash the blackcurrants and put them, still wet, into a bowl or dish that will fit into your steamer basket. Sprinkle the sugar over the top of them and steam for 15 minutes or until the juice is running and the blackcurrants are soft and cooked. Sieve the stalks and pips from the blackcurrants and keep the purée. Steam the nectarines for 30 seconds, then skin them and remove the stone. Cut the nectarine flesh into cubes and stir them into the blackcurrant purée.

Measure the mixture to determine the amount of gelatine needed. Blackcurrants take quite a lot of setting and you will need 2 teaspoons gelatine for ½ pt/300 ml. Increase or decrease the amount according to the volume of purée.

Put 3 tablespoons water into a small bowl and sprinkle over the gelatine. Place the bowl with the gelatine in the steamer and leave for a few minutes for the gelatine to melt. Stir the gelatine, then pour it into the blackcurrants and stir it in. Pour the mixture into the prepared tin or mould and leave in the refrigerator to set while you make the fluffy custard topping.

In a small bowl whisk the cream, egg yolks and sugar together and put it in the steamer. Stir it frequently and when the custard has thickened enough to coat the back of a wooden spoon, remove it and leave it to cool.

You can now use the same small gelatine bowl without having washed it up. Put 2 tablespoons water into it, sprinkle over the gelatine and place it in the steamer for a few minutes. When it has melted, remove the bowl and turn off the steamer. Stir the gelatine and pour it into the custard. Mix it well and leave until it is just on the point of setting. It will need watching carefully as there is a very narrow margin between warm and liquid and set solid! Whisk the egg whites until they are stiff and fold them into the setting custard. Spoon the mixture on top of the blackcurrant jelly and leave, covered, in the refrigerator until needed.

To serve, turn the jelly out onto a piece of cling film and peel off the cling film. Very gently, perhaps using two fish slices, turn it back into the centre of a dish.

Rhubarb

Steaming brings out the very best in rhubarb, and leaves you with whole tender pieces, rather than with a mush or little woody sticks. Steaming keeps the pieces whole by cooking the rhubarb slowly and without agitation, but if you want to make a fool just cook the rhubarb for a little longer before fluffing it up with a fork.

Below I give simple instructions for cooking rhubarb with golden syrup and an orange. If you don't have an orange you can use a couple of tablespoons of packet orange juice or water with perhaps a sprinkling of powdered ginger. The use of golden syrup is a personal preference of mine, but you can substitute any caster or brown sugar or use half-and-half syrup and sugar. How much you sweeten rhubarb is also a matter of preference and I find that some people like to leave it fairly sharp, so that, just before eating it, they can cover it with cream topped with crunchy demerara sugar.

1½ lb/750 g rhubarb
zest and juice of 1 orange
3–4 tablespoons golden syrup

Like rice, rhubarb needs to be steamed in a dish inside the steamer so choose the biggest you can find to fit your basket but be sure to leave a small gap round the edge to enable the steam to escape.

Trim the rhubarb, remove any stringy skin and cut it into pieces. Put the rhubarb into the dish together with the orange zest and juice and the golden syrup. Cover the dish with foil and steam it for about 30 minutes or until the pieces are tender when pierced with a sharp knife. At about 10 minute intervals lift off the foil and gently turn the rhubarb round to help it cook evenly, otherwise the sticks on the bottom will cook too quickly for the top ones. When you turn the rhubarb taste the syrup and if it is too sharp, add more golden syrup or sugar.

Tipsy Pudding

A traditional English tipsy cake or pudding is a trifle which has been exceptionally well laced. This pudding, which is a great favourite with my family, was, when I first gave it to them, christened 'tipsy pudding' and although it might not be strictly accurate, for want of anything better I have kept the name.

The pudding should be steamed in a 2 pt/1.2 litre basin and if your steamer is too small you could cook it in a large saucepan. If you do that, try to keep the basin off the bottom of the saucepan by standing it on some sort of trivet—crossed teaspoons work very well. Cover it with a lid and look at it occasionally to make sure that the water is not boiling away.

serves 6
4 oz/125 g wholemeal bread
12 fl oz/350 ml milk
3 oz/75 g sultanas

4 fl oz/125 ml rum, whisky or orange juice
4 oz/125 g granulated sugar
3 eggs
4 oz/125 g demerara sugar

Tear up the bread and put it into a bowl with the milk. Put the sultanas into another bowl with the rum, whisky or orange juice and leave both bowls to soak for at least 2 hours.

Make a caramel by slowly dissolving the granulated sugar in ¼ pt/150 ml water and then bringing it to the boil. Boil fast until it reaches 174° C/345° F on a sugar thermometer. If you are not using a thermometer watch the pan very carefully and take it off the heat the moment the mixture has turned to a good rich brown colour. Pour the caramel into the pudding basin and swirl it round to cover the sides, then leave it on one side until needed.

Mash up the bread with a fork and stir in the eggs, demerara sugar and soaked sultanas. You can whiz it all up in a food processor, but if you do so add the sultanas right at the end, just briefly pulsing them in without chopping them.

Pour the mixture into the prepared basin, cover it with foil and tie it on with a piece of string; if the basin is fairly full put a pleat in the foil so that it can expand during cooking. Steam for 1 hour and then turn the pudding out onto a plate. It will be a lovely brown colour with all the sticky caramel juices dripping down the sides. Serve it hot with a large bowl of double cream or Greek yoghurt.

Sussex Pond Pudding

One of the most unctuous of British steamed puddings, which is also very dramatic in the way that the wonderful yellow pond flows out when it is cut. Many recipes use 1 large whole lemon, but to cook it properly needs about 6 hours steaming, which then leaves you with an empty lemon shell with a thick layer of pith, so I prefer to make it with 2 or 3 small, thin skinned lemons which are sliced before cooking.

8 oz/250 g self-raising flour
4 oz/125 g suet
½ teaspoon salt
¼ pt/150 ml mixed milk and water
2 or 3 lemons
6 oz/175 g butter, roughly chopped, plus extra for greasing the basin
6 oz/175 g caster sugar

Well grease a 1¾–2 pint/about 1 litre pudding basin. In a mixing bowl stir the flour, suet and salt together and using a small spatula mix in the milk and water to make a soft dough. Turn the dough out onto a floured board, put one third on one side for the lid, and roll the rest into a circle with a diameter of about 2 in/5 cm more than the basin. Line the basin, letting any extra dough hang over the edge.

Wash and scrub the lemons, then cut off and discard the ends, cutting the rest into medium thick slices, and throwing out any pips you find. Layer the lemon slices and the roughly chopped butter in the pudding basin, sprinkle the sugar over the top and fold in the overlapping edges of dough. Roll out the remaining dough, moisten it round the edge, place it on top of the pudding and seal it tightly. Grease the inside of a large piece of foil, make a pleat in the centre, put it over the pudding and tie it down tightly using some extra string to make a handle for lifting the pudding.

Cook it over fast bubbling water in the basket of a steamer or on a trivet or saucer in the bottom of a deep saucepan which is filled with enough water to come halfway up the pudding basin. Steam the pudding for 4 hours. Check at intervals to make sure that the water is at a constant boil and replenish it with boiling water if the level starts to drop.

Turn the pudding out onto a large dish, making sure that it has a lip to retain the juices, and serve it immediately with lashings of thick cream.

Apple Suet Pudding

This is much the same as Sussex Pond Pudding in that it has a suet crust encasing a surprise filling. I like the addition of some wholemeal flour but if it is made with it entirely the crust will be on the heavy side.

crust

4 oz/125 g wholemeal self-raising flour
4 oz/125 g self-raising flour
4 oz/125 g suet
½ teaspoon salt
¼ pt/150 ml mixed milk and water

filling

8 oz/250 g cooking apples, peeled and sliced
5 oz/150 g demerara sugar
1 oz/25 g currants
1 oz/25 g sultanas
3–4 knobs stem ginger
1 tablespoon syrup from the stem ginger mixed with 4 tablespoons water

Make the crust and line the pudding basin following the instructions for Sussex Pond Pudding (p. 197). Fill the basin with layers of apples, sugar, dried fruit and chopped ginger and drizzle over the syrup before sealing with the lid.

Follow the instructions for Sussex Pond Pudding to cover the basin and cook it. This pudding will cook slightly more quickly and 3½ hours should be enough. If at any stage during the steaming the water needs replenishing be sure to add boiling water, otherwise the crust will start to become heavy the moment you let the water go off the boil.

Jam Roly-Poly

This is made from a simple suet dough which is spread with jam, rolled up, wrapped and steamed. It is very easy and quick and makes a good warming winter pudding.

4 oz/125 g self-raising flour
pinch of salt
2 oz/50 g suet
12 oz/375 g jam

Sift the flour and salt together, stir in the suet, and using a fork mix in 3–4 tablespoons of hot water. Stop adding the water when the mixture holds together and comes away from the sides of the bowl. Knead the dough lightly and then roll it out into an oblong of about 8 × 15 in/20 × 38 cm and ¼ in/5 mm thick.

Spread half the jam over the dough, leaving a margin all round the edge. Roll it up and, using a little water, pinch and seal the edges. Wrap it loosely in a double thickness of greased foil. Steam it, over fairly fast boiling water, for 1½ hours. If necessary top up from time to time with boiling water, remembering that suet puddings start to become heavy the moment the water goes off the boil.

Serve the roly-poly by unwrapping it, transferring it to a dish and pouring the rest of the jam, which has been gently heated, over the top. It can be accompanied by the traditional custard or with cream.

Treacle Duff

A duff is the Scottish name for a hot steamed suet pudding, plum duff, made with prunes, perhaps being the best known variety. All suet puddings are traditionally served with hot custard, but I am inclined to think that they are already sweet enough and prefer to hand round a jug of plain cream.

4 tablespoons golden syrup
2 oz/50 g self-raising flour
3 oz/75 g fresh white or brown breadcrumbs
4 oz/125 g shredded suet
1 teaspoon ground ginger
1 oz/25 g soft brown sugar
pinch of salt
2 tablespoons black treacle
1 egg
4 tablespoons milk
butter for greasing the pudding basin

Butter a 1½–2 pt/about 1 litre pudding basin and put 2 tablespoons of the golden syrup into the bottom.

Sift the flour into a mixing bowl and stir in the breadcrumbs, suet, ginger, sugar and salt. Warm the treacle and the remaining golden syrup and stir them in together with the egg and milk. Pour the mixture into the prepared basin and cover with a loose, doubled piece of cling film or with a piece of foil, pleated in the middle. If you are going to cook it in a deep saucepan tie a looped string handle over the basin.

Steam the pudding in a steaming basket or on a trivet in a large saucepan for about 2 hours. Top up the water level with boiling water as necessary during cooking. Turn the cooked pudding out onto a warmed dish and serve immediately.

Cherry and Almond Sponge Puddings

If you have no small moulds these little sponge puddings can easily be steamed in teacups. Serve the puddings with custard, which, in an extravagant mood could be laced with an almond liqueur. I give instructions for making the sponge quickly in a food processor, but if you do not own one just make up the mixture as you would an ordinary sponge cake.

serves 6
1 oz/25 g split almonds
4 oz/125 g glacé cherries

3 oz/75 g self-raising flour
1 oz/25 g ground almonds
scant 4 oz/125 g caster sugar
4 oz/125 g butter, softened
2 eggs
butter for greasing the moulds or teacups

Grease 6 little moulds or teacups and line them with cling film.

Grill the split almonds until they are browned, being careful not to let them burn.

Put a few pieces of almond and a halved cherry in the bottom of each mould. Roughly chop the remaining cherries and almonds and reserve.

Place the flour, ground almonds and sugar in the bowl of your food processor and process briefly to mix them. Add the butter and eggs and process for a further few seconds to just mix them in. Finally add the cherries and almonds and pulse the machine once or twice to distribute them through the mixture.

Spoon the mixture into the prepared moulds, cover each one with another piece of cling film and steam them for 40 minutes or until they are springy and light to the touch. Turn them onto individual plates, peel off the cling film and serve them very hot.

Creamed Rice

Rice pudding with a lovely brown skin on top is not a candidate for the steamer, but cold creamed rice is. I give the basic recipe below and for rice pudding addicts it is good just as it is. You can also serve it with either fresh or stewed fruit, or with a sauce made of dried apricots with a touch of cinnamon. If you have a couple of spare egg whites, whisk them up, fold them into the cold creamed rice, spoon it all into a shallow dish and sprinkle demerara sugar over the top. Leave it covered, but not refrigerated, for several hours and the sugar will melt into the top of the pudding.

2 oz/50 g pudding rice
scant ¾ pt/450 ml milk
1½ oz/40 g caster sugar (or to taste)
a few drops vanilla essence
¼ pt/150 ml double cream (optional)

Wash the rice and put into a dish that will fit into your steamer. Add the milk, sugar and vanilla essence. Stir it, cover it and steam it for 1¼ hours or until the rice is soft and has absorbed most of the milk.

When the rice is cool stir in, if you are using it, the cream. Refrigerate until cold.

Eight Treasure Rice Pudding

A classic Chinese pudding which is made for the New Year. The treasures are said to represent the eight lotus petals of Buddhism and therefore banish evil spirits throughout the coming year—they are red bean paste, 6 different types of dried or crystallized fruit or fruit seeds and one nut of any sort.

In the ingredients I give two suggestions; the first is for a genuine Chinese pudding and the second for a European pudding on the same theme. For the Chinese version you will have to pay a visit to a Chinese shop and, if some of the treasures given below are not in stock, you could always ask them to suggest substitutes. There is nothing to stop you mixing the ingredient lists and using what you have or what you find is easily available.

Chinese Pudding

8 oz/250 g glutinous or sweet rice

1 oz/25 g lard or margarine plus extra for greasing the pudding basin

2 oz/50 g sugar

1 oz/25 g sultanas

4 pieces dried mango

8 preserved red dates

6 glacé cherries

1 tablespoon crystallized pineapple pieces

1 tablespoon canned lotus nuts

1 heaped tablespoon walnut pieces

3 oz/75 g red bean paste

European Pudding

8 oz/250 g risotto rice

1 oz/25 g lard or margarine plus extra for greasing the pudding basin

2 oz/50 g sugar

1 oz/25 g sultanas

4 dried apricots

1 tablespoon melon seeds

6 glacé cherries

1 tablespoon candied orange or lemon peel

1 tablespoon canned lychees

1 heaped tablespoon flaked almonds

3 oz/75 g sweet chestnut purée

for the syrup

2 teaspoons cornflour

1 oz/25 g sugar

Soak the rice in water for 30 minutes, wash it very thoroughly and put it in a dish with ½ pt/300 ml water. Place the dish in your steamer, steam for 10 minutes, fluff it up with a fork and steam for a further 15 minutes or until cooked. Remove it from the heat and immediately stir in the lard or margarine and the sugar.

While the rice is cooking, thickly grease the pudding basin. Soak the sultanas, apricots, preserved red dates or any other dried fruit you are using in hot water to soften them and let them swell. Dice the bigger pieces of fruit and roughly chop the nuts: the Chinese would peel the walnuts first by pouring boiling water over them and then removing the skin with a cocktail stick or something similar, but I find this time-consuming and fiddly job can be omitted. Arrange the 'treasure' pieces prettily on the bottom and up the sides of the basin, then mix any that are left over in with the hot rice.

Spoon half the rice, or a bit more, into the bowl and make a small well in the centre. Fill the well with the bean paste or chestnut purée, then spoon on the remaining rice. Cover the basin loosely with a double layer of cling film and steam it for 45 minutes.

While the pudding is steaming make the syrup sauce. Put the cornflour into a cup and stir in 2 teaspoons water. Place the sugar in a small saucepan with 7 fl oz/200 ml water and slowly bring it to the boil, stirring until the sugar has dissolved. Pour in the cornflour mixture and stir until the sauce has thickened. Turn the pudding out onto a plate, pour the syrup over it and serve immediately.

INDEX